The Alienated
War Veteran in
Film and Literature

The Alienated War Veteran in Film and Literature

EMMETT EARLY

McFarland & Company, Inc., Publishers

Jefferson, North Carolina

LIBRARY OF CONGRESS CATALOGUING-IN-PUBLICATION DATA

Early, Emmett, 1939–
    The alienated war veteran in film and literature /
    Emmett Early.
        p.   cm.
    Includes bibliographical references and index.

    ISBN 978-0-7864-7499-8
    softcover : acid free paper ∞

    1. Veterans in motion pictures.   2. Veterans in literature.
I. Title.

PN1995.9.V44E269 2014
791.43'6581—dc23   2013048689

BRITISH LIBRARY CATALOGUING DATA ARE AVAILABLE

On the cover: Bruce Willis as Emmett Smith in *In Country*, 1989
(Warner Bros./Photofest)

Manufactured in the United States of America

*McFarland & Company, Inc., Publishers
    Box 611, Jefferson, North Carolina 28640
    www.mcfarlandpub.com*

To my son,
Liam Early

Contents

Preface

This book is a product of four primary sources. The first source is derived from my own personal contact with veterans from various wars as I worked for more than 30 years as a psychotherapist. The second source is the archive of scientific publications, mainly psychological research into posttraumatic stress disorder. My third source comes from reading the accounts of other veterans, personal memoirs, biographies, fiction, and historical and sociological literature concerning veterans of various eras. My fourth source is derived from my perspective of popular American culture, particularly movies about (and, in some cases, made by) veterans. Because I teach an occasional course in veterans' culture I am acutely aware of various sources of information about war veterans that I *don't* utilize, such as graphic arts, cartoons, music, and stage dramas. My knowledge of the experiences of other countries' war veterans is similarly scarce. I have tried to compensate by including works by Japanese, British, French, and German sources.

I have constructed this book to roughly capture the postwar eras when veterans were prominent in American culture, examining films and personal narratives from each of the more recent eras: post–World Wars I and II, Korea, Vietnam, and the wars in Iraq and Afghanistan. I have focused on several sources of literature, principally Homer's *Odyssey* and medieval myths and fairy tales, along with some modern fiction from or about veterans. I've focused on the psychological adjustment of individual war veterans with the goal of comparing the creative works with actual veterans' postwar adjustments.

It is to no one's surprise that alienation is the lot of the veteran of combat upon his or her return to home society, yet it seems that the wheel must be recreated and given expression in each cohort of veterans produced by our wars. It is seldom observed that the society is reciprocal in exchange with its veterans, that culturally the flow of influence from veteran to the greater society and back is dynamic.

"I realized close combat had changed those of us who endured it — we were just plain different from other people through no fault of our own. We saw life through a different lens and always would."
— E.B. Sledge, *China Marine*, 2002, p. 132

"I'm still around, but from here on in, for reasons I'm not at liberty to disclose, I've disguised myself so cunningly that even the cleverest reader will fail to recognize me."
— J.D. Salinger, *For Esmé: With Love and Squalor*, 1953, p. 103

"Knight: Through my indifference to my fellow men, I have isolated myself from their company. Now I live in a world of phantoms. I am imprisoned in my dreams and fantasies."
— Ingmar Bergman, the Knight's confession in *The Seventh Seal*, 1960, p. 149

"No matter where I went, I felt something was not right about me."
— Karl Marlantes, *What It Is Like to Go to War*, 2011, p. 151

"The Man who really endured the war at its worst was everlastingly differentiated from every one except his fellow soldiers."
— Siegfried Sassoon, *Memoirs of an Infantry Officer*, quoted in Paul Fussell's *The Great War in Modern Memory*, p. 90

Introduction

The five quotations opposite are meant to span time and imply that alienation is normal and common among war veterans when they return home. I certainly found it so among the veterans I knew. For a little over 29 years, from 1979 to 2008, I functioned as a psychotherapist for war veterans. During that time I had contact with many other war veterans who were not therapy clients, but were in other ways associated with the treatment of veterans, such as attorneys, firemen, journalists, politicians, corrections officers, craftsmen, other health professionals, friends, maintenance and construction workers. By the term "war veteran" I mean a veteran of military service who was engaged in fighting the enemy in a combat zone. Some clerks, cooks, truck drivers, medical staff, or aircraft crew chiefs may not think of themselves as combatants, and that is for them to decide. I found that war veterans, whether clients or not, all reported a remarkable level of social and cultural alienation following their return from combat. Some, who were otherwise successful in their adaptation to civilian life, revealed in candid moments that they experienced alienation or estrangement, even when among family and friends, who were not themselves war veterans. And while my comments are not based solidly on objective scientific measurement, and acknowledging that I probably have a clinical skew in my perception, it has been my observation that alienation in some form is common among war veterans. Ray Scurfield, who was an army social worker in the Vietnam War and went on to work with veterans for the rest of his professional career, described this element of the veteran population.

> And, there is a third sub-group of veterans who are seldom recognized — and who are mistakenly lumped in with the "successful" majority group. This sub-group is comprised of veterans who have made a successful postwar recovery and yet still are troubled to some degree or a considerable degree. They have

felt a profound and indelible impact, both negative and positive, from their war and postwar experiences; they lead relatively or substantially satisfying lives; and they continue to experience war-related demons and hauntings that remain "unfinished" or unresolved. These can include sporadically felt and sharply painful war- and postwar memories and nightmares from time to time, or fairly regularly, and/or vague or pervasive and chronic under-currents of pain and malaise [Scurfield, 2004, p. 6].

To be an alien is to be from a different culture and speak a different language; to feel separation and detachment from others. The culture of the military, particularly that which engages the enemy in foreign combat, is quite different from the home-based civilian culture, having its own language, jargon, and customs. The word "estrange" is derived from the Latin *extraneus*. One feels estrangement when one is removed from a customary environment or associations. "Alienation" is derived from the Latin *alienus* and refers to a withdrawing or separation of a person, or his or her affections, from an object or position of former attachment, from the values of one's society and family. Much of the alienation for the war veteran appears to occur when the veteran returns to a familiar surrounding and is aware that he or she has changed significantly due to experiences not had by others. The veteran may come back from the war looking the same as when he or she left, but with many ineffable changes in his or her personality: changes in attitude toward safety, comfort, pain tolerance, death, authority, trust, loyalty, duty, order. The veteran's family may feel the change as estrangement; certainly the veteran will. Ben Shephard writes of the British veterans of World War I: "They put on civilian clothes again and looked to their mothers and wives very much like the young men who had gone to business in the peaceful days before August 1914. But they had not come back the same men. Something had altered in them" (Shephard, 2001, p. 144, quoting Philip Gibbs, *Realities of War*).

Alienation does not necessarily entail violence, hostility, or aggression. At the root of alienation, and reasonably at the root of many veteran suicides, is the loss of attachment that first takes place when the recruit leaves his or her home community and enters military service; then, following the intense bonding that takes place in the rigors of training and work, and especially under combat conditions in a foreign land, or the experience of in-service sexual trauma, the veteran is discharged and put back into society without much process that would help with the transition.

It is quite possible that my observations are biased by my own experience with alienation, which I grew up with and found enhanced by being a psychotherapist for veterans with posttraumatic stress disorder (PTSD). I know that I empathically bonded with the veterans collectively, and at times found myself standing alongside many of them in attitude, at odds with the government and the dominant values of the society. McGilchrist (2009, p. 28) asserts that this is not unusual: "By attending to someone else performing an action, and even by thinking about them doing so — even, in fact by thinking about certain sorts of people at all — we become objectively, measurably, more *like* them." So, the validity of what I report should be taken with this grain of salt.

Probably 70 percent of my clinical practice over 30 years was devoted to talking with veterans, mostly of the Vietnam War. During that war, the years from 1962 to 1975, I was myself a military veteran, going to college, traveling and working at blue collar jobs. I thought of myself as a writer, albeit unpublished, and largely detached from politics. I was engaged in finding myself and achieving some direction in a career. I discovered the writings of Carl Jung in the mid–1960s and finally landed in graduate school in psychology in 1972. In 1979, after an internship at the Seattle VA hospital, I was offered a peach of a job, starting up the city's first Vet Center. However, my training had not really prepared me to deal with what I encountered. Theories about psychological trauma were not then well formed. My chief clinical mentor in graduate school had seen his extended family largely devastated in the Holocaust and avoided the topic. Even during my year-long internship at the Seattle VA hospital in 1976 to 1977, psychological trauma was not explored as an important topic, which seems incredible in retrospect. I do not remember a lecture devoted to the topic. VA psychology and clinicians were wary, I think, of conducting outreach to the veterans. There was a sense, similar to what we have now as a result of our several wars on terror, that the United States had overreached its capacity fighting in Vietnam. It seemed that none of the VA in-house psychologists wanted the job that I was hired to do. The Vet Center program had been forced upon the VA by Congressional mandate. PTSD as a diagnosis had only just been introduced with DSM III (the Diagnostic and Statistical Manual) in 1980 (Figley, 1978, Scurfield, 2004, pp. 90ff). Psychological trauma was scantily understood in 1979 when we opened the Vet Center doors. Kardiner's 1941 text about World War I Shell Shock casualties was not helpful to me. The most useful literature, besides Figley's 1978 text, came to me via the Holocaust in Henry Krystal's *Massive Psychic Trauma* (1967). My first glimpse at a copy of *The Diagnostic and Statistical Manual for Mental Disorders*, third edition, was when I was on the witness stand in Seattle Superior Court, when the prosecutor at a felony trial of a client waved it dramatically in front of the jury.

Ben Shephard, in his history of the psychiatry of wars, is critical of the Vet Center effort: "The Vet Center programme was probably the most ambitious attempt at collective psychotherapy in history, based on an idealistic hope that mass treatment could transform the lives of up to half a million people" (p. 396).

I was stunned emotionally by listening carefully to the Vietnam War veterans. I approached the job optimistically. The VA in its collective wisdom had hired a solid professional staff who were themselves war veterans and provided support, but our first year of operation confronted me with an intense energy that seemed, at times, chaotic. We were successful, in a sense, because we gave a forum to combat veterans who had not talked about their experiences in the war with anyone and had mostly not associated with other veterans. It was as if I had taken the cap off a pressurized container and it exploded in my face. Our groups were intense. Jung's concepts helped me formulate some idea of what was happening, and I was sensitive to the imagery, which I was able to write about later (Early, 1992, 2003). William Rivers reported the influence of Freud in Rivers's efforts to heal the impact of psychological trauma among the British veteran officers of World War I (Shephard, 2001, p. 87), selecting what worked of Freud's theory. For me it was Jung's theory of the psychological complex that allowed me to conceptualize the impact of psychological trauma. Conceptualizing gave me an intellectual distance from the strong emotions elicited in psychotherapy.

What the veterans told me about the realities of combat in Vietnam widened and darkened my consciousness. Their treatment by U.S. society I could see in Jungian terms, as a projection of collective shadow. Jung, himself, put it best: "Since it is universally believed that man *is* merely what his consciousness knows of itself, he regards himself as harmless and so adds stupidity to iniquity. He does not deny that terrible things have happened and still go on happening, but it is always 'the others' who do them" (1964, p. 296, emphasis in the original). I connected this collective shadow projection to our heritage, what I knew about the negative side of America's history: racism, the vestiges of slavery and anti–Asian prejudice, and the genocidal treatment of Native Americans. I felt I was living in the wake of a major historical event.

When I write about the war veterans' alienation, I regard it as a universal phenomenon that is the lot of almost every veteran of every war returning home from foreign combat, even under good conditions, but during the Vietnam War era, the conditions were especially destructive. I was subject to a collective social naiveté, exemplified by the following scene. One evening, after my work at the Vet Center, I went to pick up my wife at a dance studio in Seattle's Belltown District. The dancers were gathered together having refreshments after their workout. As I approached them, fey as they were in their tights and leotards, I felt like Dr. Frankenstein's Creature with flesh dripping from my teeth. I felt that I had to censor my language in order to protect them when I mentioned what I'd done in my work. As Clarissa Dalloway said (in voice-over) in the film *Mrs. Dalloway*: "Don't talk about death in the middle of my party."

I recall putting up posters in the Vet Center. We had decorated most of the walls with framed pictures the veterans had brought in from their service. But in one corner, next to the bathrooms, I stuck up two posters that seemed be appropriate: one was of a movie that had just reached Seattle, Werner Herzog's *Aguirre, The Wrath of God*, about a mad Spanish Conquistador in South America, and another poster of Washington's own Mount St. Helens, that had just erupted.

My anger finally became manifest. I turned it toward the government that employed me and I finally had to resign, much to the displeasure of the hospital administration. This occurred after a dissociated veteran, one I had not seen before, with a pistol came into the center and held me captive at gunpoint and finally shot at me as I escaped. The hospital officials, including my boss, were not sympathetic (similar events had occurred at other Vet Centers), but talked to me on the telephone as if it were a minor incident. I exploded in rage: "I'm not your cannon fodder!" I shouted. In rational retrospect, of course, I was identifying with the veterans I was treating. I'm not sure what the hospital officials thought, but I knew I was, as it were, going to go off the deep end. I felt my colleagues and peers at the Department of Veterans Affairs hospital showed little understanding of what was happening — but then, to be fair, I wasn't a good communicator. Although it was their job to understand the effects of psychological trauma, few of them at that time really did. (Scurfield, 2004, pp. 73–4, saw this, also.) I was like the foolish World War I veteran in *The Last Flight* (1931) who, attending a bull fight, leaps from the stands to challenge the bull and is immediately gored.

Fortunately for me and my career, I was able to continue working out of my own office in Seattle as a therapist for veterans (because, although it seems contradictory, I enjoyed working with veterans), when, in 1983, the state of Washington, as a part of its own Department of Veterans Affairs, in a unique period of enlightenment, in a veritable alchemist's crucible, formed a PTSD treatment program for veterans who were outside the reach of, or avoiding, the federal VA, and I am grateful for the chance they gave me to continue the work. (Thanks to a Vietnam War veteran, then the WDVA director with a name out of *Parsifal*, Randy Fisher, and a Vietnam War veteran former navy corpsman, Mike McWaters.) The state project has been remarkably successful in funding counselors and therapists to work in the veterans' communities. When they have an annual meeting for contractors in the spring, the counselors seem like trappers coming out of the mountains.

It appears that about one third of those involved in combat are traumatized and develop symptoms of PTSD, although not necessarily the full disorder. Statistics tend to vary depending on a number of factors having to do with how the data was gathered, but that about 30 percent of returning veterans report symptoms seems to be a current consensus (Hoge, 2010). The U.S. Department of Defense Task Force on Mental Health in 2007 reported "postdeployment health assessment surveys indicated that more than a third (38 percent) of soldiers return from deployment with 'psychological problems'" (Bell, et al., 2011). Hoge, et al. (2004) put the rate of diagnosable PTSD in returning Iraq and Afghanistan war veterans at 13 percent, but this figure is probably artificially low, given that the veterans were answering computer questionnaires while still on active duty, where fears were expressed that positive answers might lead to delays in further processing for discharge or influence future assignments or promotion. The army has not solved the problem of stigma associated with a psychiatric diagnosis, although it is clearly working on the problem (Corman, Matthews, & Seligman, 2011). Veterans may be willing to acknowledge specific behaviors that the mental health profession would identify as symptoms, yet the veteran avoids the label of the disorder. This may well be true of most veterans of most wars. It is quite possible that stigma associated with PTSD will never dissipate so long as "illness" is attached to the disorder. Therapists may be contributing to the perception of stigma with their pathology-oriented intake and outcome questionnaires and where formal diagnoses must be made to justify fees for treatment.

Whether or not PTSD is involved, my belief is that combat in wartime, particularly wars fought on foreign soil that are far away from home, generates alienation on the part of the returning war veterans attempting to adjust to civilian life. While academics may quibble about the issue of causality, it is a repeating experience across wars that the soldier departs from home with attachments, values, and identifications that are changed with the experience of prolonged combat or military sexual trauma. While the experience of alienation may dissipate over time, many veterans proceed into old age still conscious of its influence. I speculate that combat, in any prolonged form, offering repeated exposure to potential traumas, causes a change in the values of the combatant. The person who goes into combat is changed by the experience, and evidence for that change is in the veteran's hierarchy of values. Attitude toward death, for example, is changed by the time the recruit becomes a veteran. Probably the change in personality wrought by combat is in proportion to the magnitude of the trauma(s) and the identity of the individual.

The wars fought by the United States in the 20th century and the first decade of the 21st century were all fought in foreign countries. The experience of fighting abroad is important, because the combatant experiences harsh and traumatic conditions that are often prolonged and repeated and, most importantly, are not shared by the homebodies. The so-called wars against terrorists, guerrilla wars where combatants hide among civilians, appear to aggravate alienation. The comparison might be made to western Europeans fighting colonial wars or engaged in crusades. Combatants in the current U.S. all-volunteer military are liable to experience repeated deployments and some have taken medicine to suppress post-traumatic symptoms while deployed (Calohan, et al., 2010). One observer, Madelyn Hsiao-Rei Hicks (2011), noted, citing an army mental health advisory report, that 15.8 percent of previously surveyed soldiers in Iraq reported suicidal ideation within the previous four weeks of 2007. The intense experiences that combat conditions entail lead the combatants to form attachments to the customs, artifacts, and symbols of the land in which they fought, and likely will increase the alienation felt at home.

The War Veteran Depicted in Film and Literature

The homeland culture takes the war veteran back into society and we have a record of how they are regarded in the form of the motion picture. The motion picture (movie), which first became popular in the beginning of the 20th century, has since depicted the challenges facing the war veteran in his or her adjustment. As a popular art from, the motion picture has gradually displaced literature as a cultural resource, and tends to reflect both how society views the veteran and the culture of his or her era, as well as the current culture in which the film is made. An example of this can been seen in the movie *M*A*S*H* (1970). The film, directed by a World War II veteran, Robert Altman, concerned a mobile medical unit in the Korean War, and has been widely regarded since its release as a contemporary cultural comment on the conduct of America's war in Vietnam (Zukoff, 2009).

A second example of a movie reflecting the culture in which it was created is the Elmore Leonard story *3:10 to Yuma*. Delmer Daves, who directed the first version in 1957 starring Glenn Ford as the robber and Van Heflin as the rancher, delivered the story in a fairly straightforward manner. The rancher has to escort the bandit to the train and face threats and attacks from the robber's gang. In the 2007 remake directed by James Mangold, Christian Bale plays the rancher and Russell Crowe the robber. The rancher in this version is a wounded Civil War veteran (the best shot in his regiment), and the robber quotes the Bible. Added to the remake, along with an arsenal of fireworks special effects, are scenes of torture using electric shock, the element of racism, and an added maturity and heroism to the rancher's son, suggesting that the values and awareness of the movie-viewing public has changed in the interim.

Movies during the 20th century frequently made significant comments on modern life. Cecil B. DeMille stated that there are 2,000 people who will see a movie to one who will see a play (Thomson, 2010). By 1930, 90 million Americans were going to the movies at least once a week (Dixon & Foster,

2008). Movies today are dispersed outside the theater as part of the many electronic media that are commanding increasing attention of the populace. Digital processing now allows veterans to make their own movies at reasonable cost.

A movie can be a statement about collective culture. Making a full-length movie is itself a collective enterprise, although often dominated by and reflecting the director's personality, involving artists, craftsmen, producers, publicists, costing today usually millions of dollars, the cost of which forces everyone to fashion a product that is attractive and saleable to the public. Lillian Ross (1997) gives a vivid journalist's description of the collective process of filmmaking with the production of *The Red Badge of Courage* (1951), starring the war veteran-turned movie star, Audie Murphy. Another example is provided by historian Michael Adams, who observed, "When the film *Glory* [1989] appeared people said they had never heard the story of the black regiments [in the U.S. Civil War]. There had been scholarly studies, but only with *Glory* did black soldiers enter mainstream awareness" (Adams, 1995, p. 200). A third example is from Jean Cocteau's diary of the making of *Beauty and the Beast* in 1945 in the environs of Paris, amid labor unrest and daily power failures, when it seemed that French national prestige in cinema was at stake in the quality of the outcome (Cocteau, 1972).

Thus the movie, created to be embraced by a large collective audience, becomes a reflection of that audience and a subject worth examining for what it expresses of the culture itself. Therefore, in this book I will refer to movies made about or featuring war veterans, film actors playing veterans, their friends and family members, to provide examples of what veterans and their families go through, always with the understanding that the movies are fictional stories, even if based on facts, embellished with enough drama to attract an audience. I will also include works of literature, when relevant, to enhance the presentation and with due respect for the knowledge that the literature of war veterans is extensive and beyond my ability to encompass. And I will look at the influence of war on the works of movie directors and writers who are veterans.

The war veteran has been a character common in most of the world's cultures since oral epics have been recorded in writing and it seems the influence of the veteran grows as the culture becomes more warlike. The Greek poet, Homer, in the *Odyssey*, and the Roman poet, Virgil, in the *Aeneid*, wrote of the veterans of the Trojan War and dramatized their attempts to settle in a homeland. ("Homer" may not necessarily be an individual, but the name of a collective effort, much as we think of Walt Disney today.) Jonathan Shay demonstrated this homecoming masterfully in his *Odysseus in America* (2002). Robert Penn Warren (1998, p. 82) wrote that the U.S. Civil War was "our Homeric period, and the figures loom up only a little less than gods." Veterans of wars, discharged soldiers, prove often to be influential in shaping cultural tastes and politics in their homeland. They have been incorporated into fairy tales and novels as romantic or demonic characters. War veterans in every culture range in influence from populating the homeless shelters in cities as transients to the decision-making offices of government and commerce.

The war veteran is also found in folk literature and the mythology of Western culture. The Brothers Grimm gave us "Bearskin" and "Brother Lustig," about the discharged war veteran vying with the devil. The anonymous medieval epic *Sir Gawain and the Green Knight* presents the knight who fights in the place of the king and is fated to fight again on the anniversary of the battle. War veteran authors tell their tales in fiction of the trials of adjustment to civilian life: Erich Maria Remarque's *The Road Back*, Ford Madox Ford's *Parade's End*, as well as those who associate with veterans and record their postwar adjustment experiences in fiction, such as Virginia Woolf's *Mrs. Dalloway*, Bobbie Ann Mason's *In Country*, and Somerset Maugham's *The Razor's Edge*. Other novels leave a record of the war veteran's attempts at adjustment to civilian life: Sloan Wilson's *The Man in the Grey Flannel Suit*, David Gutterson's *Snow Falling on Cedars*, Newton Thornburg's *Cutter and Bone*, Cormac McCarthy's *No Country for Old Men*, and William Wharton's *Birdy*. War veteran writers have laced their fiction with the influences of their war experiences, as have war veteran movie directors with their films: Ambrose Bierce's ghost stories, J.D. Salinger's *For Esmé with Love and Squalor*, Raymond Chandler's *The Long Goodbye*, James Jones's *Whistle*, Kurt Vonnegut's *Slaughterhouse-Five*, Joseph Heller's *Catch-22*. William Shakespeare dramatized the challenges of the returning war veteran in *Coriolanus*, which was adapted to film by Ralph Fiennes in 2012.

In my earlier work, *The War Veteran in Film*, published in 2003, I selected films in which war veterans were depicted as a measure of how the society at large viewed the wars and veterans they produced. The broad categories into which the films were clustered suggested how the veterans were portrayed: as action heroes or anti-heroes, as the wounded war veteran, the veteran aging within family, or the veteran as a disguised or comic figure.

The U.S. has been a nation at war, arguably since 1941. The Cold War was one of posturing and border wars that kept the armed forces at levels of high strength with the leading nations of the world on alert for sudden attacks and impending nuclear destruction, for such was the trauma of World War II. James Hillman (2004, p. 17) counts two wars for every year of man's historical existence. Films are being produced at this writing that concern wars that are in progress. Films about veterans of past wars often say as much about the cultures that produce the film as they do about the eras they seek to represent.

For the sake of continuity, I have relegated the synopses of the films under discussion to the second section of this book.

The Washington State Department of Veterans Affairs PTSD War Trauma Program and the federal Department of Veterans Affairs are not responsible for the content of this book. "The Odyssean Man" was originally presented as a workshop to a conference sponsored jointly by WDVA and the federal Department of Veterans Affairs in Seattle, Washington, in 1999, and has since been greatly revised.

No doubt the 21st century will produce more art forms in the protean nature of electronic media. Digital animation now makes it possible for a veteran to tell his or her own story, as we shall see. (For example, film student and Iraq War veteran Kyle Hausmann-Stokes's short movie *Now, After*, concerns his problems with adjustment to civilian life.) I here present a sampling of the movies and stories I know of and offer my observations as a clinical psychologist with a history of treating veterans.

CHAPTER 1

Kurosawa's Masterless Samurai and the Modern War Veteran

The warrior who is discharged from duty and must function without a master or source of income is on his own in a world where he has but few other marketable skills. He can fight, provide security against enemies, and perhaps offer some sage advice, but he has little interest and few means by which to earn a living. He is depicted as disconnected from the world in which he lives, with no regular residence or family. Film director Akira Kurosawa captured in his films about the Japanese samurai a character who has worked as a professional warrior and who, when the battles are over, is "discharged" from military service and left to survive on his own. The war veteran in Japan in the period following the end of World War II, when Kurosawa made these films, was forced to adjust to the reality of defeat. Stephen Prince wrote in *Warrior's Camera*: "Kurosawa's contemporary films are attempts to redefine the cultural boundaries of modern Japan by dramatizing the emergence out of the ashes and wreckage of war, of a new type of individual, whose example is tested in confrontations with contemporary ills" (1991, p. 200).

In Japanese society, particularly under the militaristic wartime government, the individual existed for the emperor. Emphasis on individual happiness was censored as unpatriotic. In the tradition of the masterless samurai, when that devotion was broken, the individual samurai was free to direct his loyalty to the group of his choice. The tradition of the devotion to the collective continues in Japan, now more as loyalty of the worker to his or her employer, or the ballplayer to his team, even at the sacrifice of individual happiness (Buruma, 1996, p. 246). However, the question of individuality itself is complex, as McGilchrist (2009, p. 456) elaborates: "The Japanese word for self, *jibun*, implies a share of something which is both separate and

13

not separate, individual and yet still shared. It is a common Western misconception that Japanese culture does not value the individual."

Kurosawa made the following three movies about masterless samurai at a time when Japan was occupied with integrating a large population of veterans of their defeated armed forces: *Seven Samurai* (1954), *Yojimbo* (1961), and *Sanjuro* (1962). Samurai films were not made during the period of the American Occupation of Japan from 1945 to 1952 due to censorship of films having to do with feudalism or swordplay (Hirano, 1992, pp. 67–70; Buruma, 2003, p. 135). (Films mentioned here and elsewhere in this essay are reviewed in the second half of this book.)

The key to the connection of the modern war veteran and the masterless samurai is their mutual status as disconnected from society. While many veterans successfully reintegrate in some fashion, through work, school, church, sports (or most often through relationships, as Ray Scurfield observed), there is yet a loss of connection for many others who appear successful. The loss of connection is in the veteran's frame of reference, which for the veteran has been changed by the experience of foreign war, an important referent not shared with fellow citizens. The values learned in combat may be applied in civilian life, but they are seldom met. The early scenes of *Seven Samurai* mimic scenes of war veterans passing in the streets, unemployed yet still primed for combat. When the seven samurai are recruited by farmers whose village is threatened by a roving gang of bandits, Kurosawa clearly defines each samurai as an individual who is recruited not for material reward, but for the honor of fighting again. The samurai organize the defenses of the village. When the bandits return to the village in the driving rain for the final battle, the samurai respond and take charge of the anxious villagers. It is what the samurai are fated to do, to fight and die, without reward. Kambei (Takashi Shimura), the samurai leader, identifies himself as a *ronin*. He states, "I'm not a man with any special skill but I've had plenty of experience in battles, losing battles, all of them. In short, that's all I am."

In Japanese culture the term *ronin* implies shame. It is currently applied for those who fail exams, but in medieval times it was applied to the warriors who were no longer employed, but whose skills were regarded in peacetime more often as threat than as security. In Japanese tradition, the defeated nobility committed suicide. Their warriors became *ronin* who shared the shame of the defeated.

For most of recorded history discharged soldiers, the veterans of wars, have been regarded with anxiety by the society that no longer needs their services. Upon their retirement, the veterans of the Roman Legions who survived their years of military service were given plots of land on the borders of the empire, serving the purpose both of stabilizing such regions as well as keeping the retired soldiers far away from Rome (Webster, 1981, p. 24). Jonathan Sumption in his comprehensive history *The Hundred Years War* gives many examples, from 14th century Europe, of the havoc created by discharged soldiers forming marauding companies to pillage the poorly defended villages and towns. For many farmers and villagers of that era, the most dangerous times were the periods of truce. Between the soldiers and the plagues of that era, some areas of France were reduced in population by 90 percent (Sumption, 2009). Although the comparison is to very different cultures, the Japanese society of 1954, when *Seven Samurai* was released, had the task of absorbing discharged veterans from a defeated militaristic dynasty. Ian Buruma (2003, p. 169), upon visiting Japan in 1976, reports, "Small traces of war were still visible then. Veterans without arms or legs, dressed in white kimonos, sat outside the railway stations, playing sad wartime tunes on their keening accordions."

Yojimbo establishes the theme that Kurosawa developed early in his career, depicting the samurai warrior as a man who does not belong to the community, which, in this case, is fraught with bad characters on both sides. The town merchants and their henchmen are corrupt and their destructive end seems deserved. That Kurosawa struck a chord with the public is indicated by *Yojimbo*'s popularity in Japan and its continued international acclaim. *Sanjuro* continues the saga of the vagabond warrior, played by Toshirô Mifune, helping young affluent samurai reform corruption in their clan by engaging in combat and feats of daring. In *Yojimbo* and *Sanjuro*, the masterless samurai departs the community, as he entered, alone. Again, he gives his loyalty to the group of his own choosing, in the case of *Sanjuro*, to young samurai who are fighting injustice.

In *Seven Samurai*, the character Kikuchiyo, played by Toshirô Mifune, is an offspring of peasant farmers; he is also a bawdy, rude character who becomes a warrior before he is killed. In *Yojimbo* and *Sanjuro*, Mifune plays a samurai warrior who, although a member of an elite profession, is impoverished and rough, but a man free of obligation. What Kurosawa has captured in his samurai films, and what the American Western has so frequently captured, is the alienation of the war veteran attempting to survive after the war. Ted Kotcheff famously portrayed Sylvester Stallone as Vietnam War veteran John Rambo in *First Blood* (1982), walking down a country road dressed in an army fatigue jacket, carrying only a sleeping bag, unjustly harassed by the town's lawman.

Archetypes are formed through the ages as warriors return home after the war and repeat similar experiences (Jung, 1971, p. 48: "There are as many archetypes as there are typical situations in life"). Alexander (2009, p. 95) writes that folklore heroes "tend to stand out as lonely wanderers as folk from far away or from nowhere." The inviting opportunity in film storytelling is the social commentary of society viewed from the isolation of a man who is living where he doesn't feel he belongs. Prince, in his review of Kurosawa's films writes: "Referring to the chaotic condition of Japan's culture and economy immediately following the second world war, Kurosawa remarked, 'I believe at that time that for Japan to recover it was necessary to place a high value on the self'" (Prince, 1991, p. 29). Kurosawa's films of the masterless samurai stress the survivor's individuality after the fall of his master.

The symbol of the masterless warrior who does not belong to the community captures the feeling of estrangement in the modern war veteran. The symbol today has to do with habitual ways of thinking and behaving; the veteran's frame of reference being influenced by memories of combat conditions, all of which constitutes a difference, distinct or ambiguous, between the veteran and his home community, a difference that was not present before deployment to the combat zone. This complex mix of estrangement and feelings of strong potential are subsumed in the romance of the masterless samurai.

Jean-Pierre Melville, who was himself involved in combat in the French Resistance of World War II (see his 1969 autobiographical film, *Army of Shadows*), directed the 1967 noir film *Le Samourai*. He wanted to give his nameless hit man a schizoid personality (Melville called him schizophrenic), that was unresponsive to most relationships and who, wearing white gloves, killed remorselessly. Melville's stylized hit man mimics the masterless samurai. The director exaggerates the symbol for illustration and flat effect is taken as cool.

The contemporary combat veteran is not necessarily schizoid; in fact, he or she may relate competently and functionally in the community, yet *feel* estranged, impatient, annoyed, and more or less vaguely in peril, as if the veteran were unconsciously expecting something dangerous to happen. The opening quote by E.B. Sledge, is by a war veteran of Pacific island battles of World War II, who returned to a welcoming family and went on to college and an academic career, yet *felt* the estrangement. Joseph Heller, author of *Catch-22*, beautifully described this sense of impending peril lingering in the war veteran in his second novel, *Something Happened* (Daugherty, 2011, p. 320).

The compatibility of the samurai of Japanese culture with the American West of the 19th century makes the Western movies of John Ford, Sam Peckinpah, Clint Eastwood, and others, attuned across cultures with Kurosawa, Melville, and Sergio Leone. Lately, film director Clint Eastwood has adapted the theme of the estranged war veteran to modern times with his films *Absolute Power* (1997) and *Gran Torino* (2008), both of which concern Korean War combat veterans who remained maladapted and estranged into old age after suffering the loss of their spouses. This theme was captured nicely in a 1995 low budget film *Lonely Are the Brave*, also about a Korean War Veteran. Victor

Nuñez's *Ulee's Gold* (1997) and Daniel Barber's *Harry Brown* (2010) also capture this theme; again, the aging veteran's isolation after the loss of his spouse.

The anonymity of the samurai represents the duality of the war veteran who has adopted a persona of adjustment, but whose strong memories are of a combatant who is now hidden and more or less secret. This sense of dual identity can be integrated by a number of creative techniques, not the least of which is the commitment to a relationship with a person of trust. Hoge (2010, p. 177) advocates for establishing a narrative that incorporates the veteran's combat into his civilian identity. This duality may also be revealed in creative works other than films, as exemplified by a rich history of combatants who became artists. (See Chapter 7.)

Early postwar estrangement may also be made worse by maladaptive personality style and the formation of habits for coping that perpetuate the feelings, what Briere, Hodges, and Godbout (2010) term "dysfunctional avoidance." The veteran may find more solace in a subculture, such as law enforcement, a trade of physically demanding perilous work, or an outlaw club membership, where the warrior's estrangement is understood and even honored, and where relationships may be formed in a particular environment that itself never integrates fully into the dominant culture. J.D. Salinger's biographer, Kenneth Slawenski (2010, p. 321n) relates a pertinent observation that Salinger's World War II combat partner in the 12th Infantry, John Keenan, who went through all the traumas that afflicted Salinger, went on to become chief of homicide detectives in the NYPD. So while Salinger was baring his soul and withdrawing from society, which, one could argue, proved for him dysfunctional, Keenan was grappling with society's worst stressors, as Slawenski writes, continuing "the career he had begun with the Counter Intelligence Corps."

The theme of the war veteran as masterless samurai is exploited for many action films. War veterans are hired for criminal capers and for the protection of citizens in John Frankenheimer's 1998 film, *Ronin*, which is pure action, exploiting the idea of ex-soldiers who are for hire. *Ronin* begins with a solemn reference to the samurai of medieval Japan, where "the warrior class of samurai were sworn to protect their liege lords with their lives. Those samurai whose liege was killed suffered a great shame, and they were forced to wander the land, looking for work as hired swords or bandits. These masterless warriors were no longer referred to as samurai. They were known by another name: such men were called Ronin." The remainder of the film, however, which seems more inspired by auto racing, makes no further reference to the Japanese tradition.

John Sturges's *The Magnificent Seven* (1960) is an undisguised imitation of Kurosawa's *Seven Samurai*, exploiting the romantic formula that worked so well in Japan of action and nostalgia with a group of distinct individuals. It was Kurosawa's desire to make films that displayed a sense of individuality as a way to adjust in a postwar Japan that was having democracy and American values imposed (Prince, 1991, p. 200). Shortly after his last film, *Dreams* (1990), was released, Kurosawa made a trip to the U.S. to accept an award. The film he wanted to see first when he arrived was Martin Scorsese's *Taxi Driver* (1976), which depicted the urban plight of the isolated discharged war veteran. In *Dreams*, as mentioned in my previous work (Early, 2003), Kurosawa has a short film, *Tunnel*, devoted to a Japanese army officer returning home after his incarceration as a prisoner of war. He had sacrificed his company in battle and had been captured. Kurosawa's war veteran is followed through the tunnel by the ghosts of his dead soldiers. Kurosawa was never in the military, therefore this short film, if it is indeed a depiction of his dream, perhaps represents how he, as a citizen, felt about the war. Kurosawa was an art student and apprentice director during the war, although his father was a strict military influence as a graduate of a military academy (Kurosawa, 1982). His postwar (1949) *Stray Dog* portrays a young policeman (Toshirô Mifune), whose pistol has been stolen, wandering through the crowded streets of Tokyo, disguised as a war veteran in search of his lost weapon. The disguise he chose was apparently a common sight on the streets of the city. (The bombing of Japanese cities left nine million homeless at the end of the war.) The policeman whose pistol was stolen is shamed and he anticipates guiltily that harm will be committed with his weapon, which becomes a profound symbol for occupied Japan in defeat. In fact, both the policeman and the criminal who winds up with the pistol are war veterans, both of whom were robbed on their return home after repatriation. One of the veterans turned to crime upon discharge; the other, to law enforcement. Their final deadly struggle captures, symbolically, the conflict of postwar adjustment (Hirano, 1992, p. 78; Prince, 1991). Hirano writes of the American postwar occupation censorship of that period in relation to *Stray Dog*.

> Repatriated POWs and veterans experienced many difficulties, financial and psychological alike, in adjusting to the postwar life of their homeland. However, these difficulties could not serve as an excuse for repatriates turning to crime, according to the [American] censors. They therefore excised from a film a line of dialogue concerning a returning soldier taking up black marketeering because he could not find a job. In the script of another film, a black marketer character was permitted only after the army uniform he was originally to wear was changed to civilian clothes.
>
> The type of treatment given this issue in Kurosawa's *Stray Dog* [*Norainu*] (1949), written by Kurosawa and Ryuzo Kikushima, must have been exactly what the American censors wanted [p. 78].

The theme of the good veteran versus the bad veteran and the fight over a gun was examined again, this time by American film director Lewis Allen, in *Suddenly* (1954). The good veteran is the town sheriff, while the bad veteran is a mentally ill former infantry sniper, who is trying to assassinate the president of the United States. The battle over the gun is accented by a war widow who forbids her son to have a toy gun or to see war movies. The bad veteran, played by Frank Sinatra, claims he won the Silver Star for killing in Italy, but it appears he was sent home and discharged before the end of the war for reasons due perhaps to mental illness. The sheriff (Sterling Hayden) is in love with the widow and the sniper picks her home from which to shoot the president, whose train is due to stop at the town of Suddenly. The gangsters disarm the sheriff and shoot him in the arm, but in the final struggle over the control of guns, the boy shoots and misses, the widow shoots and hits the sniper, and, finally, the sheriff kills him with a pistol shot. The parallels with *Stray Dog* are remarkable. Both films show the wounded good veteran, the one representing authority, as finally prevailing. One doubts if such a struggle would have the same outcome during the Vietnam War era, for it seems that two large factions were spawned in America as offspring of the World War II generation. One faction represented the authority as legitimate, the other challenged authority in the form of political activism in Civil Rights and Women's Liberation movements, and came to clash over the legitimacy of the war American troops fought in Vietnam.

The theme of two veterans fighting can also be seen in the 1962 film *Lonely Are the Brave*. A veteran of Okinawa (where he lost an arm) and a recipient of the Purple Heart for his duty in Korea, start a brawl in a tavern. The one-armed World War II veteran was described as "a tough hombre" by the police and seemed deadly serious in his anger. The Korean War veteran, a cowboy, played by Kirk Douglas, seems motivated toward a higher goal, but also seeks the fight.

There is a relationship between the Toshirô Mifune character, Detective Murakami, in *Stray Dog*, and the characters he plays in the three movies that feature the masterless samurai. In *Seven Samurai* the principal samurai, Kambei (Takashi Shimura) is noble and dignified, whereas the Mifune character, Kikuchiyo, is earthy and clownish, representing the split of characters in *Stray Dog*. The two sets of characteristics are combined in the earthy samurai, Sanjuro Kuwaratake, in *Yojimbo*, and Sanjuro Tsubaki, in *Sanjuro*, both played by Toshirô Mifune. In the latter two films he maintains his noble performance while displaying earthy qualities: scratching, yawning, disdaining form for substance (performance) when he goes into combat. It can be said of Kurosawa, that he spoke to the West of Europe and the United States, which shows the combat veteran as an ordinary person who is capable of extraordinary performance.

CHAPTER 2

Films Featuring Veterans
of the Wars on Terror

Veterans of foreign wars have a particular challenge when they return home. Many are still young and have yet to start a civilian career. They have been part of an intense subculture with its own jargon and values. They have witnessed and participated in the brutalities of war, while their fellow citizens have lived in a land at peace. American veterans of the First World War were greeted at home by a worldwide economic depression with very high unemployment, while being a step behind their civilian brothers in terms of career and more or less isolated from fellow veterans because of their dispersal across the nation and the lack of opportunities for communication. The Second World War was a part of a worldwide social and economic upheaval and the mass of returning military men and women were partly absorbed by the liberal federal legislation assisting veterans with education and housing (Mettler, 2005). The veterans of the Vietnam War were met with anti-war protesters and social upheaval (demonstrations for racial equality, women's rights, and vehement antiwar sentiment) at home, and although they did have the GI Bill, they had to tolerate the sometimes hostile campus culture to take advantage of the benefits that had been reduced since World War II. Veterans of the Wars on Terror, involving mainly wars in Iraq and Afghanistan, have returned to a land still at war with no clear end in sight in an electronic age of mass communication, Internet connectedness, and a staggering economy with high unemployment. These are also the first wars fought with PTSD in the psychiatric diagnostic manual. The combatants grew up accepting that PTSD was a fact and a risk of war along with physical injury. PTSD was introduced following the Vietnam War and those veterans were viewed by the public for the first time as a group potentially disturbed by combat. Previously, war veterans who were shell-shocked or burdened with combat fatigue were more often than not deemed to be the product of disturbed childhoods. The 1954 movie *Suddenly* was an example of depicting the disturbed veteran along-side a solid veteran; the former was, as a child, raised by bad parents and dumped into an orphanage. As the wars on terror continue, veterans of those wars are shown struggling to adjust to civilian life with knowledge of PTSD in the background.

At the time of this writing, there are 13 films that feature veterans of the Wars on Terror: *The Dry Land* (2010), *Oliver Sherman* (2010), *The Messenger* (2009), *Stop Loss* (2008), *In the Valley of Elah* (2007), *The Hurt Locker* (2008), *Brothers* (2009), *The Lucky Ones* (2008), *Restrepo* (2010), *The Veteran* (2011), *Jarhead* (2005), *Taking Chance* (2009), and *The Jacket* (2005) (if we count the first Gulf War as a war on terror), and the short film *Now, After* (2010). In different ways, several of them (except for *The Dry Land*, *The Lucky Ones*, and *Oliver Sherman*) have a way of showing us the battlefield through tech-nology that puts the viewer at the forefront of combat while, at the same time, creating a safe distance. The use of video-phone cameras has become the action photography of this age, as the post-election demonstrations in Iran and other anti-government demonstrations in the Middle East have recently shown. *Stop Loss* shows the GI-made video, what used to be called home movies, featuring the soldiers' lighter side in Iraq. *In the Valley of Elah* presents the forensic reconstruction of cell-phone video of GIs in combat that is central to the plot. *The Hurt Locker*, like *Jarhead*, creates false intimacy at a distance through sharpshooter scopes. IEDs (improvised explosive devises) are command detonated by cell phones. *Brothers* puts the video equipment into the hands of a Taliban recorder, leaving the terrorist dead and the equip-ment smashed when Americans raid. In *The Messenger*, the soldiers who carry news of combat casualties to the next of kin are on call and notified by cell phone and pager. Their rigid adherence to protocol protects them from grief-sharing empathy. This protocol is followed in *Taking Chance*, which follows the escort of a Marine casualty from Iraq. In *The Dry Land* the veteran sadly views a video sent to him when he was in Iraq, showing a cheery birthday party for him in his absence. Being home, he soon realized, was not at all cheery. *Restrepo*, which is a non-fiction documentary that devotes most of its attention on a U.S. 173rd Infantry company in Afghanistan, and which follows some of the men after discharge, has the video combat action recorded by professional cinematographers, and captures the combatants between firefights on their cell phones, calling home, and playing hand-held video games in their bunker. *The Jacket* shows the battlefield of the 1991 Gulf War in a mon-tage of confusing, surrealistic video images.

These films about veterans of the Wars on Terror are signaling that war-fare is in the electronic age. In Vietnam it seemed bizarre that grunts carried radios and cameras into the bush. In World War II, a soldier might come across a Victrola or music box in a blasted building and play a record. (Film director Samuel Fuller, as a World War II infantryman, drew cartoon pictures of his war [Fuller, 2002].) Current warriors play video games when they're off duty. In these Wars on Terror the grunts make their own movies and talk to their friends back home before they go out on patrol. This ease of electronic communication is a two-way street, and for the veteran it means that he or she is never far away from the war even when back home, and, conversely, potentially saddled with mundane problems from the homeland while in combat. Kyle Hausmann-Stokes is perhaps unique in making his short movie, *Now, After*, about himself attempting to adjust to college life after combat deployment in Iraq.

All of these recent films depict the veteran as being impacted by the war; most profoundly in *In the Valley of Elah*, which is based on a true story, in which veterans kill one of their own; in *Brothers*, where torture in captivity has caused the veteran to inhibit his ability to relate to his family; and in *Oliver Sherman*, where brain injury and cognitive damage appears to have limited a veteran socially. One veteran in *Stop Loss* commits suicide, while the other, who has been "stop-lossed," futilely seeks redress from his senator in Washington, D.C., against forced return to combat. The veteran in *The Hurt Locker* cannot relate warmly to his wife or child and returns to combat. The veteran in *Brothers* wants to leave his family and return to combat, where he thinks he can relate, although his CO wisely thinks otherwise. The veteran in *The Dry Land* is wracked with guilt about surviving the ambush of a Humvee he realized he may have caused by his compassion (stopping to help wounded civilians). The Marine veterans in *Jarhead* are paraded in a bus when they return, but the viewer is left with a feeling that it was a huge anticlimax that will always be a source of guilt for not getting into the fray, after spending months in staging awaiting combat. In *The Messenger* the soldier is recovering from wounds, particularly affecting his vision. Sherman Oliver, in the Canadian film about an Iraq war veteran *Oliver Sherman*, has been brain injured by a blast, and finds he cannot fit in, even with the help of the veteran who saved him. Similarly, the Gulf War veteran in *The Jacket* is brain-injured with retrograde amnesia that causes him to lose his identity. The three veterans in *The Lucky Ones* are all wounded, two with wounds from combat, and one with a back injury from a combat zone accident, and find they do not fit in civilian life and return to the army and Iraq.

In the Valley of Elah and *Stop Loss* are blatantly political anti-war messages. *In the Valley of Elah* depicts the veterans just back from Iraq as irreparably damaged by their combat experiences. *The Hurt Locker* depicts the veteran as addicted to the excitement of his work to the extent that he is unable to tolerate peaceful domesticity. In *Brothers* the veteran's traumas at the hands of the Taliban caused his consciousness to constrict and the veteran to lose his emotional flexibility, and, as tends to happen in such cases, paranoia results for that which is outside the emotional range. The veterans of *Stop Loss* are depicted as finally accepting their fate. They are being forced to return to combat against their will, while at the same time the film ducks the contentious question of the contract that the enlistee's signed which informed them of the possibility of just such treatment. Veterans of the Second World War encountered a similar fate when the Korean War began in 1950. William Styron was among those caught up in the recall as a Marine reservist (Styron, 2009). Melinda Pash (2012) records the desperate call-up of World War II reservists during the Korean War. Fate seems to similarly work in the message of *The Hurt Locker*, when the veteran goes back to work at the job he knows will eventually kill him. The politics of *The Messenger* is eloquently expressed by the intense and sometimes explosive grief of the next of kin, similar to the stoic grief of the kin at the funeral in *Taking Chance*. *The Lucky Ones* is mixed about the reception the veterans receive from civilians, but shows empathy of other veterans for those who have just returned.

Brothers gives us hope of, if not recovery, at least readjustment. In that film, Sam, the veteran, confesses his traumatic deed to his wife, after much urging. He has been hospitalized after his destructive rage, and meets his wife on a day pass from the VA hospital. *Brothers* doesn't overplay the scene, but cautiously hints at optimism. The political appeal of the films is not generally overplayed; the focus on the costs of war on the veteran makes sufficient statement. *The Messenger* gives a similar glimmer of hope as the veteran, Will, wins an invitation to write to Olivia as she leaves town. *The Dry Land* speaks directly to the family and friends who attempt to relate to the veteran who is struggling to adjust to his memories of trauma in Iraq. *Oliver Sherman* depicts the brain-injured veteran as lost without hope, while the veteran who saved him proves he is adaptable. The horror of sadistic mental health treatment seems torturous for the veteran in *The Jacket*, yet he is able to prevail and survive with a positive outcome.

America has been at war since the Japanese attack on Pearl Harbor, it seems, and this latest war, the so-called War on Terror (particularly the wars fought in Iraq and Afghanistan), has the ambiguity that offers no foreseeable end. The wind-down of the U.S. commitment in Iraq has a tentative feel to it, with combat troops staged nearby. The United States seems staggered by the impact of the wars, which populate our culture with a steadily increasing number of affected war veterans and their families in stress, and the old debate reemerges: Do wars cause emotional trauma or are posttraumatic symptoms encouraged by the potential for compensation? *In the Valley of Elah* hits this subject with a hard hammer blow, telling its story, based on fact, that veterans just returned from a combat tour in Iraq, still on active duty, murder their friend and attempt to destroy his body without expressing any true remorse. The Vietnam War veteran father of the murder victim (he was an MP in Vietnam), pursues the investigation of his son's murder with an ideal about how combat veterans are supposed to care about one another. In the final scene of the film, he flies his flag, the one he carried in Vietnam and gave to his son to fly in Iraq, not at half staff, but upside-down, a signal of a nation in distress.

The 11 films that have made it into the first-run theaters (*Now, After* was never theatrically released, and *The Dry Land* and *Oliver Sherman* have had, so far, only film festival showings) have not done well at the box office, with the possible exception of *The Hurt Locker*, a tense tale of hazardous combat work disarming IEDs, which earned an Academy Award for Best Picture. Its hero is a soldier portrayed as locked in his work as the doomed suicide bomber he attempts to disarm. Tim Robbins had an insight into why movies about war veterans don't do well in time of war when he was interviewed about being approached for the lead role in *The Player* (1992): "It was kind of a critical time for me when I met Bob [director Robert Altman]. *Jacob's Ladder* had just come out and tanked. No one saw it. It was as if the universe conspired to create the worst possible environment for a movie about a Vietnam veteran who was having hallucinations. It was two or three weeks before we went into the Gulf the first time, the Gulf War. So the country was not in the mood for a movie that was in any way critical of the military or in any way questioning the military" (Zuckoff, 2009, p. 407). Robbins fails to mention that *Jacob's Ladder* was a horror film, a very scary tale of war veterans doomed by unknowingly participating in a government experiment, depicting with bizarre flourish perhaps the ultimate in postwar alienation. It may also be true that the public is not ready for the psychological dimension of postwar adjustment. World War II Hollywood filmmakers had the business savvy to perceive that the public wanted dramatic action and gave them the contest of the veteran versus the corrupt society as a metaphor for psychological conflict.

One wonders if this is the collective message the films convey about our country's Wars on Terror: that we are locked into a battle that is ill-defined and bound to be repeated. Our soldiers are valiant and heroic in their work, and technology, hard-learned battle tactics, medical intervention, all produce gains, gems found in the mud, but the cost is prohibitively expensive in both dollars and collective identity. In *Brothers*, the Vietnam War veteran father struggles to express empathy to his Iraq War veteran son. It is sad for old veterans to see the perpetual wheel roll on.

Oliver Sherman, *Brothers*, and *The Dry Land* are movies about family relationships. The directors present their movies as not political, yet the atmosphere of the films is all about death and as grim as *In The Valley of Elah*, which was directly political. It is a wonder how any film about veterans returning home could not be political if it is intimate enough to show war's tragic effects.

The Dry Land portrays the veteran in this film as vulnerable and not yet defended by methods of coping. The veteran, James, admits that he lied about symptoms on his post-deployment screening because he didn't want his discharge to be held up. To the ER doctor at the army medical center where he gets his head wound (from a drunken brawl) treated, James admits with manly understatement that he's "been on edge." The doctor gives him an appointment with a psychiatrist for the next week, which does not seem as immediately helpful. The doctor also gives James a prescription, "Something for anxiety," and we see James periodically for the rest of the picture quaffing pills from the amber plastic container, in a manner reminiscent of Travis Bickle in *Taxi Driver*.

How many films about agony and discomfort of war veterans can be made before becoming, as a critic of *The Dry Land* opined, generic "echoes of every stress disordered vet movie in history"? I would suggest that the "generic echoes" are, in fact, archetypal motifs played out in 21st century dress. The conflict depicted in the films about veterans of the Wars on Terror are indeed quite similar to the Vietnam War era, and the post–World War II era. The spouse and friends of the veteran struggle to understand. Parents want the veteran to get on with life. Veterans bounce like those stainless steel pinballs, from one clanging barrier to another, reacting with sometimes accelerated motion. The difference of this new crop of war veteran films is that they are largely psychological struggles rather than dramatic struggles against the evil in society.

Yet for all the films and stories about veterans of other wars, dating back to Erich Maria Remarque's thoughtful *The Road Back* (which was made into a film in 1937), the director of *The Dry Land*, Ryan Piers Williams, acknowledged that he only just discovered PTSD as a problem for veterans. A big difference this time around is that the military is supporting a film that depicts with dramatic candor the perils of postwar adjustment. The shift is seen in the federal government's attitude toward the reality of the difficulty that veterans have when they return home, which is reflected in Charles Hoge's book, *Once a Warrior Always a Warrior*, and in the army's confrontation with PTSD (Casey, 2011), that argues for the broader perspective that postwar adjustment struggles are normal and expected, and that help is available. Yet James's memory block is not normal, but rather posttraumatic psychopathology that should warrant a diagnosis of PTSD. And if PTSD is normal in a society, it is surely an indication that the society is under great stress.

Iraq War veteran Brian Castner (2012) addresses this issue candidly in a scene in his memoir, as an explosive ordinance expert in Iraq who attempts to adjust to civilian life. His psychotherapist decides after talking with him that he does not have PTSD:

> "Just because you feel all those things doesn't mean you have PTSD," she chides gently.
> "So if I'm not Crazy, then what's wrong with me?"
> She laughs a silver waterfall of ringing bells.
> "You're human," she says [Castner, 2012, pp. 218–219].

Sherman Oliver's brain injury impairs his ability to be a contributing member of society. He becomes a drag on the veteran who has found a way to fit, through family. The story reminds us that follow-up of therapy is essential to postwar adjustment, and very often the intervention that is least thought through. Kyle Hausmann-Stokes's *Now, After* is a short film that he made as a student. It dramatizes his difficulty as a veteran of the Iraq war adjusting to civilian life as a student. The veteran suffers from a sleep disturbance and, on waking and packing to go out of doors, he is shown going in and out of intrusive memories of combat. The film ends with the veteran going to a VA hospital and being supported by other veterans of various ages in the hospital waiting room. The film has been widely praised in veteran mental health circles and adopted by the Department of Veterans Affairs.

In *The Lucky Ones*, the returning army reservist is met with rejection from his wife and learns that his job has disappeared because of a factory closing. He becomes depressed and suicidal, but, with the help of his veteran friends, manages to regain his spirit. He then re-enlists to get a bonus to pay for his son's education. Still, there is a sense that his option is one of choosing without regard for his own well-being.

The Wars on Terror, of course, have not been exclusively American, nor even exclusively involving military. *Oliver Sherman* is Canadian, although the production crew did its best to obliterate nationality. *The Veteran* features a UK veteran of the war against the Taliban in Afghanistan who returns to a violent life in his homeland. The alienation in his mind is more than matched by the alienating violence in his neighborhood. The nation of Israel has fought terrorism from hostile states on its borders since its U.N. founding mandate (see *Waltz with Bashir*). And the U.S.-Mexican border has experienced a recent upsurge of violence that has come from criminal gangs organized around drug trafficking, who have taken up the tactical use of campaigns of terror that mimic organized terror movements in other countries, and seems to be a 21st century repeat of the legacy of early 20th century Prohibition (see *No Country for Old Men*).

CHAPTER 3

The War Veteran
in a Dark Time

The victorious U.S. veterans of World War II experienced, on the one hand, unprecedented GI benefits. The veterans of World War I, who marched to Washington, D.C., during the Great Depression seeking the small bonus that had been promised them, had no inkling that their government would later be capable of bestowing such largess, although it was probably their demonstration of activism, the notorious Bonus Army, which led the government to be concerned about the prospect of angry war veterans organizing after the ending of World War II hostilities (Dickson & Allen, 2004, Mettler, 2005). Ben Shephard wrote, "American veterans of World War II are generally regarded as the most fortunate in history" (2001, p. 329). Films featuring war veterans during the Depression era were gloomy: *The Last Flight* (1931), *I Am a Fugitive from a Chain Gang* (1932), and *Heroes for Sale* (1933) show the war veterans much abused and misunderstood, fading into the darkness at the end of their struggle to survive.

Injustice dominates *Heroes for Sale*, directed by William A. Wellman. Richard Barthelmess plays Tom Holmes, who performs heroically in the trenches but is wounded and captured, while his cowardly friend takes the glory and is promoted and lauded as a hero. After the armistice Tom is repatriated dependent on morphine to treat intractable back pain. He develops a heroin habit, apparently because he is cut off from treatment, is fired from his job at a bank, incarcerated at a treatment farm, and improbably cured in a few months (no further mention is made of his back pain). He succeeds at another job but is caught up in a workers riot, which he was trying to stop, and is sentenced to prison again, this time for five years of hard labor. When he is released, he is wealthy because of his investments, but gives all his money to a soup kitchen and goes on the road with jobless men. His acts are saint-like and he is a martyr to injustice, his veteran status ignored. He complains to a railroad cop as they are driven in the rain out of the railroad yard: "Who're you calling hoboes? We're ex-servicemen." (The origin of the word hobo is attributed to transient Civil War veterans looking for work with garden hoes [Shay, 2002].)

On the other hand, veterans of World War II were thrown into a dark time of world reclamation of war debt, both literal economic worldwide debt, massive population disruption that had been caused by the wartime industrial boom, paranoid fear of the repetition of war manifested as anti–Communism and the polarity of the Cold War, symbolic exhaustion from the energy expended in the war, and fear of the potential of the A-Bomb. Hollywood had participated in the war, in its own way, and endured the restrictions. The shortages of lighting, set materials, and personnel led to a tendency to shoot dark, low-budget films that reflected the mood of the times (Doherty, 1993). The French, during the German Occupation, had no exposure to American film while the war was waged. After the war, the French critics saw a half decade of Hollywood productions in the course of a short time and some critics were struck with the style of a genre they termed *film noir* (Borde & Chaumeton, 2002). The French critics made special note of the influence of war veterans in American film: "There was, however, another aspect to this work: the difficulty soldiers have in readapting to civilian life, their disarray when faced with the new responsibilities that are their lot, and the uncertainty of their status" (p. 115). French film critic Robin Buss writes: "The historical moment [of the post–World War II *film noir*] also accounts for the fact that many of the protagonists of American *film noir* are war veterans, often scarred by their experiences or, at least, alienated from the cozy small-town environment to which they return" (Buss, 1994, pp. 25–6).

A sampling of films of this dark era depicting war veterans are *The Blue Dahlia* (1946), *Till the End of Time* (1946), *Crossfire* and *Ride the Pink Horse* (1947), *The Third Man* and *Thieves Highway* (1949), *In a Lonely Place* and *The Men* (1950), *Kansas City Confidential* (1952), *Human Desire* and *Suddenly* (1954), *Nightfall* (1956), and *Elevator to the Gallows* (1958). Carol Reed's *The Third Man* is listed here among films about returning war veterans, although its plot features the search for a black marketer in bomb-ravaged Vienna, who was a product of the war, and the movie sets the dark mood of the war's influence perhaps better than any other film of that period. Originally the protagonist, Holly Martins, was depicted as a war veteran, but that attribution was dropped in the film (Greene, 1977).

The returning veterans run into trouble. Mark Halprin (2012), in his romantic novel about a World War II veteran, *In Sunlight and in Shadow*, makes a case that the underworld gangsters had a resurgence of organized activity during the war. Thieves harm those close to the veteran and he has to take revenge to set the record straight. The screenplay for George Marshall's *The Blue Dahlia* was written by World War I veteran, mystery writer Raymond Chandler. It concerns a discharged navy pilot, Johnny, played by Alan Ladd, who returns home to find that his wife has caused their son's death by her drunken driving. He is accused of her murder when she is found shot to death after his visit — shot with his pistol. The original screenplay had one of the navy crewmen (Buzz, played by William Bendix), who was drinking with Johnny, committing the murder in a blackout caused by his wartime brain injury. The censoring board of the Breen Office, however, refused to allow a war veteran to be depicted as committing such a heinous act, and the plot was changed, and weakened, by having the murder committed by the local hotel detective with the chilling nickname, Dad.

Hollywood did take racial and ethnic prejudice seriously and, in Edward Dmytryk's *Crossfire* (1947), World War II veteran, Montgomery (Robert Ryan), is revealed as the killer of another medically discharged combat veteran in civilian clothes, who seemed to be killed because he was Jewish, although he was labeled by others as a draft dodger. Interestingly, in the novel by Richard Brooks, *The Brick Foxhole*, upon which the screenplay was based, the murdered combat veteran was killed because he was homosexual. In *Crossfire*, Montgomery was depicted as virtually psychotic with his paranoid hatred.

Two noir films about World War II veterans have an important common motif. In *Ride the Pink Horse* (1947) the war veteran, Lucky Gagin (Robert Montgomery), is motivated to seek vengeance against a gangster who caused the death of his buddy. He travels to New Mexico and boldly challenges the realm of the gangster. With the aid of a local native girl who nurses him back from a beating, he is able to prevail. In *Thieves' Highway* (1949), the veteran is Nick, played by Richard Conte, who takes over his father's trucking business when his father is injured as a result of sabotage on his truck, injured by gangsters who control the San Francisco produce market. This veteran is also aided by a local woman, Rika (Valentina Cortese), who is herself a war refugee working as a prostitute. In neither movie is the veteran's wartime record discussed, other than to declare its existence. Both movies rely on the veterans' innate determination and courage to prevail.

The veteran who is wrongly accused and driven into hiding, described in *The Blue Dahlia*, is also found in *Kansas City Confidential* (1952), in which John Payne plays a World War II veteran who is just out of prison, having been convicted of a gambling beef. He is framed for a bank hold-up while working as a florist truck driver. The thieves wore masks that concealed their identities, and the war veteran, in his search for the real thieves, dons a mask to infiltrate the gang. This theme was adopted over and over, from *I Am a*

Fugitive from the Chain Gang, to more contemporary perils of a Vietnam War veteran, as in Richard Rush's *The Stunt Man* (1980), in which Steve Railsback plays a veteran on the run from the police, who happens upon a location shooting of a war movie, is transformed into a stunt man, replacing the one he accidentally killed. He is nicknamed Lucky by the director of the movie within the movie. The archetypal variation of the unjust treatment of a wandering war veteran is picked up in *First Blood* (1982) and given mythical play in which the veteran John Rambo (Sylvester Stallone) takes refuge in a cave and emerges as a fighting hero. (See my *Raven's Return* for a discussion of *The Lone Ranger* theme of a survivor nurtured in a cave.) Such treatment is itself a variation of the archetypal war veteran, Odysseus, who returns home disguised as a transient beggar.

This theme of the veteran wrongly accused and driven into hiding is repeated in Jacques Tourneur's *Nightfall* (1956), in which the alienated veteran has to reclaim his integrity, and speaks to the injustice that seems to be inherent in becoming a war veteran, but not necessarily shared by those of the world in which the war veteran lives. From the civilian perspective, the war veteran is honored in parades and Veterans Day interviews. His war memorabilia is tucked into drawers or trunks. The fact that he had his life on the line and could have died, and did, in fact, suffer greatly to defend his country, is not kept central in his life. He anticipates a homecoming that proves to be anticlimactic. To be wrongly accused is to experience injustice, a violation of one's honor.

Fritz Lang's *Human Desire* (1954), a remake of Jean Renoir's *La Bête Humaine* (1938), has a veteran (Glenn Ford) just back from Korea as a railroad engineer who is drawn into a murder plot, but finally (and righteously) refusing to participate. "It's all wrong," he said. "I feel dirty." When the noir temptress, played by Gloria Grahame, says, "You killed before." The veteran replies, "The war. You thought I could do it because of *that*? It takes a different kind of killing ... a different kind of man."

Lewis Allen's *Suddenly* featured Frank Sinatra as Johnny Baron, who is an army veteran who was a sniper in Italy during World War II, liked killing and brags about winning a Silver Star. He might have been discharged on a "Section Eight," at least that's what the sheriff suggests. Johnny is setting up to kill the president of the United States. The sheriff is also an army infantry veteran. Johnny explains that he was nobody before the war, the son of a "dipso" (alcoholic) who was put in an orphanage. He claims to have no feelings: "They were taken out of me by experts."

Censors were reluctant to allow a war veteran, who is not mentally ill, to be depicted as having a dark side caused by the war. In 1950, Nicholas Ray directed *In a Lonely Place*, a complex film that portrayed the army infantry veteran, also wrongly accused of murder, as having a dark, paranoid personality. He drives away those who love him with his anger.

France did not have the shackles of censorship as tightly bound as the U.S. and, by 1957, Louis Malle directed a veteran of the French colonial wars as engaged in a vengeful murder in his excellent *Elevator to the Gallows* (released in 1958). Generally, it was more common in Hollywood of that period to depict the war veteran, consistent with the Odyssean prototype, as a more or less noble man who found himself battling the dark forces in his society.

In Jacques Tourneur's *Nightfall*, Aldo Ray plays Jim Manning, a navy veteran of Okinawa. He stumbles into a murder while camping with a friend in Montana. Bank robbers happen upon the campers, kill one, and Manning manages to get away with the loot. Stunned by a ricochet blow to the head, however, he cannot remember where he left the bag with the money. The killers pursue him, as does an insurance investigator, played by James Gregory. Manning meets a beautiful fashion model, Marie (Anne Bancroft), who is also drawn into the peril. The story is given excellent dialogue by Sterling Silliphant (adapted from a novel by David Goodis), with fine acting by Brian Keith and Rudy Bond as the robbers, but the plot ends in a contrived shootout. Jim Manning, the navy veteran, gives us little insight on the impact of the war. He tells Marie, "I'm just back from the wars, honey. I'm a vet." As with *Human Desire, Ride the Pink Horse*, and *Thieves' Highway, Nightfall* merely uses the war veteran status of the hero to give us a sense of his righteous, solid character caught up in a situation depicting alienation. In *Nightfall*, as in *The Blue Dahlia*, the circumstances force the honest veteran to go into hiding until he can prove his innocence.

The anger that is blatant in the war veteran in Nicholas Ray's *In a Lonely Place* is suppressed in *Elevator to the Gallows* and its energy channeled toward self-serving revenge. He is killing the war profiteer, yes, but it so happens that the war profiteer is the husband of the veteran's lover (played by Jeanne Moreau). The veteran of *In a Lonely Place* has a loose-cannon kind of anger that attacks whoever is near. The veteran of *Elevator* is calculating and his angry energy is narrowly channeled. He would never blow up with road rage, but he would kill by climbing through the window. The veteran of France's colonial wars is also falsely accused of multiple murders; the crimes, in fact, were committed by a young man using his identity, who, in a neat ironic twist, finally has to confess.

A bright light in that dark time came from the celebrated *The Best Years of Our Lives*, produced by Samuel Goldwyn and directed by William Wyler. During the war years Wyler had made two well-received war documentaries, *The Memphis Belle*, and *The Fighting Lady*, both released in 1944. *The Best Years of Our Lives* was an "A" film with top stars and a real disabled war veteran in a lead role, Harold Russell, who had both hands amputated and wore prosthetics. He played Homer, a navy veteran, who returned to his home in Boon City, along with two army veterans, an air corps navigator, Fred (Dana Andrews), and an infantry sergeant, Al (Fredric March). They fly into the Midwest town in the belly of a B-17 that is going to be retired. Each of the veterans has been changed by their time at war, and is experiencing the alienation in different, interesting ways. The brilliant screenplay is by Robert E. Sherwood, from a novel by MacKinlay Kantor. The plot cuts among the three as they try to return to their prewar lives. Fred had just been married before he left for the war and his wife, Marie (Virginia Mayo), went on an independent way, working in a nightclub, and proved to be intolerant of her husband's postwar difficulties. When he had nightmares, she snarled, "Snap out of it!" Fred worked in a drug store before the war, and he tries to take his old job back as a soda jerk, (now referred to as a server). He becomes one example of the change brought about by the momentous responsibilities required of combat. Fred had guided flights of B-17s on bombing missions and returned to serving sodas and being supervised by a "jerk" who never served. (An equivalent in the era of the Wars on Terror, an army reservist serving in a combat capacity, operating a machine gun in a Humvee, returns to her prewar job as a corporate receptionist.)

Al, the infantry sergeant, presents another homecoming example: he worked in a bank before the war. He returned to the same bank and was put in charge of GI loans. However, several changes have taken place for Al. He now drinks a great deal. He gives his adolescent son a Japanese officer's sword as a war souvenir, and his son wonders about the atomic bomb. But, more importantly for his career, Al now has a newfound empathy for veterans, which leads his boss at the bank to question his judgment. Al argues that because they're veterans they can be trusted. That his values have changed is indicated by his complaint: "Last year it was 'kill Japs'; now it's 'make money.'"

The situation of the amputee veteran, Homer, is even more difficult. Homer is upbeat, practicing, what we'd call today, the principles of positive psychology. He returns to his old room upstairs in his parents' house. He assures everyone that he is not as disabled as it may seem. He lights his own cigarette, pours a drink and holds the glass, even plays a tune on the piano, and is clearly making the best of a difficult situation. He also returns to his childhood sweetheart, his neighbor, Wilma (Cathy O'Donnell). She still loves him, but he can't return her acceptance until he shows her what it's like for him when he is helpless in his pajamas with his prostheses removed. The movie reaches its emotional climax when Homer and Wilma are married.

The veterans congregate at Butch's Tavern, with Hoagy Carmichael, a popular jazz pianist and composer, playing the tavern owner, Butch. They enjoy the cultural camaraderie of veterans, which they cannot find among civilians, sharing the difficulties of renewing their old lives. Fred is fired from his job at the drug store when he comes to the aid of his buddy, Homer, who was sitting at the drugstore lunch counter when a wise guy talked to him about how maybe Hitler wasn't all that bad and the war that was fought was a mistake. Homer is angered and takes him to task, ripping off the man's American flag lapel pin with his prosthesis. Fred leaps over the counter to help and is fired.

Homer's anger can be appreciated because of the significant sacrifice he has made and the importance that he must give to the meaningfulness of the war effort. The harmfulness of the proto-fascist is not so much his politics as the implication, even if it is coming from a fool, that his sacrifice was not worthwhile.

Al has the task of separating from his idealism about veterans when Fred and Al's daughter, Peggy (Teresa Wright), strike up a romantic relationship. Al has to tell Fred that he, Fred, isn't right for his daughter, being a married man, albeit estranged from his wife who is divorcing him. Al's wife, Millie (Myrna Loy), is a cheerful, tolerant woman who supports her husband, even during his bouts of excessive drinking. (The dance scene she has with her drunken husband at Butch's is a memorable scene.) She presents an iconic example of the thousands of tolerant spouses of war veterans who return from the battlefield chaos to a more or less orderly home life. The recent film of the Iraq War veteran, *The Dry Land*, presents a more contemporary example of this spousal test of tolerance in which the wife leaves the veteran after becoming fearful of his violence, only to support him after his crisis and arrest.

Edward Dmytryk's *Till the End of Time* (1946), released just a few months before *Best Years*, features two Marines who are discharged after combat in the Pacific during World War II. In a sense, it is an addendum to *The Best Years of Our Lives* and, although it is much darker in terms of production values, it is not considered part of the noir genre. It features Cliff (Guy Madison) who, like Homer, returns home to his parents' house and his old room. Cliff is whole in body, but his values have changed as a result of his combat, and the alienation from his parents is portrayed by his disinterest in finding a civilian job. His father, a World War I veteran, is understanding, but urges Cliff to get on with his life. Cliff becomes friendly with a widow of an army air corps pilot who was killed in action. (The widow is played by Dorothy McGuire, who received the film's top billing.) The Marine buddy, with whom Cliff was discharged, is William Tabeshaw (Robert Mitchum), who had a combat brain injury for which he refuses compensation, but who finally ends up being hospitalized after a bar fight. These veterans seek out another discharged Marine, who is paralyzed and discouraged about his rehabilitation until the film's robust finale, which involved a barroom brawl with the racist veterans' organization recruiters. Both films, *Best Years* and *Till the End*, echo the fear in the nation, especially in Hollywood, that fascism, here couched in racism, was still an infection that had to be actively fought and suppressed.

The dark period of American cinema during and after World War II tended to put the war veteran at odds with a criminal and corrupt society, which made for good entertainment, given the built-in attributes of a war veteran trained for combat. *The Best Years of Our Lives*, and its "B" movie counterpart, *Till the End of Time*, presented the war veteran facing the darkness within the less melodramatic confines of domestic adjustment.

An important film that took on the issue of the permanently paralyzed veteran was Fred Zinnemann's *The Men* (1950), featuring the passionate and articulate Marlon Brando in the lead role as Ken, a paraplegic infantry officer shot through the spine in Germany. Also featured as paralyzed patients were Jack Webb as the sarcastic Norm, and Arthur Jurado as Angel, a patient who seems to be the most successful and advanced in his rehabilitation, but who suddenly dies, drawing attention to the precarious nature of their recovery process.

The Men focuses on Ken's recovery and struggle to reintegrate into society and his relationship with his patient and nurturing wife, Ellen (Teresa Wright). It is worthwhile to draw attention to the integrity and empathic authority represented in the behavior of the lead doctor, Dr. Brock (Everett Sloan). He encourages the patients with a pragmatic realism, and counsels the wives regarding the sobering task ahead in supporting a paraplegic veteran in his long-term recovery. By the end of the film, Ken, although he has rebelled and expressed his despairing anguish, reconciles to plodding and coping with his condition, a resignation that is shared by the double amputee, Homer, in *Best Years*, and the paraplegic Marine veteran, Perry, in *Till the End of Time*. Contrast these presentations with the later study of the treatment of the paralyzed Marine veteran in Oliver Stone's *Born on the Fourth of July* (1989), which was based on the autobiography of the same title by Ron Kovic. Stone's version is a bitter rendition of VA treatment of the paralyzed veteran, showing neglect of the patient in an overcrowded ward. Although Stone can be criticized as being hyperbolic (Davis [2000, p. 136] writes that Stone reverts to sensationalism), *Born on the Fourth of July* represents a vitriolic criticism of the medical treatment of veterans. Davis notes that, although *Born* drew "lukewarm reviews," it achieved box-office success and awards, indicating a popular reception. Davis draws a comparison of Stone's film with *The Men*: "The rat-infested, filth-ridden facility, the uncaring orderlies, and the uncertain

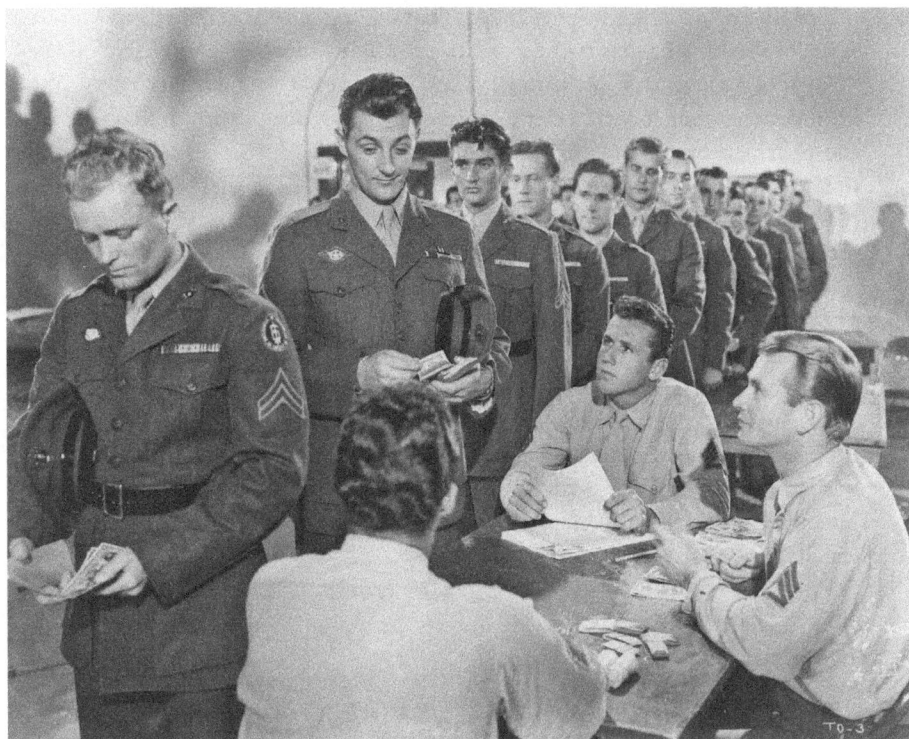

Till the End of Time (1946), Edward Dmytryk, director. **Processing out of the Marine Corps at the end of World War II is Cliff, played by Guy Madison, in line in front of his buddy, William Tabeshaw (Robert Mitchum). Both will have challenges in their adjustment to civilian life. (RKO Radio Pictures, Dore Schary Productions, Vanguard Films.)**

physicians are a chilling opposite to the efficient, antiseptic VA hospital depicted in Brando's *The Men*. Stone's 'choking close-ups' of Kovic struggling to recuperate under the horrid conditions heighten the audience's own sense of agony" (Davis, 2000, p. 142.) Davis, an historian, attributes Stone's lurid rendition of VA hospital treatment to his anti-war sentiment (p. 147), although, when looking at the horrific hallucinations in the 1990 *Jacob's Ladder* and the 2004 *The Jacket*, I am inclined to think that these later films mark a change in respect to how the public thinks veterans are treated by American medicine. *Born on the Fourth of July* and *Jacob's Ladder* are distinctly critical of U.S. policies of resorting to military enforcement of its foreign policy. That criticism did not exist in any remarkable way in the period during or following World War II. But the criticism may be more profound than just being opposed to war policy and may represent a decline in respect for authority in

general, and medicine in particular. That change was articulated by Marcia
Angell's scathing criticism of psychiatric medicine in a two-part article in *The
New York Review of Books* (Angell, 2011). She argues that psychiatry, and by
implication other mental health professions, have been overly influenced by
the pharmaceutical and insurance industries. I think that she would argue
that veterans with postwar behavioral disturbances have their recovery complicated by medication, when psychotherapy and counseling may be the treatment of choice.

The 1998 drama *Coming Home* takes a neutral stand about VA treatment
of paraplegic veterans. The movie depicts the rage in Jon Voight's character
as he strives to regain mobility. He expressed his rage, not so much at the VA,
but at the U.S. government's war policy in Vietnam. Jane Fonda plays the
spouse of a Marine officer who is serving in Vietnam. She comes to love the
righteous paralyzed veteran and engages in passionate love-making until her
husband comes home, alienated and enraged at her infidelity. Fonda was instru-
mental in producing the film, which cannot but be taken as an anti-war political statement.

CHAPTER 4

The Vietnam War Veteran as America's Shadow

The Vietnam War Marine combat veteran and author Karl Marlantes refers extensively in his philosophical study *What It Is Like to Go to War* to the topic of C.G. Jung's concept of "shadow." Marlantes writes about coming back to the U.S. as a Marine, still on active duty, stationed in Washington, D.C., and discovering that he was, at times, the subject of vilification. He writes with poetic license: "*Somebody* had done something quite bad in Vietnam and it must have been us since we were the only ones there" (2011, p. 41). Jung, himself, puts it succinctly: "The shadow is a moral problem that challenges the whole personality, for no one can become conscious of the shadow without considerable moral effort" (1959, p. 8).

The veterans of the Vietnam War were identified as participants in a controversy about the purpose of America's war overseas. Many of the veterans had been drafted, or were influenced to enlist by the indication of an eventual draft. Anti-war activists seemed to think the veterans should have avoided military service or resisted serving in Vietnam, but, for most, that option was never seriously considered. Not only did the veteran return from Vietnam with the memories of combat zone activities, he (or she) was associated by others, civilians, with the government's decisions to conduct the war, and the veteran was labeled with the moral judgments. A collective shadow projection was created by a large segment of the population, which said, "We did not choose to fight the war, you [the veteran] did. You were wrong to do it, and by extension, you deserve the wounds and disorders that come from combat." The righteous citizens were joined in an odd coalition by those, usually the more conservative, who assert that combatants who break down, for whatever reason, do so because of weak character. Such citizens then get to avoid responsibility for the wounds and deaths, and the long tail of consequences that follow in society.

In my previous work (2003), I listed and reviewed a host of movies that had been made about the Vietnam War veteran. I have added a few since. Almost all of them feature the veteran in a state of alienation. Here I can list some of the best feature films that were made during or about that era, all depicting the Vietnam War veteran in a state of alienation:

Taxi Driver (1976). The veteran as paranoid urban isolate who becomes psychotic as a result of amphetamine abuse.

The Deer Hunter (1978). A veteran, tortured as a POW, is depicted as a suicidal heroin addict with his veteran buddy trying to help in his recovery.

Cutter's Way (1981). A severely wounded veteran who is also alcoholic, reckless, and suicidal, sets out to solve a murder mystery.

The Stunt Man (1980). A veteran is on the run from police and caught up in the production of a war movie, posing as a stunt man.

Dead Presidents (1995). Unemployed urban black veterans opt for violent crime.

Alamo Bay (1985). Texas crab fisherman veteran loses his livelihood and opts for committing a hate crime against competing Vietnamese emigrants.

The Big Lebowski (1998). A bombastic, comic veteran threatens violence.

Birdy (1984). A psychotic, comatose, hospitalized veteran is being helped by his childhood buddy, who was also wounded in service to his country.

Born on the Fourth of July (1989). A paralyzed veteran, alienated from his family, participates in political activism after a self destructive, alcoholic binge.

Coming Home (1978). A Marine veteran, who is cuckolded by a paralyzed army veteran, commits suicide.

Distant Thunder (1988). A "tripwire" veteran is depicted as a social isolate who avoids family and grapples with the more extreme violence of fellow veterans.

Land of Plenty (2004). A veteran adopts inappropriate post–9/11 vigilante antiterrorist surveillance activity.

Missing in America (2005). A veteran, who is a social isolate, takes on the responsibility of caring for a Vietnamese-American child and struggles with the more extreme violence of fellow veterans.

First Blood (1982). A veteran is persecuted by a local sheriff and opts for violent retaliation.

Indian Runner (1991). An antisocial veteran avoids family responsibilities and commits a brutal murder.

Jacknife (1989). A recovering veteran helps his alcoholic veteran buddy and falls in love with the man's sister.

In Country (1989). Avoidant, depressed veteran takes on family responsibility in response to his inquisitive, persistent niece.

Rushmore (1999). A successful but alcoholic veteran falls in love.

The Spitfire Grill (1996). A socially avoidant veteran is lured to return home by a traumatized girl.

Ulee's Gold (1997). A work-oriented veteran fights to protect his family.

The Visitors (1972). A pacifist veteran is harassed and assaulted by antisocial veterans after testifying against them.

Who'll Stop the Rain? (1978). An opportunistic veteran steals drugs and fights for survival against bad cops.

The War (1994). A guilty veteran with PTSD struggles with unemployment while attempting to provide for his family.

No Country for Old Men (2004). An opportunistic veteran steals drug money and fights to survive.

In my opinion these are the best of the films of the Vietnam War era in that they all give a view of the veteran that is worth discussing. There are many more movies featuring the Vietnam War veteran, many of which show the veteran as a heroic character of action drama (such as *Gordon's War, Lethal Weapon, Born Losers, Mr. Majestyk*), and some that depict him as a disturbed criminal (*To Kill a Clown, Motor Psycho, Black Sunday*). During the Vietnam War era Hollywood tended to exploit the controversy of the war for drama, almost always showing the veteran as emotionally disturbed by his war experience. This trend has been continued with the veterans of the Wars on Terror, but the later movies, as I have indicated above, tend to better recognize the emotional disturbance as an inner struggle.

Americans seemed to have learned a lesson from the errors of the Vietnam War regarding the harsh treatment of returning veterans. Although it did not stop the U.S. government from going to war again, American citizens during the Wars on Terror (including the First Gulf War, Iraq, and Afghanistan) did not blame the warrior or the war veteran. The heritage of World War II led the warriors of the Vietnam War period to expect gratitude for doing a dirty job that had to be done, but it was soon clear that a significant and vocal segment of the population did not think the Vietnam War was necessary or even moral, indicating a significant disagreement with their democratically elected members of Congress and occupants of the White House, who initiated and maintained the Vietnam War for all those years. The damage done by the error of blaming the warrior for the war has been terrible, leading many veterans to suicide, unemployment, homelessness, marital disharmony, and persistent mental disorders. It had the effect of unjustly blaming the victim for the trauma, while not taking the collective responsibility for creating the traumatic conditions. Karl Marlantes, to his credit, writes with candor about his feelings as a Marine combat veteran: "No matter where I went, I felt something was not right about me." ... "I needed desperately to be accepted back in [to American society]. I think I ended up assuming unconsciously that I must have done something wrong to have all this rejection happen" (2011, p. 151). In a language that suggests dissociation, he writes vividly about his condition upon returning to the U.S. after doing what he thought was right: leaving a comfortable academic life to serve his country.

> That body had suffered. It was covered with scars from jungle rot. It had had dysentery, diarrhea, and probably a mild case of malaria. It had gone without fresh food for months at a time. It had lived on the knife edge of fear, constantly jerked from an aching need for sleep with all the cruel refinement of the best secret police torturer. It had pumped adrenaline until it had become addicted to it. There were scars where hot metal had gone in, searing and surprising in its pain, and scars where a corpsman had dug most of it out.... The inner ears rang with a constant high-pitched whine that ceased only in sleep, when the nightmares started" [Marlantes, 2011, p. 152].

It is interesting to examine why the psychological and emotional traumas of combat got lost in the fog after World War II. It has been observed that as the Second World War was looming on the horizon of history, the British government elected to ban discussion of shell shock (Jones, et al., 2007; Shephard, 2001, p. 328). After World War II ended, psychiatry elected to discard the category of trauma neurosis that had prevailed, including the concept of hysteria as a product of the suppression of psychological trauma (Lifton, 1978; Hyler & Spitzer, 1978). Psychologist Carl Rogers, in his 1946 book of advice to counselors treating "returned servicemen," never mentions the word trauma or deals with the subject (Rogers & Wallen, 1946). Wilson, Friedman, and Lindy (2001, p. 4) regard it as "a puzzle that a 'cloistered' group of mental health professionals charged with the responsibility of revising the psychiatric criteria of (DSM-I, 1952, and DSM-II, 1968) would have difficulty in recognizing and accepting the necessity of scientifically classifying PTSD as a distinct psychiatric disorder, especially given the profound worldwide and historic traumatic events which punctuated the 20th century." Ben Shephard in the introduction to his 2001 A War of Nerves, writes: "PTSD is a cumbersome phrase devised by a cumbersome committee" (p. xxii). Yet psychologist John Wilson, who was one of the pioneers who lobbied for the PTSD category in DSM-III, might have recognized that it was the very nature of the "historic traumatic events" that obscured the judgment of the "cloistered" committees. Jung had predicted this in his reaction to the rise of Nazi Germany. It took the advocacy of mental health professionals like John Wilson, Charles Figley, Robert Lifton, and Chiam Shatan, most of whom were influenced by their contact with Vietnam War veterans, to reestablish psychological trauma as a diagnostic category in DSM-III. It may be that, similar to the individual's tendency to cope with traumatic circumstances, the nature of psychological trauma on a collective level is to be suppressed in the absence of inspired leadership to keep it in the forefront of consciousness. Certainly the Holocaust and the calamities of World War II were universal collective traumas. If that has been the case, we can predict that there will, in the coming years, be another collective discrediting of PTSD, leading to new controversy.

It remains unclear in psychology literature why the one-third rule seems to apply, at least to combat forces. About one-third of the troops engaged in combat come out with reported symptoms of PTSD, and probably more have symptoms that go unreported. The Vietnam War was a product of World War II in many respects. The Korean War set a precedent for U.S. intervention to curb the expansion of Soviet-Chinese Communism. It was thought by many at the time to be an unwanted war, burdening those who had already been threatened by World War II. Korean War veterans are often depicted as forgotten, standing in the shadow of the larger population of World War II veterans (Pash, 2012).

The Vietnam War was a product of World War II in several ways beyond the geopolitical rearrangement of boundaries. The film legacy of World War II, including censored newsreels, created a false impression of the action as romantic, and won for actor John Wayne, a man who never served in the military, a heroic image (Doherty, 1993). And, more importantly, the Vietnam War veteran was a product of the so-called World War II Baby Boom generation, when the families separated by war were reunited and made up for their long separation. Their offspring, that generation that came of age in the 1960s, proved to be an activist cohort, giving rise to the Civil Rights Movement, the Women's Movement, and the Anti-War Movement, each with its own roots, yet triggered by America's involvement in Vietnam and blossoming at the same time, as though World War II mobilization had shaken the society and produced an excitement that was expressed in their offspring 20 years later. A large and vocal swath of the public did not like the U.S. policy in Southeast Asia and, in their vigor, they marked the soldier as the villain, and it was that vilification that, if the veteran felt guilt at all coming from combat, drove him into exile. The war veteran, fresh from the service, was easily identified in public places and associated with the war. His negative emotions and mistakes in civilian life were attributed to his participation in the war. He found that he had a better chance at a job if he left his military service off his résumé, unless, of course, the job was an extension of his military role. The emotions of witnessing the traumas of foreign combat became associated with the citizens' projections. Sensational news stories reported the Vietnam War veteran driven into exile and living in isolation, creating a legend out of a small segment of the veteran population.

Movies like *Distant Thunder* and *Missing in America* portrayed the Vietnam War veteran in an extreme state of alienation, living in the mountains among a disorganized group of similar isolates. In both films the veteran is presented as suffering from guilt about deaths that occurred in combat and both are challenged by young persons, innocents of a new generation, coming into their lives. In *Distant Thunder* the veteran living in the mountains of Washington State's Olympic Peninsula, played by John Lithgow, is contacted by his son whom he has not seen for many years. In *Missing in America* the veteran, played by Danny Glover, also living on a remote Northwest mountain, is visited by a former squad member, who asks him to care for his daughter while he goes off to die of cancer. In both films the veteran has to deal with other veterans who are living in even more isolated conditions (and not given any depth as characters), are less amenable to outside intrusions, and, in fact, prove to be dangerous.

Both films were independently made: *Distant Thunder* by Rick Rosenthal in 1988, and *Missing in America* by Gabrielle Savage Dockterman in 2005. They depict the Vietnam War veteran protagonist as hyper-alert and guarded, but not pathologically paranoid. Those veterans associated with the protagonist, however, are paranoid and prove to be violent. The viewer gets the message that the Vietnam War veteran was damaged by his service and, for good reason, driven into social isolation, and that he represents others even more damaged. This plays on a very common sentiment among war veterans, that although they are wounded and suffer, there are many other veterans who are worse off, so that they dare not complain.

Both veterans in these films are stirred into action by youths who enter their lives. In *Distant Thunder* the veteran, Mark, discovers through a letter that his son, who has just graduated from high school, is coming to visit him and meet the dad he never knew. In *Missing In America*, Jake must now care for a nine-year-old Vietnamese-American girl, Lenny, played by Zoë Weizenbaum. *Distant Thunder*, the earlier film, is the less romantic and acknowledges the unlikelyhood that the relationship between the veteran and his adolescent son would thrive. *Missing* sacrifices the girl, but culminates in the romantically portrayed trip to the Vietnam Memorial Wall. Both films depict the veteran as having to cope with associates who are living in greater isolation.

Another independent movie, *In Country*, made about the same time as *Distant Thunder* (1988), culminates the intrusion of a high school graduate's inquiry into the death of her father, with a similar sentimental visit to the Memorial Wall as a healing pilgrimage.

A good illustration of this form of alienation can be found in another film about the Vietnam War veteran: *Spitfire Grill* (1996), directed and written by Lee David Zlotoff. The story concerns a young woman, Percy (Alison

Elliott), being released from prison, where she was sent for murdering her father. Her father had forced her into incest and, when she became pregnant, caused her to abort the fetus. She seeks a job in a remote Maine mountain town at the Spitfire Grill, the owner of which is an arthritic woman (Ellen Burstyn), who has a son who came back from Vietnam and chose to live in the woods on the mountain, eschewing society. He comes at night to split firewood for his mother and she leaves out supplies for him. Percy romanticizes the veteran in her mind while reading a tattered paperback of Homer's *Odyssey*. Percy seems to have filled the need left from losing her baby with the mute image of the ragged veteran, whom she calls Johnny B. Percy becomes fascinated with the reclusive veteran and finally attracts him into approaching her in a field as she sings.

These films show the war veteran driven into exile in his own land, not completely out of touch, but representing those veterans who are lost. War veterans may seek isolation because they feel guilty, or irritable, or are hypersensitive to noise. (Griffin, et al. [2012] found that successful psychotherapy for PTSD reduced sensitivity to noise among veterans.)

The veterans who go to remote areas to live in isolation may provide dramatic material for movies, but most veterans withdraw in a more subtle manner. Perhaps the most common veteran is the one who returns home after the war and takes up his life as before, except that there is no forgetting. One of the most successful of the dramas is the 1993 film *Ulee's Gold*. The Vietnam War veteran works hard as a beekeeper in the manufacture of Florida's tupelo honey. Ulee, played with quiet restraint by Peter Fonda, works with his body. He is caring for his two granddaughters. His son, the girls' father, is in jail for theft. Their mother, Helen, is on a drug binge in Tallahassee. Ulee is compelled to care for his granddaughters (well played by Jessica Biel and Vanessa Zima).

Ulee, the veteran, has to carry his solo business on a bad back, which hurts so that he has to lay prone on a wood floor to relax. His world is threatened by two criminals who contact him. It seems they have Helen in Tallahassee, where she's been on a drug binge. Ulee's son is in prison on a robbery charge, and the criminals were his henchmen who believe he hid the stolen funds.

Ulee's isolation is his work, his dedication to duty. He has tried to avoid violence since Vietnam. As he tells his youngest granddaughter, Penny, he alone of his squad survived a firefight. There is guilt in his voice when he tells Penny that he survived because he was tricky. Adaptability is a key to the war veteran's adjustment to civilian life. Ulee had extensively withdrawn from society, but was forced to adapt when he had to help his daughter-in-law recover from drug toxicity, and he had to deal with the criminals who accosted

Ulee's Gold (1997), Victor Nuñez, director. Peter Fonda plays Vietnam War veteran Ulee Jackson, a Florida beekeeper, shown here with his granddaughter, Penny, played by Vanessa Zima. The beekeepers' screened hood is like a veil used for hiding grief. (Orion Pictures. Photo by John Bramley.)

them. The key for the veteran is not to let his alienation make him unadaptable. Ulee's name is short for Ulysses, which the director admits is a barely disguised reference to Homer's epic.

The Vietnam War veteran who was 19 in 1972 would be 60 in 2013. Other wars have intervened and his own war is fading from public (though not his own) memory. Unless he declares it on his apparel in the form of a pin or button, his veteran's status is not apparent. Long-term sequelae of a stressful life may be a factor in his health. VA hospital patient census increases for war veterans when they enter the age cohort of 50–60 years. Details of the Vietnam War can be found in new archives and on library shelves, but memories are not so easily catalogued and filed away. I once likened the phenomenon of the war veteran's awareness to Christmas lights in January — the event is over, but still aglow to some.

Films, like the 2008 *Land of Plenty*, written and directed by Wim Wenders, takes the troubled Vietnam War veteran as a seriocomic character and makes him into a kind of quixotic urban vigilante, who, after 9/11, hunts in the streets of Los Angeles for potential terrorists. John Deihl plays Paul, the army Special Forces veteran who is sick from defoliant sprayed in Vietnam. He is serious in his mission, but portrayed as deluded and is brought to a more realistic perception by his peace-loving niece, Lana (Michelle Williams, in her first screen role), the young daughter of missionaries, who seeks out her uncle. In helping him pursue the solution to a mystery she guides him to a new realization with a broader worldview.

Wim Wenders is a German-born filmmaker with an international reputation. He made the film himself when his big-budget film was put on hold for the summer. His depiction of a Vietnam War veteran is not flattering. The sympathetic, non-violent Paul is driven by his own imaginings, in the manner of Don Quixote, and seriously intent on helping his society.

Of course, profiling a Vietnam War veteran in a film does not describe any other veteran. Movies feed off stereotypes, some say archetypes. Yet movies also feed on the public. The producers make movies that sell tickets at the box office. If they exploit the veteran, however crassly or thoughtfully, it is because the images are there to be exploited.

CHAPTER 5

The Odyssean Man

But my heart breaks for Odysseus,
that seasoned veteran, cursed by fate so long —
—*The Odyssey*, Book 1:56–60, Fagles's 1996 trans.

In a variety of ways every war is a cultural as well as an historical event. The U.S. Civil War is still having its long-term cultural impact of a collective trauma (at least 750,000 dead with many more among the wounded and disturbed) in four years of internecine fighting. In 1865, the U.S. population was around 35.2 million. A 21st century proportional equivalent to impact of the Civil War death toll, based on a 2012 population of 311.6 million, would entail 6.6 million combat deaths. A century and a half later movies and books about the Civil War still fascinate our populace, as evidenced by the comet-like return of the long-standing hit book and movie *Gone with the Wind*; the recent, mesmerizing PBS TV documentary history by Ken Burns; and the Pulitzer Prize-winning best seller, the 1997 Civil War road romance *Cold Mountain* by Charles Frazier. The award-winning 2012 dramatic film by Steven Spielberg, *Lincoln*, has been realistically compared to the 21st century U.S. political divide. Robert Penn Warren (1998) wrote of the Civil War as being our Homeric period. A subculture thrives of Civil War re-enactors, cultists who gather and try to replicate the campaigns and mimic the suffering (Horwitz, 1999). Movie directors John Ford and Howard Hawks capitalized and romanticized the westward migration of Civil War veterans. The 2007 remake of the 1957 film *3:10 to Yuma* adds to the plot the fact that the righteous but desperate rancher is a Civil War veteran, a wounded amputee who was "the best shot in his regiment."

The impact of World War II has yet to be fully absorbed. We have recently seen the cultural impact of Steven Spielberg's *Saving Private Ryan*

(1998) in reviving memories of the World War II D-Day invasion. The traumas of Nazism continue to haunt us as it did for the survivors as the unexpected knock on the door: the dreaded rise again of fascism and race hatred. Claude Lanzmann's epic 1985 *Shoah* disturbed the Western world with its unflinching scenes of calamity.

In a similar way the Trojan War and the return home of the war veterans was transformed from song to the written text and has become part of the heritage of Western culture through its epic poetry.

Nóstos — The Warrior's Return

Some time around the eighth century BC, Homeric oral tradition became recorded in fragments with the new Phoenician alphabet. The tyrant Peisistratos finally collected the fragments of Homeric texts and had them rendered into a formal volume around 550 BC (Nagy, 1996, p. 65). The collective oral tradition then became captured in writing and formalized at a time of so-called Pan-Hellenism, when the major city states were increasing their communication with each other. But, while the tradition stopped evolving in one sense when it was written and collected, it continued in folk tradition, as through the ages warriors kept on returning home estranged from their loved ones, influencing cultures with their various quests, and, as Stanford (1992) demonstrated, authors and poets kept repeating the Odyssean theme.

The *Odyssey* is the myth of *nóstos*, the return home, repeated every few generations in the fate of war veterans. It is a tale about alienation and the restoration of power. Its collective repetition through time and across cultures attests to its relevance. Hexter, in his introduction (1993, p. *lxv*), refers to Homer's *Odyssey* as "the quintessential postwar epic," depicting an archetype in the sense of the basic pattern, the first written form from which all others grew. Carl Jung would argue that there is a physical reason for the pattern of repetition in the warriors' return (Jung, 1971, p. 48).

The *Odyssey*, employing a very modern style, convolutes time, first picking up Odysseus's son Telémachus as he comes of age, engaged in a search for his father. The first four books are concerned with setting up the current dilemma in Ithaca, with a hundred or more rude suitors vying for the hand of Odysseus's faithful and circumspect wife, Penelope, and occupying Odysseus's palace. The story shifts in book five to Odysseus himself as he is about to be released by the goddess Calypso and journey to Phaeacia, the threshold ground between the gods and men, and between reality and fable, which rather resembles a university campus.

The chronological tracking of Odysseus's journey then begins with his own rendition to the Phaeacians of his journey from the time he left Troy. What follows in his narrative is an account of the war veteran Odysseus as he gradually loses his power, depicted as material possessions, ships and crew, through misadventure in a mythical world. He gradually loses his fleet of 12 ships and his estimated seven hundred men with his cargo of the plunders of war, including slaves, as he journeys off course over mythical seascape and is finally flung ashore in Phaeacia, alone, naked, without a single possession. There, on the threshold of reality, his wealth is reconstituted through gifts from the Phaeacians, amounting to a treasure more magnificent than he had lost. He is sent home to Ithaca with full honors.

When Odysseus's story is brought up to the narrative present, he departs Phaeacia in a magical boat, known to read men's thoughts, and travels home. When he finally reaches Ithaca, however, he must hide his power and wealth until his household is restored and the threat to his throne is defeated. All along, throughout the epic, reference is made to the sad fate of his fellow warrior, the returning commander Agamemnon, who was killed by his unfaithful wife and her lover upon reaching his home.

Murnaghan (1987, p. 235) put it nicely when she observed that the theme of the *Odyssey* "is asserted through its portrayal of Odysseus' unique success, the contention that the mind and will are sufficient to win out against circumstances, that Odysseus can control events through his strategic plotting of them." It is this theme, calling for a suppleness and malleability of the mind, that makes the tale applicable to the modern survivor of trauma. The symptoms of PTSD tend to cause the personality to narrow, influencing the survivor to withdraw, literally or figuratively, from social stimulation and other stressors, and by lapses into obsessions and compulsive behaviors related to coping with trauma memories that are arrested in time. This tendency of the personality of the survivor to form habits and styles of coping with primitive emotions and feelings of threat, leading to hypervigilance, makes the way to recovery a challenge of adaptability.

After combat, the returning war veteran, leaving the military behind, is figuratively sapped of the power of his military identity. But when he returns home he finds that he must fight again, but in a different way, to restore his power and fortune. In peacetime the war veteran must survive and prevail without the force of arms and the bravado of the warrior, but rather with tact and inventiveness. The chief difference between the *Iliad* and the *Odyssey*, as Clay (1983, p. 101) observed, is the difference between the Greek words *biê* and *mêtis*. *Biê* is used in war, referring to force, power, battlefield fury, and things to do with physical strength, whereas *mêtis* concerns the use of the intellect, trickery, adaptability, and artifice. *Biê* is featured in the *Iliad*, although Nagy (1999) refers to the *Iliad* as a contest between Achilles (*biê*) and Odysseus (*mêtis*). Nagy's point is worth observing that *biê* (force) got the Achaeans to the walls of Troy, but *mêtis* (trickery) won the war in the *Iliad*, whereas *mêtis* got Odysseus home, while his *biê* won the day against the suitors.

We saw in Jonathan Shay's *Achilles in Vietnam* (Shay, 1991, 1994) that Achilles's anger could *not* be brought home, any more than the angry combat veteran could survive at home with his anger undisguised. Achilles could not tolerate Odysseus's talent for deception. He hated anyone who said one thing and thought another.

Certainly *mêtis* dominates the work in the *Odyssey*. In Homer's *Odyssey*, *mêtis* is the way of adaptation, and the poem itself, as Vidal-Naquet (1996, p. 39) put it, is the story of Odysseus's return to normality, of his deliberate acceptance of the human condition. Although, to be fair, a hero like Odysseus can hardly be considered normal, in the collective sense, or even in the sense of what was normal for the individual. The criteria for normalcy change for the combat veteran. The question becomes, rather, what is normal for a combat veteran?

Athena's *Mêtis*

Athena is the prominent divinity of the epic. Her role in influencing and aiding Odysseus is central to his success. She advises him, she lobbies on his behalf before Zeus, she helps him hide his treasure, she disguises him, makes him seem familiar even though he is a stranger. She shields him from attack, aids him in battle, gives panache to his image and adds prowess to his feats of athleticism. She also counsels and protects his wife and son. Of course, there are times in the poem when she is prominently *not* helpful, most notably when the elder god, Poseidon, is involved.

Athena is the goddess who most appreciates *mêtis*, which may explain her affection for Odysseus. In fact, she, in her genesis, is the offspring (of sorts) of the goddess Metis (Schmidt, 1980). Hesiod (Lattimore, 1959) tells of Metis's birth to the ancient gods Tethys and Oceanus: "She knew more than all the gods or mortal people." She was Zeus's first wife and, when it was prophesied that their offspring would destroy Zeus, he swallowed Metis, developed a whopping headache, and, with the assistance of Hephaestus and Hermes, Athena was born, fully armed, from his head wound.

Otto (1954, p. 184) argues for Athena as symbolic of thought and describes how she plays the role of inspiratrix. She seems indeed to represent a higher form of consciousness, one in which sheer physical power and force are not always necessary, but which comes into play when adaptation is required for survival. If she is queen of battle, she is also the queen of adaptation after battle. In dealing with the symptoms of PTSD, instead of spontaneity, circumspection and deliberation are often the desirable processes to aid the survivor in drawing a distinction between salient trauma memory, with all its influence, and the contemporary event.

Odysseus: The Hero with Courage and *Métis*

Odysseus has the courage of a hero to fight against great odds, to never give up, and the wile to win in ways other than with power. As noted above, a chief message of the *Odyssey* is the contention that the mind and will of the hero are sufficient to win out against circumstances of fate. He was the one who designed the Trojan Horse as the ruse that won the war after the failure of sheer power applied by the armies assembled by the combined forces of Menelaus, Agamemnon, Achilles, and the other Achaean heroes. He has the craft to tell a great variety of stories, to charm and entertain others, such that his storytelling is compared to bardic song. Alcinoüs, the Phaeacian king, and a semi-divine celebrant who draws gods to attend his feasts, compares Odysseus's rendering of his tale to enchanting song.

Odysseus has the practical craft to design and build a sea-worthy raft, not to mention a marriage bed within a living tree. Odysseus has the strength to string a bow that is beyond the power of almost everyone else, although we note he signaled his son, Telemachos, to cease *his* attempts. We also see evidence of his power when he throttles the bullying beggar, Irus. His prize example of *métis* and courage is when he tricks the Cyclops Polyphémos with the potent wine, given him by Maro, a Cíconian priest of Apollo, during his raid. Athena refers to Odysseus in the beginning of the poem as a poisoner of enemies, for he was known to add deadly compounds to the tips of his arrows.

Disguise and Recognition

Half of the *Odyssey* describes the hero's return to Ithaca. He arrives at the midpoint of the story. During most of this second half, Odysseus is in disguise as a transient old man dressed in rags. Nothing is ever as it seems with the returning hero. He tells different stories to different people. He even (perhaps) fools his wife regarding his true identity. (The content of the poem is sufficiently vague regarding Penelope's complicity that the doubt survives.) While disguised, Odysseus tests the loyalty of his household staff as he endures ignominy at the hands of the suitors and others.

The need for the war survivor with PTSD to be in disguise is similar to Odysseus's. A few examples, not uncommon in kind, describe the veteran in disguise. The first is the story of a combat veteran who, after returning home from Vietnam, was attending a party when a discussion about the war became heated. People were talking emotionally and animatedly, yet the veteran remained quiet, even though they were arguing about facts of which he had first-hand information.

Other examples illustrate the veteran in disguise. There is the veteran who sits in the classroom as his professor expounds on the wrong-headedness and atrocities of the war. The veteran does not reveal his identity and does not return to the class. There are also those veterans in disguise who do not list their military record on job applications, on insurance applications, and live with their wives and children in secrecy regarding what they experienced in combat.

The return of the war veteran in disguise is an Odyssean theme that repeats through the war veteran sagas of various cultures. The return of Martin Guerre from foreign war was a popular courtroom phenomenon in France of the Middle Ages, which resulted in a trail, conviction, and execution of a man who returned disguised as a war veteran, fooling perhaps even the veteran's wife (Davis, 1983). This idea was repeated with a curious twist with the 2001 film, *The Majestic*, directed by Frank Darabont, in which Jim Carrey plays a non-comedic role of a Hollywood writer being investigated by the House Un-American Activities Committee (HUAC), who incurs amnesia in a drunken auto accident, and is mistaken by the citizens of a California coastal town who mistake him for a local World War II hero who has been reported missing in action. Peter was in the army during the war but never left the States. But, with amnesia, he's not sure who he is.

Other works of the war veteran sagas contain certain patterns that are consistent. The war veteran returns disguised as a pilgrim or anonymous dark knight in Sir Walter Scott's *Ivanhoe*. Another film about the Crusades veteran, Ridley Scott's *Robin Hood* (2010). Made during these Wars on Terror, Robin Hood returns home posing as a knight. In Homer's *Odyssey* the war veteran is disguised as an impoverished and aged transient. In Western folklore, probably influenced by the long wars of the 16th and 17th centuries, there were folk tales (e.g., the Grimms' *Bearskin* and *Brother Lustig*) of the war veteran disguised by the devil as a beastlike wanderer. The *Martin Guerre* story was adapted to the U.S. Civil War by French director Jon Amiel in *Sommersby* (1993), with Richard Gere as the trickster who pretends to be a returning Confederate war veteran. Across centuries the theme takes an ironic twist, that the veteran of war returns disguised as himself but is really a changed man, not to be mistaken for the one who left.

Perhaps the most entertaining and intriguing study of the war veteran in disguise is presented in *The Stunt Man*, a 1980 film by Richard Rush, which features a Vietnam War veteran (Steve Railsback) on the run from California Highway Patrolmen. In fleeing the police he finds himself accidentally causing the death of a stunt man during the making of a movie. The eccentric director of the movie within the movie (Peter O'Toole) is interested in the fugitive and hires him to replace the dead stunt man. He calls the veteran "Lucky," and transforms the scruffy guy into a handsome Hollywood player and inserts him into a movie about the folly of war as a World War I aviator shot down and chased as a fugitive. *The Stunt Man* thus becomes a movie about war veteran alienation with extra dimensions added: the police are still looking for the veteran and the movie demands dangerous stunts while mimicking the casualties of war. The movie also deals with the issue of the cultural exploitation of war and war veterans for the purposes of entertainment and profit. *The Stunt Man* plays up the war veteran, disguised or not, as being caught up in a fate virtually out of his control.

Power

When Odysseus arrives on the island of Phaeacia he is cast ashore in a storm and, naked and without possessions, exhausted, he crawls up the outlet of a river and settles under the eroded roots of an olive tree. Homer notes conspicuously that the tree has both wild and domesticated roots (5:525–528, Fagles' 1996 trans.).

Legends and epics are formed around archetypal, oft-repeated human situations. One such archetype is the return of the warrior after years of struggle, a profoundly changed man, who must re-establish his power and win over his household, passing on his power to his son as his own father fades. The diminution and the re-establishment of power has caused some to view the *Odyssey* as a solar myth and Odysseus as a cultural hero representing all true combat veterans of his time (Nagy, 1996, p. 21), as one who has expended power in warfare, been drained, and yet thereafter must cope with an over-producing capacity for alarm and rage. Recent scientific evidence (Southwick & Yehuda, 1997) now points to a dysregulation of the brain's HPA (Hippocampus-Pituitary-Adrenal) axis and an over-responding emergency system, causing the war survivor with PTSD to become uncomfortable living an ordinary life, the proverbial southpaw in a land of right-handers. Such a person, more or less, has learned to distrust authority, responds poorly (if at all) to mundane problems and, in seeming paradox, over-reacts unpredictably. For the person who has been traumatized, it doesn't just rain, it threatens to flood.

The man or woman who should be dead, isn't. Civilian identity must be re-established somehow, because wartime identity and pre-war identity no longer apply. Neither is appropriate or even reachable, except as memories. And, indeed, memory of trauma vies for prominence with the contemporary events, changing focus, and motivating behavior. In the life of the war survivor there isn't much sure ground. Upheaval is the perpetually anticipated next shoe to drop.

Odysseus: The Reckless Adventurer

We see this odd mixture of recklessness, unconsciousness, courage, and cleverness in the hero fated to return home from the war and restore his power. Ahl & Roisman's (1996, p. 129) discussion of the *Odyssey* refers to Odysseus as a reckless and destructive man: "The most terrifyingly consistent feature of Odysseus in the *Odyssey* is his ability to bring death and destruction, not life and new hope, upon everything he is associated with." He loses his entire crew to poor judgment and mismanagement. Whatever the metaphorical role his crew plays in the symbolism of a modern individual in postwar adjustment, he loses them all to situations that are reckless or foolish. The first adventure they have as soon as they leave the battlefield is to raid and sack the neighboring Cíconës. We know from the *Iliad* that Odysseus was in command of the "high-hearted Cephallenia" in 12 ships. In their ill-considered raid they lose six men from each of 12 crews, for a total of 72, which is a considerable loss even if we don't know the total number of each crew. Hexter (1993, p. 142) estimates crew strength as 58 per ship, or a total of over 700 in Odysseus's fleet when they left the battlefield. (Homer puts the Phaeacian crew at 52.) Odysseus is unable to control his men in the raid. They linger too long and are attacked by an avenging regrouped Cíconës army.

Escaping that peril, Odysseus then loses 11 of his 12 ships when they are allowed to sail into a harbor of the Laestrógians. The giants bombard the ships with rocks. Odysseus's own ship escaped because it had not sailed into range.

One crew member is killed on Circe's island in a drunken accident. Odysseus loses six crew members to the dreaded Scylla, who snatched them from the last remaining ship during a moment of foolish heroism by Odysseus. Circe had advised Odysseus to avoid rather than fight the Scylla, but Odysseus could not resist taking up his sword and, despite Circe's admonition not to fight the dreaded sea goddess, he challenged the Scylla and lost six crewmen.

Odysseus almost makes it home, when, with the aid of Áeolus's winds, he sails within sight of Ithaca. Then, strangely, he falls asleep like a guilty man about to succeed and his remaining crew ruin the homecoming. They are swept out to sea when his crew open Áeolus's bag of winds and a storm ensues. The rest of the crew are lost after their foolish adventure with Hélios's cattle. On Hélios's isle, Odysseus is meditating and again dozes when the crew eat the cattle of the sun god and Hélios appeals to Zeus to destroy them. Bad things happen when the hero sleeps, it seems. Earlier in the epic, Odysseus himself brings about the crew's near demise when he taunts the blinded Cyclops as he sails away. The blinded giant is able to fix on their location and lobs boulders, almost hitting the ship, because Odysseus impulsively shouts out his real name. He had earlier told the Cyclops that his name was Otis (Nobody). Just as they are escaping in their ship, Odysseus shouts out his real name, taking responsibility for his deed (injuring the giant) to ensure his fame (*kléos*). Cyclops appeals to his father, Poseidon, who takes up the anger and vows to make Odysseus's homecoming hard. And we note in the last book of the *Odyssey* that the townspeople and relatives of the suitors were not only angry about those slayings, they were also relatives of friends of the destroyed Cephallenian contingent (Fagles' 1996 trans., 24:472–475).

We see in PTSD the untamed nature of suppressed trauma memory and the inevitable compulsion to repeat when what is suppressed, when projected, engages the veteran in battle. An example of this projection is the Vietnam War veteran who had repressed the memory of taking part in a battle that killed most of his company. He had been sent to battalion to direct artillery fire and had been happy to work on safer turf. However, while he was on the radio at battalion his company was ambushed and, in the ensuing battle, his company command center had been hit by friendly fire and destroyed. He listened on the radio as his friends screamed and died. After the battle, he went on R&R. He subsequently remembered that he had been on R&R *during* the battle. It is only 30 years later, when he was sorting his late father's possessions, that he read his letters from Vietnam and realized the truth. This man had worked for years as a low-level clerk whose job it was to field phone calls from dissatisfied customers and listen helplessly as they pleaded their cases, knowing his company would do nothing to help.

One explanation was that, while not remembering his profound guilt, he nonetheless acted it out by holding himself in the job that was far below his potential, yet symbolically captured the emotional essence of his trauma. Odysseus repeatedly falls asleep and that allows his crew to commit their foolish acts, which is a metaphor, in this case, for the unconscious influence of repressed trauma memory.

Odysseus Aided by Gods

Odysseus functions best when aided by the gods. Hermes fortifies Odysseus with holy *moly* to neutralize Circe's power and Odysseus is finally able to restore his men to human shape. After Odysseus lingers a year with the enchanting goddess, his men have to urge him to leave. We know from the epic of Jason and the Argonauts (Rhodios, 1997, p. 168) that Circe is a cleanser of nightmares, nocturnal fears, and haunting memories.

Odysseus is kept by Calypso for seven years. Calypso, daughter of Atlas, the foundation of the world, is known as The Hider. She lives in a magnificent cave. She only releases Odysseus when directed by Hermes, who is acting as Zeus's messenger. The cave is a place for hiding and probably functioned as a safe place for primitive man, and for the modern veteran, the cave is a symbolic way to hide from recognition.

Odysseus is concealed in helpful ways by Athena; when he is entering the Phaeácian capital she covers him in a mist of invisibility that hides his estrangement (the citizens view him as familiar), and when he lands on Ithaca's shore, Athena, in the guise of a shepherd, first shrouds his homeland in fog. Then, in her epiphany, she changes him into an old beggar to allow him to arrive home in disguise.

Ino, Poseidon's daughter, helps Odysseus survive the storm that strips him of his last possession, casting him ashore on the Phaeácian coast. Athena helps Odysseus throw his discus at the Phaeácian games, battles with him against the suitors, argues for his release from Calypso before Zeus, and finally ends the poem with intercession to halt the outraged vengeance of the suitors' relatives and friends. She also gives assistance and advice to Telemachus and protects Penelope with sleep and an inspiring dream.

Circe helps Odysseus with advice about surviving the Sirens' sweet but deadly call to the past, and the perilous navigation between the Scylla (Nightmare) and Charybdis. What the Sirens offer Odysseus and his crew are songs about their war, tales of times in combat. Songs, however, suggest a romanticization of the events (Fagles, 1996, 12:197–208, p. 277).

Calypso supplies Odysseus with the stuff to build his raft and gives him treasure and precious clothing that he quickly loses in the storm. She even offers him immortality if he agrees to stay with her.

One does not fail when aided by divine intercession. With the help of Athena, the goddess of *mêtis*, Odysseus accomplishes deeds that become legend. But, as Homer points out, the gods don't help just anybody (16:182, Fagles' 1996 trans.). To be aided by a goddess is to leap out of the ordinary, beyond expectation, compulsive habit, and stereotype. It is to be able to think creatively and survive by artifice: the very qualities of the adult forebrain's so-called executive function which is influenced by PTSD. (Psychiatrist Jonathan Shay, [2002, p. 141,] did not believe that Odysseus had PTSD.)

Odysseus: The Trickster of Grief

Pucci (1987, p. 61) writes of Odysseus: "How this trickster can at the same time be represented as the most lamenting and troubled hero remains an intriguing and difficult problem for the *Odyssey*. Yet the *Odyssey* successfully attempts this feat: to make the trickster and the sufferer one person. The result is an odd economy in which Odysseus' brushes with death and his familiarity with anguish and grief conspire, always, with his survival and his final pleasures."

The survivor with PTSD is not who he seems to be. In *The Raven's Return* (Early, 1992), I wrote about the superhero as trauma survivor in disguise as a mild-mannered person, an analogy that was perhaps the most applicable for the war veteran in his twenties and thirties. A more contemporary example is the person touched by grief with the protean symptoms of PTSD disguised as an ordinary adult.

Odysseus's maternal grandfather was Autolycus. We learn of him when the old nurse sees Odysseus's scar and the poet recalls how Odysseus had been gored by a boar while hunting with his grandfather. It was Autolycus, a favorite of Hermes, who gave Odysseus his name, which means "son of pain." Hermes is an apt god for the nature of adaptation. He is the god of the borderland, of the thief, and the masquerade. Tracy (1990, p. 117) points out that Autolycus's name means "angry."

Naming Odysseus as one scorned by gods refers to his suffering nature, being long aggrieved and alienated. For although he is befriended by Ino, Hermes and Athena, he is punished by all-powerful Zeus and his brother, the seagod Poseiden, who is himself not to be ignored. They affect the warrior's fate in the mythical lands on the way home. The god of wind, Áeolus, scorns Odysseus's second entreaty for help like a frustrated mental health professional, referring to the hero as one who is afflicted by gods.

Grief and Vengeance

Even the most mundane formula of oral lore seeks aesthetic form [Austin, 1981, p. 20].

The most poignant picture of prolonged grief is the sight of Odysseus on Calypso's isle, weeping and pining for home. Shay (2002) comments that *nostalgia* is a word composed of the Greek roots *nostos* (return) and *algos* (pain). When he does finally return, we can appreciate his fury when he realizes that his palace is under siege. Hillman (2004) suggests that grief is a manifestation of Aphrodite.

Odysseus next expresses his grief during Demódocus's first song in King Alcinoüs's court. Demódocus sings of the Trojan War and Achaean victory. Odysseus weeps and hides his face. He is only seen weeping by the king, who mistakenly thinks he merely knew the ill-fated warriors. Demódocus's second song, interestingly, is a tribute to love and war combined. He sings of Hephestos capturing his spouse, Aphrodite, copulating with Arës, the god of war. He traps them in coitus in an unbreakable net and suspends them, calling on his family of Olympian gods to witness. The male gods assemble, while the goddesses retire to their chambers. Hermes and Apollo joke with Hephestos as they watch. This song of the entanglement of love and war appears to be an abstract of the whole Trojan conflict in which Menalaus rallies an army to retrieve his wife from Troy. Alexander (2009) demonstrates how Achaean leaders were bound by treaty to aid the aggrieved Menalaus, and were reluctantly drawn into fighting an otherwise meaningless war.

The slaughter of the 108 suitors is remarkable for its ferocity and unyielding vengeance. Odysseus, after revealing his identity, virtually seals off his palace and kills his wife's suitors like pests as they had gathered to celebrate the feast of Apollo, the Archer. Odysseus's feat follows a test put forward by Penelope in which she said that she would take as her husband the man who could string Odysseus's bow and shoot an arrow through a row of ax heads. Only Odysseus could succeed, and he then proceeded, utilizing his powerful bow, to kill the suitors. After the slaughter, Odysseus dispatches Telémachus to render justice to the disloyal servants. His son has them clean up the carnage, and then mercilessly has them hung by their necks in the courtyard. And even after all of his accomplishments, Odysseus still must pass a final test by Penelope, which he does when he describes the wedding bed that he himself fashioned within a living tree.

The slaying of the 108 suitors is an odious task. There is no fine distinction between good and bad suitors — all are slain quickly. This is a symbolic act that must be analyzed closely because so much of the *Odyssey* is devoted to the restoration of the palace of Odysseus. This is not the "Berserker" state described by Shay (1991, 1994), where fury takes on a life of its own. The oral tradition from which the tale is drawn represents a tradition of vengeance, suggesting that the story was meant to be taken as literal, premeditated vengeance that is conducted efficiently. Odysseus, in fact, stops his loyal servant from gloating in victory over the corpses of the suitors.

Age and tradition, however, cause us to take such grisly action symbolically as well. Odysseus's slaying of the suitors and execution of the disloyal maids is an act of vengeance that personifies what mental health professionals who work with combat veterans perceive as extreme anger. One can also assume that there are many more combat veterans of the angry ilk who are not likely ever to be included in epidemiological surveys, who avoid mental health professionals because they do not trust them. The veterans have anger that is manifested with a vengeance, i.e., an anger delivered with a vehemence that is forceful in extreme. Trauma in the area of trust, especially trust in authority, is why they do not trust. If they do happen into the psych ward of a hospital, they bounce out like a flat rock thrown into a pond. The stress of listening to such anger in close proximity is proportionally great, and too many mental health professionals (psychiatrists, nurses, psychologists, social workers, counselors, technicians, etc.) become quickly judgmental about the morality and correctness of such spoken vengeance and fail to respect it. An example of this rage-filled anger (often self destructive) can be seen in war veteran films, such as *The Searchers, Harry Brown, The Veteran*, and *Cutter's Way*. This anger, when tempered with artifice, results in more subtle forms of revenge, as in the battle for truth —*Absolute Power*.

In even more abstract terms, in modern language the odious work of killing the suitors represents a huge unpleasant task, nothing less than the restoration of one's authority. It is a task which cannot be accomplished alone and which takes wiliness, patience, and strength to pull off. In keeping with Murgnaham's assessment, quoted above, the *Odyssey*, in final analysis, describes the war survivor adapting to circumstances and with force of will, taking advantage of opportunity and working strategically toward a goal. An important distinction between the first and second halves of the *Odyssey* is that Odysseus, when he finally returns home, is no longer thoughtless or impulsive; he is, rather, patient and clever. He is more concerned about his reputation (*kléos*) and future, than about the past. For instance, we note the only exception in the killing of the suitors was the bard, who, as a latter-day news reporter, would add to Odysseus's *kléos*.

The Trickster Hero in Hiding

Working toward a goal is no simple matter for the survivor, for goal implies a concept of future. After spending seven years hidden by a goddess who offered him immortality if he agreed to stay with her, Odysseus chooses to return to his wife and declares his choice to Calypso by his mournful tears. Whereas, before, Odysseus was contemplating suicide, he finally chooses his family over joining forces with a goddess, giving his story a modern sensibility.

One combat veteran exemplified this choice when he sought treatment *because* he was recently married and expected soon to father children. His alternative was to leave his wife and return to the northern wilderness where he had been largely living since returning from Vietnam. His intelligence directed his choice, to learn how *not* to pass on his very obvious paranoid style of PTSD, and to, at the same time, opt for the relationship and family.

The myth of the return of the hero shows the war veteran both in disguise and in quest for the safety of his home. His struggle to control his emotions leads to various changes in temper and mood. If he learns to contain and cope with the symptoms, he will be, at best, an adroit manager of civilized demeanor, as well as a deceiver who longs for candor. The fate of Odysseus, as Tirésias relates it to him in the Land of the Dead, is that the war veteran, who didn't want to be drafted in the first place, will go on wandering, even after his homecoming and reunion with his wife. Tirésias predicts Odysseus will wander until he finds a people who do not recognize the oar. He will then plant it and return home to have a comfortable death. A restless fate at best to never be close to anyone for long, as if participating in war has cast a bell jar that separates the survivor from his world.

The people who do not recognize the oar must be out of the influence of Poseidon's vengeance, suggesting the calm that, hopefully, comes with old age. The problem of survival is the problem of coping and adapting to the high levels of stress brought on by this disruptive, primitive god who was offended on the battlefield and, therefore, demands foresight and circumspection from the veteran.

Many modern movies depict the war veteran from various cultures returning home to fight against great odds, whether it be during the Middle Ages, returning from the Crusades (*The Seventh Seal, Ivanhoe, Robin Hood*), in post World War I spiritual or spirit-driven quest (*Razor's Edge, The Last Flight, Heroes for Sale*), or dark mid-century America (*Key Largo, Nightfall, Bad Day at Black Rock*), or quixotically battling dark forces in a post–Vietnam society and government (*Absolute Power, Dead Presidents, The Stunt Man, First Blood, Taxi Driver, Conspiracy Theory, Cutter's Way*). The 1997 independent film gem *Ulee's Gold* represents a look at a modern Odyssean character some time after his return, with Telemachus in jail and Helen addicted to drugs. These are the ongoing, mundane, modern renditions of a classic epic created in the minds of the divinely inspired bards of ancient Greece. They show us that the war veterans' return is rarely quiet or peaceful, but a continuation of battle, both inside and outside, in myth and in society (16:233–6, Fagles's 1996 trans.).

CHAPTER 6

The Creature and the Child: Postwar Adjustment Through Relationships

> Children believe what we tell them, they believe that a rose plucked from a garden can bring drama to a family. They believe that the hands of a human beast will smoke when he slays a victim, and that this beast will be ashamed when confronted by a young girl. — Jean Cocteau, in the introduction to his 1946 film, *Beauty and the Beast*

The Big Red One, 1980

In Samuel Fuller's *The Big Red One*, war veteran actor Lee Marvin plays a nameless, weary World War I veteran in the throes of another European world war. He plays the unnamed infantry sergeant leading the squad of inexperienced young white men into their first combat. We follow these men over years and many battles through Europe on a path first experienced by director Samuel Fuller as a young private. Interspersed amid the scenes of combat and tension in North Africa, the sergeant is repeatedly approached by a pretty, long-haired Arab child of ambiguous gender. In Sicily, a ragged boy totes his dead mother in a cart. He bargains with the sergeant to help bury his mother in exchange for leading the squad to a German gun. A Sicilian village girl sticks flowers on the sergeant's helmet, which he wears incongruously into the next battle. Finally, in Czechoslovakia, he carries a starved child out of Falkenau concentration camp. Despite his attempts to nurse the child back to health, she dies. The gray-haired director, Fuller, can be seen in the role of an army newsreel cameraman, filming German children. He seems to be striking a theme in contrasting age and experience with innocence by juxtaposing the war veteran and the child. (In every one of Fuller's war movies, there is an abandoned or orphaned child.)

Fuller writes about his experience and what he witnessed at Falkenau in his 2002 autobiography, *A Third Face*.

> On a final inspection of the camp's buildings, our sergeant heard a moan behind a pile of worn clothing. He whirled and almost shot the ghastly girl who slowly raised her head. Her black and sunken eyes were frightened. She seemed about eighteen because she was so fragile and gaunt. She could have been younger or older. The sergeant picked up the young girl in his arms and carried her to the SS commandant's ex-quarters.
>
> The girl died a few days later.... For all of us, however, she remained a symbol of those mournful times filled with incomprehensible suffering and loss [pp. 217–218].

Children are the most helpless and the most common victims of war and, for many combatants, their tragic deaths remain the veterans' darkest memories. This dark memory, which I have here labeled "Creature" should not be confused with the veteran per se, but rather as an *influence* upon his or her identity after combat.

It is a theme, like a vein in a formation of rock, that runs through war veteran films, and the opening quote from Jean Cocteau sets it off smartly. The Creature tainted by death meets the child. It is a basic scene played out every New Year's Eve when old man Experience meets the innocent child fresh with hope. Here, however, it is not just experience, it is the traumatic experience of combat, and the child, for the war veteran, is more than innocence personified. As can be seen by Fuller's several examples in *The Big Red One*, the child is often also the victim of traumas (which is sometimes a key to the relationship,) and yet retains the substance of hope. Sometimes the child is a resource and a key to the war veteran's return to society, and, sometimes, the child and the veteran are worse off because of their encounter.

The first example of this theme that I know of is in Homer's *Odyssey*, when Odysseus, veteran of the ten-year Trojan War, a sea-battered derelict stripped bare of all things, a beast of nature, after ten years of wandering since the war, desiring desperately to return home, flounders ashore on the Phaeacian coast of Scheria. Athena has preceded him. She has enticed the Princess Nausicaa in a dream to go to the ocean to wash the family's laundry. Nausicaa is described as an adolescent girl, an unwed virgin. They encounter each other at the mouth of the river. Odysseus begs the young Princess to have pity on him, to befriend him, telling her a bit of his history, all the while not really identifying himself. Nausicaa describes the history of her land, Scheria, which is isolated at the end of the earth where no one visits. Nausicaa gladly aids Odysseus, as it seems the obligation of her countrymen, and he is returned to his homeland with a king's treasure, and, it is important to note that Athena sent Nausicaa, setting her up as a marriageable virgin princess vis-à-vis the battered warrior.

It is with the assistance of the adolescent girl that the war veteran manages to reach home. Odysseus himself is described in Fagle's translation as a "Man of misery" who awakens with a start "his heart pounding." The princess thinks his appearance is "appalling," but, then, after he describes his history and predicament (albeit ambiguously) and bathes in the river and rubs oil on his body, he is perceived by Nausicaa as a god and a potential husband. (Or, as she might say today, totally awesome!)

Outside the city, Odysseus is left by Nausicaa in a grove, which the Princess identifies as dedicated to Athena. Nausicaa doesn't want to be seen bringing a stranger home. Athena speaks to him through the rustle of the wind in the trees. The goddess casts a spell over Odysseus, interestingly for the war veteran, of making him seem familiar to the townspeople so that he is not seen as an alien — interesting because the most adaptable war veterans are usually not identified as veterans. They work and live in apparent harmony with the larger community, but they do not share the traumas of their war.

Beauty and the Beast, 1946

From a broader perspective, the Creature approaching the child is a variation of the archetypal story of Beauty and the Beast. Jean Cocteau's film is based on a 1757 story published in Le Magazin des Enfants, by Jean-Marie Leprince de Beaumont. She based her story on an earlier and much longer version by Gabrielle-Suzanne de Villeneuve, who published her Le Belle et la Bête in Les Contes Marins ou la Jeune Américaine in 1740. Both young women were married briefly to much older men. Mme. de Villeneuve was married to an army Lt. Colonel, who died within four years, and Mme. de Beaumont to "a dissolute libertine" (Zipes, 1989, p. 231). Cocteau himself was an ambulance driver in World War I.

Cocteau chose Mme. de Beaumont's shorter version, which was more easily adapted to cinema. He made the Beast (Jean Marais) seem romantic and suffering, drawn to carnage by enchanted animal instinct. Cocteau beautified the Beast, whose love for Beauty (Josette Day) was his redemption. Her acceptance of his bestial ugliness transformed him into a handsome (if less interesting) prince.

Cocteau's 1946 film version is magical. It mixes human features and artifice, as men's arms protrude from walls holding torches that light the way through the dark castle halls. Sooty faces stare and belch smoke from fireplace ceramics. Doors open automatically and a mirror portrays meaningful scenes, briefly, from another time and place. The enchanting music by Georges Euric plays in the background as Beauty dines alone.

Beauty's acceptance of the Beast is clearly her best choice: Mme. de Beaumont and Cocteau agree: the heart and soul win out over pomp and mean-spirited greed. Beauty is a heartfelt girl. As the third and most humble daughter of a merchant, she fulfills her dutiful obligations with cheerfulness. She is always faithful to her father, and serves him even at her own risk. This emphasis on heart and feeling that emanates from Beauty and influences her choice is triggered by her love for her father. It is just what the Beast needs, an infusion of feeling, heartfelt caring, to transform from beast to prince.

Bearskin

This theme of the dutiful third daughter, always the youngest, is carried on in the Grimms' fairy tale of another Creature, *Bearskin*, in which the war veteran becomes the Creature after he makes a pact with the Devil.

The Brothers Jacob and Wilhelm Grimm as young men experienced Napoleon's armies overrunning their village near Kassel in 1806. The first of their collections of *Tales* appeared in 1812, the year of Napoleon's retreat from Moscow. In their story of *Bearskin* (Grimm, 1972), an unnamed veteran is discharged at the end of the war. Rejected by his brother's family, he becomes a destitute derelict sitting in a circle of trees when the Devil, in a green coat (reminiscent of a medieval chthonic deity), approaches and offers him a deal: "You shall for the next seven years neither wash yourself, nor comb your beard, nor your hair, nor cut your nails, nor once say the Lord's prayer. I will give you a coat and a cloak, which during this time you must wear." The green coat gives wealth. The cloak is the skin of the bear he slew to prove his fearlessness. By the second year "he began to look like a monster. His hair covered nearly the whole of his face, his beard was like a piece of coarse felt, his fingers had claws, and his face was ... covered with dirt."

Bearskin is wealthy, but rejected by others and forced to wander alone. He takes shelter in the outhouse of an inn and there he meets an impoverished merchant to whom he gives money to pay for lodging. The grateful merchant offers his benefactor one of his daughter's hand in marriage.

The major difference between *Bearskin* and *La Belle et la Bête* is the point of view. *Bearskin* tells the story of the war veteran beast, and the girl enters at the conclusion of the story. The older daughters reject Bearskin for his ugliness, but the youngest (and most innocent) daughter does her duty: "The youngest, however, said: 'Dear father, that must be a good man to have helped you out of your trouble, so if you have promised him a bride for doing it, your promise must be kept.'" After she accepts him, Bearskin gives her half of his ring and leaves to finish his deployment with the Devil. When he is restored as promised, he returns as a rich and handsome gentleman. In *Beauty and the Beast*, the girl is at the center of the story and accepting *Le Bête* is her dilemma of self-sacrifice and duty.

Fairy tales really have no intrinsic gender and *Beauty and the Beast* can be interpreted from a male or female perspective, as Marina Warner (1994) points out: "The journey the story has itself taken ultimately means that the Beast no longer needs to be disenchanted. Rather Beauty has to learn to love the beast in him, in order to know the beast in herself" (p. 312). And from another perspective, Warner writes: "When men adopt this material, they often introduce special pleading on their own behalf; Cocteau's entrancing film, of 1946, for all its delicacy and dreamlike seductiveness, concentrates on awakening Beauty to consciousness of Beast's goodness" (p. 295).

In this sense, these variations of the Creature and the Child are to be seen as significant for different reasons to both characters. The war veteran as traumatized Creature sees hope in the non-threatening child to rediscover his own feelings, to reach back to a state of being before war. For the child, the Creature connects with soul, and that causes a meaningful attraction. He also offers the child (or so the child hopes) protection, security, and worldly knowledge. In *Beauty and the Beast*, the girl is obeying her father's wish, and finally comes to see the beauty in the beast. In *The Odyssey*, Nausicaa is attracted to the old warrior after he cleans himself, but she also has a devilish streak that wants to make a sensation at court by helping him in his cause.

Frankenstein, 1931

The fairy-tale theme takes a perverse twist in the 20th century when we see James Whale's 1931 film version of Mary Shelley's 1818 novel, *Frankenstein; or, The Modern Prometheus*. Whale was himself a veteran of combat in World War I, where he was a young officer in the trenches. He was captured and held prisoner by the Germans (Curtis, 1998). Whale made Dr. Frankenstein's Creature a brutal beast, depriving him of language and giving him a countenance reflecting his ghoulish parentage, having been sewn together from the parts of corpses with the brain of a criminal. (Jack Pierce did the makeup for Boris Karloff's Creature in a corpse-like gray.) The Creature is rejected by his creator, escapes his confinement, and wanders the countryside, when he happens upon Little Maria (Marilyn Harris) at the lake. This scene is quite at variance with Mary Shelley's gentle, articulate novel. In her original story, the Creature tries to save the peasant girl, who has fallen into a river. His noble efforts are misunderstood by the villagers and the Creature is eventually hunted like a wild animal by the town's vengeful citizens. Ultimately, the Creature flees to the Arctic netherworld. In Whale's 20th century film adaptation, the little girl is left by her father, who has gone off to the market. She is playing on the shore of a lake when the Creature approaches. She is lonely and greets him, inviting him to play with her, tossing daisies, one by one, into the water so that they float. She hands the Creature flowers and he dumbly tosses them all in. Then, when he has no more flowers, he picks up the girl and tosses *her* in. In the next scene, we see the grim father carrying the limp body of his drowned daughter through the village, putting a damper on the festive occasion of Dr. Frankenstein's marriage.

In Whale's movie version, Little Maria is lonely and readily accepts the Creature's companionship. There is a parallel with Beauty, in that Little Maria is symbolically abandoned by her father when he leaves for the market against her wishes.

It is significant that Whale's war veteran's version has the Creature behave like a brutal criminal, as if genetically cursed, killing the girl, whereas the female author's original version (Mary Shelley was also traumatized by maternal abandonment,) gives the Creature soul and caring (as well as articulate language), that is misunderstood by the citizens. By giving her Creature language and intelligence, she creates more romantic pathos when his intentions are misunderstood and he is driven to exile and death. Whale's brutish monster is logically no more than the sum of his parts.

Travis Bickle (Robert De Niro), the veteran in *Taxi Driver* (1976), is not unlike Frankenstein's creature, an outsider looking in. His isolation with urban society is unbridgeable with the exception of one person with whom he managed to have a meaningful connection: Iris (Jodie Foster), a 12-year-old prostitute, who became a symbol for him of his renewal, saving her to redeem himself.

As I describe in *The War Veteran in Film*, Martin Scorsese, the director of *Taxi Driver*, intended Travis to be viewed as a veteran of the war in Southeast Asia who was coming apart emotionally with sleep deprivation, drug abuse, and paranoid social alienation. Travis tries to date a female his age, Betsy (Cybill Shepherd), who is working on the political campaign of a presidential candidate. Travis's inappropriate choices (including taking her to see a pornographic movie), repel her. As he grows psychotic in his thinking, he buys guns and decides to kill the presidential candidate, who is, in a sense,

Taxi Driver (1976), Martin Scorsese, director. Robert De Niro plays Marine Corps veteran Travis Bickel, here applying for a job at a New York City taxi barn. The signs above his head, packed with irony, speak to his state of mind. (Columbia Pictures Corp.)

his rival for Betsy's attention. When he is spotted lurking near the speaker's platform at a rally and is chased away, he then decides to rescue Iris. The veteran's fascination with the girl is romantic in the sense that he wants to liberate her from the bondage of prostitution. He accomplishes this by killing everyone connected with her exploitation and nearly being killed himself in a prolonged, bloody scene that could only have traumatized Iris further.

Travis sees Iris as an innocent who needs to be liberated from the men who are exploiting her. Iris seemed to like Travis for his weirdness, but she did not want to be liberated, and one wonders what her life would offer her back home after her experiences in New York City.

Travis has some of the qualities of a man with a borderline personality disorder. When traumatized, he has symptoms which play out in crude ways; when he becomes psychotic with the aid of stimulants, he acts out his quest for wholeness in the most brutal, violent, primitive (albeit direct) way — and then, in the final scenes of the movie, seems to be at peace.

To demonstrate both the machinations of Hollywood and the toll of wars on culture, contrast Travis Bickle and Iris in *Taxi Driver* with the prewar veteran and the "child" in Billy Wilder's *The Major and the Minor* (1942), in which a young lady named Susan Applegate (Ginger Rogers) tries to leave New York City after a disappointing attempt to build a career. She is unable to afford the train fare to her hometown in Iowa, and so poses as a 12-year-old girl to qualify for half fare. She takes after the early film star Mary Pickford, who made a career as an adult playing adolescents. Susan meets the major (Ray Milland) while fleeing from the suspicious railway conductors (they catch her smoking between cars) and hides in his sleeping compartment. The major, we soon learn, is an instructor at a military academy because he has a bad eye. He wants to get into "active service" but is frustrated by his influential fiancée, who wants to keep him at the academy. Susan plays into the major's poor vision and Wilder plays with the absurd idea of a mature-looking woman posing as a 12-year-old girl and fooling everybody but the major's young niece (Diana Lynn). The cadets at the military academy are infatuated in a manner that seems, at best, as naïve. The major is not a Creature, but in the final scene, he and Susan agree to marry before he goes off to the Pacific Theater to engage in "active service." She will be one of those brides who then awaits the return of her husband from the war, who will hopefully be similar to the one who left. To play out the titillation of the story, the Hollywood studio promotional trailer states salaciously: "The uproarious adventure of a big little girl who's too good to be true!"

The Spirit of the Beehive, 1973

One important film makes the connections between these disparate images of the Creature or Beast, the war veteran, and the child. The connection came in the remarkable 1973 Spanish film in which a little girl ministers to the war veteran *as* the Creature. *El Espiritu de la Colmena* (*The Spirit of the Beehive*) was released in 1973. Directed by Victor Erice, the story takes place in a small rural town "somewhere in Castile," in 1943. A truck rumbles into town, bringing film canisters. The children crowd around as the truck is unloaded, yelling, "The movie is coming!" The driver announces that the movie is "*Dr. Frankenstein.*" The screen is set up in the town hall. The children sit in front, the women occupy the middle chairs, and the men stand in back. The projectionist unscrews the light bulb and the film begins with its ominous warning to the audience by actor Edward Van Sloan who says, "I think it will thrill you. It may shock you. It might even horrify you."

Not everybody in town is at the movie. A man works a beehive and a woman in a stone house writes a letter to a soldier. We don't know who her correspondent is: lover or relative. She mourns the war's destruction. On his way home the beekeeper passes the town hall and sees the poster of James Whale's 1931 classic. On the screen is the scene depicting the Creature's encounter with Little Maria at the lakeside. Two girls, daughters of the bee-keeper and the letter-writing woman, watch mesmerized in the audience. They are "Las Niñas:" Ana (Ana Torrent), and Isabel (Isabel Telleria). Ana, the younger, is captivated by the Creature and asks her sister why he killed Little Maria. Isabel puts her sister off, and later, in a tautly sustained scene of the girls whispering in their beds, she tells Ana that the creature is real. "I've seen him alive," she says. "He's a spirit."

After school the next day, Isabel takes Ana to a deserted stone barn where she claims to have seen the Creature. Ana is in a spell, peering into a well, and then, with trepidation, into the empty barn. She finds a large boot print in the dirt by the well and it seems to be proof to her that the Creature was there.

There is a bit of perversity in Isabel. She tricks Ana and charms her with lies. In one scene she feigns death, posing limply on the floor, to be discovered by Ana. In another she squeezes the cat about the neck until it protests.

Ana, enraptured by the story about the Creature, sneaks out of the house at night. The scene cuts to that of a man jumping from a moving train and injuring himself in the fall. He appears to be an escaping prisoner, perhaps a leftist guerrilla who survived the Civil War. Ana finds him hiding in the barn with an injured leg and ministers to his needs. She helps him tie his shoe. She brings him an apple and then her father's coat — with his musical watch still in the pocket. Then, in the dark of the night, the deserter is killed in a gun battle. He is next seen laid out on a table in the town hall, feet sticking out from the covering sheet, and we are reminded of Dr. Frankenstein's Creature.

Ana's father confronts his daughter. She runs away and hides in the dark beside a glittering body of water. In a hallucinatory vision, the Creature of Dr. Frankenstein visits her, kneeling beside her as he did in the famous movie scene.

The significance of *The Spirit of the Beehive*, for our purpose, rests in the connection Ana makes between the fugitive veteran and Dr. Frankenstein's Creature. Ana is caught in the spirit of the profound image so quickly tossed off in James Whale's rendition of the deadly encounter between the malformed Creature, rejected by his creator, and the innocent girl. Ana approaches the injured fugitive as if he *were* the Creature. He stands for the veteran who has lost his innocence in war. *The Spirit of the Beehive* picks up on an archetypal theme, a variation of which is in Whale's brutal version of *Frankenstein*.

Ana's fate is unclear. She has flirted with danger out alone in the dark of night. She has been, it seems, fatally attracted to the danger implied by the Creature's strange power. The doctor reassures the girl's mother that Ana will, in time, recover.

Other films that illustrate aspects of the theme of the Creature and the Child (all summarized at the end of this essay) are: *Fairy Tale: A True Story* (1997), *Sundays and Cybele* (1962), *Ulee's Gold* (1997), *Desert Bloom* (1986), *Spitfire Grill* (1996), *Missing in America* (2005), *Distant Thunder* (1988), *Land of Plenty* (2008), *Little Lips* (1999), *In Country* (1989), *The War* (1998), *Gran Torino* (2010), *Absolute Power*, (1997), *True Grit* (2010).

Sir Gawain and the Green Knight

An interesting literary variation of the theme of the Creature and the Child deals with the aspect of shame, which appears to be a critical feeling in this discussion. The process of shame is inevitable for some survivors of the repeated traumas of combat. Shame, we know, can accompany the repeated witnessing of death, destruction, and suffering, as well as the contagion of combat action and excitement, especially, as our opening quote for this chapter declares, when the veteran is confronted with innocence. When shame occurs in a war veteran, it is a feeling that alienates the veteran from others in the society to which he returns, including, and perhaps especially, his family. Hundt and Holohan (2012) found shame as a distinguishing feature among perpetrators of intimate partner violence in U.S. veterans. Dave Grossman, in his *On Killing* (1995, 2009), renders excellent illustrations of the shame that follows killing. This is a critical issue when a country that produces the combatants denies the horrible consequences: that combat produces rage, atrocities, ugly emotions, death, and dismemberment, causing combatants, young men and women, to experience changes in their values, while the citizens at home are shielded in innocence.

Sir Gawain and the Green Knight is a rare piece of early English literature of unknown authorship. It was probably recorded from oral tradition in the later Middle Ages and has elements of folk tradition involving solstice festivals and Arthurian mythology. The story is charming for its adherence to Courtly Love and for maintaining the magic of enchantment (Merwin, 2004). The story is relevant to the modern combat veteran, particularly regarding the problems presented by adherence to duty and the emotion of shame regarding choices and circumstances of combat.

Gawain is a knight present at King Arthur's Round Table, celebrating the winter solstice when an awesome event occurs. A gigantic knight rides into the court bearing a huge battle ax. (The cutting edge is about 4.5 feet.)

Even more spectacular is the fact that the fearsome knight and his horse are both bright green. The associations are at once to death (decay) and to vegetation (life). The Green Knight challenges the king and any of his knights. He offers the use of his ax to anyone who would cut off his (the Green Knight's) head on the condition that that person must seek out the knight next solstice and accept the same blow in return. All at the court are awestruck, and as the king rises to accept the challenge, Gawain intercedes like a soldier volunteering and asks that the battle be his (Merwin, 2004, p. 25).

Gawain agrees to the fight in the place of the king. He cuts off the head of the Green Knight. However, the giant reaches down and picks up his bleeding head by his green hair, leaps onto his horse and calls out his challenge to Gawain. He will have to go to a place, The Green Chapel, a year from that date to receive his fate.

When the time has passed and winter returns, Gawain dutifully sets off to find the Green Knight. The epic emphasizes Gawain's hardship. He faces peril, loneliness, and deprivation in his search, for he does not know where the Green Chapel is located. Merwin uses a wonderfully simple line that captures the war veteran's plight: "He slept in his armor / among naked rocks more than enough nights" (p. 53).

Eventually, he arrives at a castle where he is given shelter and a promise to be taken to the Green Knight's chapel in time for his end-of-the-year appointment. In the meantime, he is entertained by the castle's lord and lady. The lord of the castle recognizes Gawain as "a prince without peer\where bold men fight" (p. 61) and proposes a game between he and Gawain: they will exchange whatever they gain that day. The lord engages in a hunt and, on each of three successive days, brings in his kill and gives it to Gawain. The poem describes each day's hunt in gruesome detail; the killing and slaughtering of a deer on the first day, the dismemberment of a giant boar on the second, and the skinning of a wily fox on the third. Gawain stays at the castle during the hunts. Each day the lady of the castle visits him in his bedchamber. Each time she visits she offers her body to the knight and each time he refuses her with such graceful courtly language that she is not offended. Each day they kiss, first once, then twice, then thrice. Thus, each time the lord of the castle returns to give Gawain his kill, Gawain kisses the lord, returning each in the number he was given by the lady of the castle.

Significantly, the lady insists on giving Gawain a gift on her last visit. She gives him her green belt, which, she claims, carries the power to prevent death to its wearer. This gift Gawain secrets on his person and does not turn over to the lord. He rides off to the Green Knight's chapel with the sash wrapped around his waist "to save himself when his time came to suffer / And wait for death with no sword to defend him or other blade" (p. 139).

Gawain travels off at his appointed time, directed to the Green Chapel, which turns out to be a cave and a mound where the Green Knight is sharpening his blade. Gawain submits to the blow. First, the Green Knight feints with his ax, and Gawain winces. The Green Knight taunts him and makes him bow for a second blow. This he delivers without Gawain flinching, but delivers only a nick on the knight's neck.

The Green Knight, who is called "a wild monster with no use for mercy," spares Gawain. He reveals himself to be the lord of the castle Gawain just left. The nick on his neck is for not giving up the gift of the Lady's green belt.

Gawain returns to Arthur's court in shame, although he is praised by everyone who hears his story. So admired was Gawain that the Knights of the Round Table thereafter wore a bright green sash as a symbol of his bravery.

> "Look, sire," he said, and held up the belt,
> "This ribbon belongs with the blame branded around my neck,
> This is the harm and loss that I have endured
> For the cowardice and coveting that I was caught in there.
> This is the token of the untruth I was taken in
> And I must wear it as long as I live,
> For no one can hide the wrong he does, nor be free of it,
> For if ever it takes hold, nothing can cut it away"
> [Merwin, 2004, pp. 170–171].

Sir Gawain and the Green Knight can be compared to the story of the war veteran who delivers the blow for the government and then must submit to his fate of dealing with the return blow, which is his life disrupted. The poem spends the heart of its story creating the sharp contrast between the lady's tender offer of love, repeated more arduously each day, with the lord's rough hunts and detailed bloody slaughters. Gawain must accept both, but must accept only the lady's kisses, not her body. When she gives him her magic belt that guarantees his well-being, he breaks his ethical code and the rules of the game. This is his shame: he has survived by protecting his life. It is a poignant truth for war veterans that those who admire the veterans' accomplishments do not comprehend their shame. I am reminded of Marine veteran Eugene Sledge's remembrance of his experience on Okinawa looking at the body of a dead Marine:

> Every time I looked over the edge of that foxhole down into that crater, that half-gone face leered up at me with a sardonic grin. It was as though he was mocking our pitiful efforts to hang on to life in the face of the constant violent death that had cut him down. Or maybe he was mocking the folly of war itself: "I am the harvest of man's stupidity. I am the fruit of the holocaust. I prayed like you to survive, but look at me now. It is over for us who are dead, but you must struggle, and will carry the memories all your life. People back home will wonder why you can't forget" [Sledge, 1981, p. 270].

For Esmé

A variation of feeling shame upon returning home after combat is survivor's guilt, which is the kind of thing that Walt referred to in Clint Eastwood's 2010 film *Gran Torino*: shooting an enemy who is surrendering. Usually the context of such events are blurred and forgotten. Like a lot of problems connected with PTSD in veterans, survivor's guilt has become a cliché. But when Walt commits suicide in a variation of Suicide-by-Cop, in this case Suicide-by-Gangsters, we really have to pay attention to the problem that some combatants survive at the expense of others, traumatized in violent acts that can only be explained in the context of combat.

Author J.D. Salinger achieved international success with his first novel, *Catcher in the Rye*. He followed up with collections of stories, among them *Nine Stories*, published in 1953. Salinger was drafted into the U.S. Army and served from 1942 to 1945. He was a member of an army intelligence team attached to the 12th Infantry Regiment that landed on Utah Beach during the Normandy Invasion of 1944. His outfit suffered heavy losses. According to biographers Ian Hamilton (1988) and Kenneth Slawenski (2010), Salinger served with the Fourth Infantry Division, then stationed in Devon, England, for training. He was with the 12th Infantry Regiment and assigned the job of interviewing prisoners and civilians in the war zone because he spoke French and German. His unit fought through France and the fierce winter of 1944, with the heaviest fighting over the battles for Hürtgen Forest and the Ardennes offensive, the Battle of the Bulge, in which everybody was thrown into line combat. Army records of the 12th indicate that the regiment (considering replacements) suffered 125 casualties. After VE day Salinger was hospitalized, apparently for exhaustion.

Salinger's short story "For Esmé—With Love and Squalor" describes a veteran, who six years later receives a wedding invitation from a girl and makes notes about meeting her in England. He writes that he was part of a 60-man intelligence unit receiving special training.

The narrator, addressing the reader in the first person, describes walking into town and stopping at a church because he heard children singing, and made note of one adolescent girl standing near him and singing better than the others. He leaves the church and goes to a teahouse and there meets the girl again, only this time she is with her little brother and her aunt. She introduces herself as Esmé. She and her brother are orphans: her father died in the war, and her mother had just died. Esmé is precocious, pretentious, and endearing. She ends their conversation with the invitation to exchange letters. She also asks him to write a story for her and encourages him to include elements of squalor, because she loves stories with squalor.

The second part of the story takes place in a barracks after the war had ended. The narrator describes a Staff Sergeant X, in conversation with a buddy who visits him. (Slawenski [2010, p. 392n] speculates that the buddy was taken after John Keenan, later of the New York City Police Dept.) They have ridden a Jeep together through the course of the European fighting. Sgt. X has had a "nervous breakdown." The narrator takes a point of view that fittingly describes dissociation: "I'm still around, but from here on in, for reasons I'm not at liberty to disclose, I've disguised myself so cunningly that even the cleverest reader will fail to recognize me" (Salinger, 1953, p. 103). Sgt. X has "the shakes" and a nervous tic. He has difficulty concentrating when it comes to reading and writing. His buddy who visits has a European Theater campaign ribbon with "five bronze stars," indicating five major battle engagements, evidence that they had been in frequent combat. His visitor informs Sgt. X that his girlfriend wrote him that people didn't have nervous breakdowns just from combat; he must have had other mental problems: "She says you were probably unstable like your whole goddamn life."

What is important in terms of this essay is that Sgt. X is unable to correspond with Esmé, whose letter has found him through a succession of APO addresses. He has lost his identity and, with it, the innocent girl, with whom he can no longer communicate.

The veteran has recovered, at least somewhat, for he has married and seems to be functioning well enough. Salinger's war record is sketchy, because he became a recluse at the height of his literary fame. He stopped publishing and declined almost all interviews. There are sufficient parallels and details in "For Esmé" that the story might very well be autobiographical. Hamilton suggests that Salinger is "a writer whose work is more than usually powered by autobiography" (p. 11). Salinger introduced his *Nine Stories* with a quote from a Zen koan, a call to meditate: "We know the sound of two hands clapping,/But what is the sound of one hand clapping?" According to his unauthorized biography (Hamilton, 1988), while Salinger didn't stop writing (he only stopped publishing), he did stop indulging his fame (clapping)—creating an enigma that lasted to his death in 2010. This veteran, who was traumatized on the job of interrogating prisoners during World War II, finds being interviewed so obnoxious that he stops the process as his fame crests. Salinger wrote in a letter that, on one occasion, when he and his partner had taken a collaborator prisoner, the enraged French citizens took their prisoner and beat him to death, while the soldiers watched. Salinger's "official" biographer, Kenneth Slawenski (2010), more thoroughly details the author's exceptional combat experiences and notes that almost 70 years later, during a deposition in a lawsuit against Ian Hamilton, that Salinger referred to himself in the third person during wartime as "the boy," which may indicate that his dissociation, suggested in "For Esmé," continued throughout his adult life (Salwinski, 2010, p. 392n).

All of these confrontations between the war veteran Creature and the child are symbolic of the problem of the war veteran living with himself (or herself) in the peacetime world untouched by destruction, when his or her spirit has been contaminated by brutality and carnage. The warrior has been made to feel the beast by prolonged combat, the "squalor" of Salinger's story "For Esmé." The warrior's identity has changed by his becoming a veteran. A few return from combat to the civilized world and cannot contain the beast. Their savagery becomes manifest in crime and brutality; they go to prison, or become ostracized, or re-enlist for more combat. However, for most war veterans this problem is not so apparent. They struggle to relate in a way that is appropriate for their society. For them, Creature is an inner state of imagery and feelings associated with memories of combat. But the war veteran also *is* the child, one who must relate to the memory of himself (or herself) as an innocent with the knowledge of the worst that is experienced in the form of cruelty and ugliness. Children are the first victims of warfare.

Demodocus Sings

The *Odyssey* episodes of Odysseus in Phaeacia are most interesting from the point of view of the veterans' postwar grief. Odysseus does something that is curious when Demodocus sings of the wily veteran's greatest accomplishments in war. When the blind bard sings of Odysseus's device of the gift horse that hides the elite warriors and brings about the Achaean victory, Odysseus, the veteran, covers his head with his blue cape and weeps (8:99–103, Fagles's 1996 trans., p.194).

There is passion in grief. Hillman (2004, p. 148) states, "Grieving in war is one of the ways the love goddess works in the soul." The bard next sings of Ares's and Aphrodite's tryst that is discovered by Hephaestus, who devises an unbreakable net to capture the lovers. The cuckolded god, the deformed god of invention, Hephaestus, caught his adulterous spouse, Aphrodite, with her lover, the straight arrow god of war, Ares, wrapped together in coitus. Hephaestus surrounded them in his unbreakable net and displayed their struggling bodies before the other divinities. Again, there is shame.

Alexander (2010, p. 116) supposes this song to have been a popular "set piece" that was a favorite of audiences of Homer's time. Yet Homer's choice and timing demands that it be taken as a comment on the war. Throughout the *Iliad* Ares was not treated well. Alexander observes that the god of war was not given "a single act of dignity" (p 111). Aphrodite, of course, was behind the momentous elopement of Helen with Paris that triggered the Trojan War.

The words *shame* and *fame* clang like opposite sides of the same bell. A stereotype describes a common behavior pattern: that veterans who have found combat daunting tend toward modesty and have a critical eye for those who boast about their time in war. It is not uncommon to hear even the wounded veterans speak of not having done much, pointing out that others had it much worse. Those with awards speak only of having done what they were trained to do. Their modesty seems to be in correlation with their time in combat.

Aphrodite is a goddess of sensual pleasure, beauty, and delight. Without her blessings life would be dull. That wrapping of the attributes of war (strength, courage, honor, duty) with sensual delight seems like a bundling of opposites (although Ares is also known for slaughter, ruin, and brutality, and Aphrodite for unchecked lust). Sage Demodocus delivers the tale as light comedy. Hermes quips how he'd love to be in bed with Aphrodite (Fagles, p. 202). It is Poseidon, Odysseus's divine nemesis, a god of primitive emotion, who finally intercedes, like a defense attorney, to free the god of war and the goddess of love, who are quick to run off in different directions.

The shame of the warrior is not of having witnessed and participated in combat, but in having to return to a peaceful civilian life with the memory of having an attachment to some of the experiences in war as evidenced by great attraction to the memories. It is virtually impossible to describe, in sensible terms, such contradiction. One doesn't love suffering, except that it is memorable for the passion in it. Most people know passion only in the experiences of love and loss (grief). Some, who are blessed, find passion in creative work, which is usually some combination of love and grief. War veterans will acknowledge the bonding that takes place when combatants (people who are selected for their youth and vigor) suffer through hardships together. In their work they are dedicated to protecting each other in combat. Some will never again know such intimacy (Shay, 2002, p. 211; Alexander, 2009, p. 147). (This close camaraderie is beautifully illustrated in the excellent 2010 documentary of the Afghan war, *Restrepo*.) Nor are they likely to be as connected with the here-and-now present as they were in their combat experiences, nor do they expect to again experience such spectacular and strange events. The veteran does not have to love war to miss it. Hillman, a World War II hospital corpsman, put it nicely when he wrote, "The world of war's horror and fear is also a world of desire and attraction" (p. 109).

Sloan Wilson's novel *The Man in the Gray Flannel Suit* presents a real wartime love affair that serves as a metaphor for the veteran's shame. Then there is the shame that causes the veteran to withdraw from civilized society in *Missing in America* and *Distant Thunder*, and the horrible trauma of leaving a wounded friend behind, which is seen in *The War* and *Jacknife*. It is the shame that often accompanies trauma where death and helplessness contaminate the memory.

In *Waltz with Bashir* the Israeli war veteran director, Ari Folman, dramatizes his shame ("We were Nazis") at the destruction of warfare, of not intervening in the slaughter of civilians as it was perpetrated by another, allied, army. War veteran movie director Jean Renoir articulates what he refers to as collective "decadence" that accompanies participation in war: "Defeat had corrupted Germany, but no more than so-called victory had corrupted France. I can see now that, win or lose, no nation can escape the decadence engendered by war" (1973, p 96). But nations that engage in foreign wars do not have a civilian population that is caught up in combat destruction. The veteran who returns from the foreign war has experienced a profound emotion that can be shared only with great difficulty, and then possibly misunderstood. This is illustrated in the surreal 2010 film *Shutter Island*, and certainly suggested in Samuel Fuller's *The Big Red One*, both concerning the GI's reaction to liberating concentration camps at the end of World War II. Often the veteran just returned is met with emotional ceremony and cheers from friends and family, very often using words like *hero* and *valor*, while death and suffering linger in the memory. Salinger commented in a letter, "You could live a lifetime ... and never really get the smell of burning flesh out of your nose" (Slawenski, 2010, p. 133). Recall the suggested shame of the Marine veterans being paraded after the First Gulf War, having never really engaged the enemy in *Jarhead*.

The scene of the gods of love and war coupled and suspended as spectacle by the crippled god of artifact is described by the blind poet perhaps as a metaphor for Homer's great epic dramatization in the *Iliad*. Alexander (2009) presents a convincing argument that it was Homer's intent in the *Iliad* to dramatize the human destruction caused by a conflict that the participants were reluctantly compelled to carry out. She refers to Homer's "insistent depiction of the war as a pointless catastrophe that blighted all" (p. 220). James Hillman (2004, p. 9) refers to "that strange coupling of love and war." He writes: "Yet where else in human experience, except in the throes of ardor — that strange coupling of love and war — do we find ourselves transported to a mythical condition and the god most real?" The Vietnam War-era peace slogan, "Make Love not War" implies there is a way of separating the two by making a choice, although it seems that since Homer's time (750 BC) it was a choice unavailable to the combatants. In many ways, that "strange coupling" describes any war veteran's account of war.

Rushmore, 1998

An instructive variation of the Creature and the Child theme is seen in the war veteran who has adapted relatively well to civilian life, made a success of his business, married, and is raising a family. In the 1998 film *Rushmore*, the veteran is Harold Bloom (Bill Murray). He is so successful with his manufacturing business that he is giving an endowment to a local private school, Rushmore. But, under the surface, he is an isolated man who is alienated from his wife, and seems to dislike his two rather oafish boys. To assuage his loneliness, he drinks alcohol and smokes cigarettes to excess. In the process of endowing the school, he becomes close to one of the strangest students, Max (Jason Schwartzman), who is the protagonist of this offbeat story. Through Max, Harold Bloom meets a school teacher, Miss Cross (Olivia Williams) and falls in love. She becomes his guiding muse, who may just help him find his way out of isolation.

Wes Anderson directed this light-hearted, deadpan comedy that has the precocious Max spouting clichés of war films as he directs a student play about the Vietnam War. Harold Bloom is a Vietnam War veteran who succeeds in his commercial enterprise and gathers about him all the prizes of material success, but his status does not cover his rough edges. An example of this comes early in the film, during which his family gathers for a party around their swimming pool. All the guests sit on one side, while Bloom sits alone, defiantly, on the other side, drinking, wearing gauche swim trunks bearing the Budweiser logo.

The demure school teacher, Miss Cross, represents the antidote for Bloom's careless cynical alienation: softness, caring, and a genuine interest in life. She is a widow who lost her husband to disease; behind her soft warmth is sadness. Both Bloom and Max fall for her, resulting in a feud. Max is an unrealistic adolescent in his ardor for Miss Cross, while maladroit Bloom sees in her a chance to escape his loneliness.

That Bloom is able to meet Miss Cross through Max is important. Max is the kid who comes to the wealthy prep school through a scholarship contest, writing and submitting a play, and is an odd but creative student. He is an outsider among the other students, and that status leads him to affiliate with Bloom and, in the process, introduce the war veteran to his muse.

The Enchanted Cottage, 1945

Perhaps the sappiest of all war veteran films is *The Enchanted Cottage* (directed by John Cromwell), made at the end of the Second World War when the U.S. was anticipating an influx of wounded war veterans. Robert Young plays Oliver, who in the beginning of the film is about to be married, but Pearl Harbor is bombed by the Japanese and he goes off, unwed, to join the Army Air Corps. The honeymooning couple was planning to stay in a cottage that carried a long-standing enchantment that the proprietor, Mrs. Minnett (Mildred Natwick), knows about. A homely local village woman who is employed as a maid at the cottage, Laura (Dorothy McGuire), also knows of the enchantment, but as local legend. When Oliver returns from the war he is maimed; one arm hangs useless, and he bears a scar from his eye to his ear. He closes himself off from his mother and his fiancée, both of whom are outwardly startled by his wounds. He calls himself a "hideous casualty." When he comes to live in the cottage, he finds that Laura accepts him, and they grow close. He asks Laura to marry him, feeling rejected by his fiancée. Laura loves him from the moment she sees him, and he learns to love her, and it happens that the enchantment of the cottage takes hold and they are transformed. She becomes beautiful in his eyes, and his wounds are unseen by her. They see each other as beautiful and whole, because their love influences their perception. Even when they discover their mutual delusion, their love persists.

The instructive part of this film, besides the truism that love influences perception, is that the wounded, alienated veteran and the homely girl are perceived more accurately by others. They remain enchanted by their feelings for each other. The world sees them differently, but that doesn't matter to the lovers themselves.

Looking back over these scenes from across the ages, we can see the theme of the difficult encounter of the war veteran and the child. The child, who is male or female, and of varying age, is metaphoric, for the important characteristic is innocence, which is not necessarily the absence of trauma. The first view of this confrontation is when Odysseus meets Nausicaa and has the task, very much like Gawain's, of pleasing the princess while she is befriending him, without introducing any manifest sexuality. Both men are lost without the help that is offered by the child.

In other variations of this story, the veteran is lost in spite of, or because of, the relationship with the child. In *Sundays and Cybele* (1962, French), the veteran, who has been brought back to feeling by the abandoned girl, is also killed because of community misunderstanding of his association with her. Similar fates await the veterans in *The Dawning* and *Spitfire Grill*.

Little Lips presents the theme in the context of the war veteran's fascination for the war-orphaned girl as both a way back into feeling and out of isolation. The suicide of the war veteran speaks to the primitive nature of the despair of living without innocence.

Clint Eastwood's Walt in *Gran Torino* also commits suicide (gets himself killed) after aiding a Hmong boy and the boy's family. It is through the boy that he breaks out of his isolation, but in doing so he gets himself into a situation in which he feels the need to sacrifice himself to make sense of his wartime trauma of killing prisoners.

Shame drives avoidance as a symptom of post-combat adjustment. It hardens over time as the veteran ages, and more of life becomes associated with the trauma. The child's acceptance and need for the veteran exposes his shame, opens the wound with feeling, as it were, and, while it fosters healing and leads to potential creativity, the open wound also makes the veteran vulnerable: opening one's self to allow feeling invites grief.

The premise of *The Enchanted Cottage* is actually true: that love is capable of transforming the veteran's environment, making the world an interesting place. The Creature, through relationship, is transformed into a handsome prince.

CHAPTER 7

Psychological Trauma and Creativity

As the *Enchanted Cottage* suggests, the effects of psychological trauma can be mitigated by allowing the mind to be creative. This chapter will explore some of the ways this is done.

Movie Directors Who Were War Veterans

San Francisco psychiatrist Lenore Terr (1987, 1990) wrote of the impact of psychological trauma on the works of various creative people. She cited, for instance, Alfred Hitchcock's trauma of being "arrested" and put in jail as a child, after his father conspired with the jailer to teach his son a lesson. Hitchcock's dominant theme in his later movies has to do with the innocent man wrongfully accused and threatened. I note that movie director Roman Polanski had survived in Nazi-occupied Poland by hiding out while his parents were killed. His movies frequently depict the characters as trapped and threatened in isolation (for instance *Knife in the Water* [1961], *Cul-du-sac* [1966], the horrific *Repulsion* [1965], *The Pianist* [2007], and his recent *Ghost Writer* [2010]). These great directors were not driven to create the subjects, but those were the subjects that attracted their attention. Combatants who become movie directors also process traumas through their works because they are interested in the subject.

The influence of psychological trauma on the survivor's artistic expression can be attributed to the strength of the artist's memory, with trauma, by definition, leaving a highly salient mark, whether it is conscious or merely an influence on the creative process. Terr (1987) shows that the trauma memory keeps appearing in the creative imagination of the survivor, in the play of children, and in the creative works of adults. The movie directors who were also combat veterans, with the exception of the early Hollywood studio directors William Wellman and James Whale, all had creative control over their films, sometimes relegating themselves to the economic fringes of the industry. Jean Renoir, by the time he got to Hollywood, had established himself as an internationally respected film director, but still had to maneuver to keep some control. He, like Altman, sought location shooting as a way to get distance from the studio's interference.

The repetition of warfare and the tremendous influence of warfare on national populations tap the combat veteran's imagery. Oliver Stone, for instance, was moved to film the autobiography of the paralyzed Marine veteran Ron Kovic (*Born on the Fourth of July*). The fact that Stone himself was wounded in the neck, nearly being paralyzed himself, must have made this project especially meaningful to him. Similarly, William Wellman's back injury and pain must have influenced his filming of *Heroes for Sale*. The histrionic melodrama of Samuel Fuller's film about treatment in a mental hospital, *Shock Corridor*, seems more understandable coming from a man who suffered from repeated nightmares of witnessing, when he was a young cub reporter, the execution by electric chair of a convict.

Wellman, Fuller, Stone, and Melville all filmed stories of their own combat experiences. There are similarities, also, in the careers of the combat veteran directors' independence, often battling the control of the studios. For instance, Robert Altman, a former bomber co-pilot, was legendary for the ease with which he seemed to share control over the movie-making process. Many observers in his oral biography comment on how flexible and open he was to the suggestions of others, although they all noted that he usually got exactly what he wanted at the end of the day (Zuckoff, 2009).

ROBERT ALTMAN

Robert Altman enlisted at age 19 in the Army Air Corps and flew 50 missions as co-pilot in a B-25 bomber in the Pacific against defended Japanese targets in the East Indies and Southwest Pacific. He was stationed on Morotai, in the Halmahera Islands of Indonesia, and flew missions over Borneo against Japanese oil fields. He was wounded by flak (the fire of antiaircraft guns), as were several of his crew.

Altman had a penchant for gambling that seems to have developed in the army during the war. He was known, at times, to gamble everything he had when he returned to the States and began his film career. Commented one observer: "He really was a man who believed in his luck." His sister reported that he had "horrible" nightmares for two or three months when he lived in the family home after the war (Zukoff, 2009, p. 52).

Altman was renowned for chance-taking in his movie work. He was loved by actors for having faith in their talents, but was at odds with studio executives and frequently defiant about meeting demands from the people who financed his films. The spirit of his rebelliousness against authority is captured early in his career, *MASH* (the later, hit television series was spelled with asterisks, i.e., M*A*S*H), which was a highly successful dark comedy about the non-comformist personnel at a mobile field hospital during the Korean War. Altman would seem the obvious choice to direct *Catch- 22*, but that assignment went to Mike Nichols. (Joseph Heller, author of *Catch-22*, flew 60 missions over Italy and France as a bombardier in a Mitchell B-25 bomber, which flew between 7,000 and 12,000 feet, making it vulnerable to flak.) *MASH* was released in 1970, the same year as the movie *Catch-22*, making comparisons inevitable because of the similar themes and styles of overlapping conversations and situational humor (Daugherty, 2011, p. 313). Although, given his relaxed style, perhaps Altman did not want to film a story that close to his wartime combat experiences. Daugherty sees Altman's great film as a descendant of Joseph Heller's novel, which was published in 1961, lampooning the mismanagement of war, which was later viewed by readers also as a comment on the Vietnam War (p. 254).

Altman made one film about a war veteran, *The Long Goodbye*, but did a poor job of it, deleting the war veteran reference entirely from the film, which is a pity, since Raymond Chandler's novel illustrates the war veteran's return in disguise and his ties to other veterans. It may be that Altman was too much in disguise as a war veteran himself to make that angle work.

WILLIAM WELLMAN

William Wellman flew for the French Lafayette Escadrille during the First World War. He was wounded and discharged. He returned to the States, joined the U.S. Army Air Corps before the war ended, and was injured in a crash while training flyers. That injury caused him back pain for the rest of his life (Thompson, 1983). His most interesting movie about a war veteran is *Heroes for Sale* (1933), which is about a World War I veteran discharged with intractable back pain. Now addicted to heroin, this placid, much misunderstood man gives away his hard-earned fortune. The hero ends up disappearing into the darkness as one of the hoboes being railroaded out of the county's jurisdiction. At the same time he is remembered as a saint-like, absent hero by his family.

William Wellman wrote and directed *Lafayette Escadrille* (1958), about an American, Thad Walker (Tab Hunter), who grew up with an abusive father, joined Lafayette Escadrille, but deserted after he struck back at an officer who slapped him. After hiding out in Paris with his girlfriend he eventually confessed to an American general and was improbably taken into the U.S. Army air corps. Bill Wellman, Jr., has a supporting role playing his father, and Clint Eastwood has a minor role playing another American flying with the French. William Wellman, carrying the nickname Wild Bill (perhaps because he carried a pistol on the set,) also directed such World War II combat epics as *Battleground* (1949) and *The Story of G.I. Joe* (1945).

JEAN RENOIR

Jean Renoir also flew for the French in World War I, but he was first wounded early in the war while with the French army cavalry. He spent most of the war recovering from his leg wound, then was retrained and returned to action as a pilot. He flew aerial observers during combat operations. His most interesting movie about the war is *Grand Illusion* (1937), which is about French aviators captured and imprisoned by Germans. It is also a film about how social class transcends wartime divisions. Renoir blamed sequelae from his old war wound with finally forcing him into retirement, ending his long filmmaking career. He wrote about fate, which may have been influenced by the scale of the First World War.

> There is a force that I give in to in my films and that I believe in a great deal, and that's fate. I really believe that you can't go against the current, that we're caught in a kind of river that pushes us, carries us, and that men are not mean or good or traitors or not traitors. They are simply playthings of destiny, and in this film I tried to show that, too [Renoir, 1989, p. 205].

Renoir saw the war as corrupting both the victors and the defeated: "No nation can escape the decadence engendered by war" (Renoir, 1973, p. 96). His other great film, *Rules of the Game* (*La Règle du Jeu*, 1939) deals with a large gathering of fated individuals just prior to the onset of the Second World War.

JAMES WHALE

James Whale served with the English army during the First World War. He avoided service as long as he honorably could, then served as a subaltern in trench combat. He was captured while leading a patrol and was held in a German POW camp, where he claims to have learned his first stagecraft while entertaining fellow prisoners. He came to Hollywood in 1930 to direct the screen version of his stage success *Journey's End*. He later adapted and filmed Erich Maria Remarque's *The Road Back* (1937), about a German World War I veteran's postwar adjustment, but the film was taken over by the studio and given to another director to cut and reshoot, effectively ruining it. The studio apparently tried to reshape the film for sale in Europe during the rise of Nazi Germany. Whale reports that he ended his version of the film with a dwarf dressed in brown shirt, leading a band of youths on a march (Curtis, 1998).

The novel by Christopher Bram, *Father of Frankenstein*, is a fictional account of Whale's last days, following a stroke. It was made into a good film, *Gods and Monsters* (Bill Condon, director, 1998), which captured a poignant look back at the traumas of his combat. The story suggests that Whale's 1931 *Frankenstein*, an image created from his model as a creature sewn together from the corpses with the brain of a criminal and brought to life, reflected a gruesome memory of the horrors of static trench warfare where corpses rotted in the wire. (Actually, the monster's make-up was the product of Jack P. Pierce, who based his design on the description provided in Mary Shelley's 1818 novel.)

SAMUEL FULLER

Samuel Fuller volunteered at age 29 to serve in the U.S. Army infantry shortly after the Japanese attack on Pearl Harbor. He fought as an enlisted man in the First Infantry Division in every major battle in which the division was deployed, including North Africa, Sicily, Normandy, and the Battle of the Bulge. He filmed the story of a crusty sergeant from World War I who leads a squad retracing Fuller's tour in *The Big Red One* (1980). He made several films about combat, including *China Gate* (1957, which featured Korean War veterans involved in the French-Indochina war), *Steel Helmet* (1951), *Fixed Bayonets!* (1951), and *Hell and High Water* (1954). He became known for his non-conformity and eccentricities, such as firing a pistol into the air at the start of shooting. He was a darling of the French New Wave. His feisty 2002 autobiography, *A Third Face*, which he was assisted in writing after a stroke, recalled that the making of *The Big Red One* caused him to experience a renewal of nightmares. According to Fuller, one of his chronic nightmares concerned the trauma of witnessing an execution of a prisoner by electric chair as a newspaper cub reporter. He writes (p. 61), "The first execution I witnessed at Ossining's famous prison [Sing Sing] is engraved forever in my brain." Fuller, from his vantage point in the front row, reported that the prisoner "actually started to burn right in front of our eyes! The odor of charred human flesh is something right out of hell. I shudder to remember it."

JEAN-PIERRE MELVILLE

Jean-Pierre Melville was in the French Army at the beginning of the Second World War and joined the Resistance movement for the remainder of the

German Occupation. After the war he changed his name to Melville, after American author Herman Melville. He built his own studio and made his first movie, a somber study of a German officer who was lodged in a home of a French family during the Occupation, *Le Silence de la Mer* (*Silence is Golden*, [1947]). By working out on his own, he bypassed the hide-bound control of the unions and the tradition of established studios, which would have required a long period of apprenticeship as assistant director. He made another somber film at the end of his career about his work in the Resistance, *Army of Shadows* (1969), which had the feel of the French gangster underworld films that he made so popular (*Bob Le Flambeur, Le Doulos, Le Samourai, Le Cercle Rouge*). These films capture the gangsters living in a dark, desperate subculture of alienation.

Melville's personal style bears some comparison with Samuel Fuller's. Fuller was very popular among the leading figures of the French New Wave, who also regarded Melville as a pioneering figure. Richard Neupert, in his *History of the French New Wave Cinema* (2002) writes: "Like Rene Claire [who was an ambulance driver in World War I and wounded in combat] Melville made a break with his own past, in part motivated by the psychological trauma of the war years, as he adapted a new name and followed his passion, trying to make his postwar life worth living" (p. 63). Resistance fighter, French philosopher, and director of *Shoah* (1985), Claude Lanzmann (2012) visited Melville and reported the director was living alone in the dark shadows in his studio. Lanzmann later reported that Melville died penniless.

Melville, Fuller, and Robert Altman have similar styles of defiance toward authority and a career-long quest for independence. They were all prone to outbursts of anger and had a fellowship with actors. Neupert writes of Melville: "Like Hollywood's Samuel Fuller, he came off as a tough veteran and interviews typically touched on his violent war background" (p. 64). The same was not true of Altman, who did not like the army and seldom mentioned his war experiences. Melville's first popular film was *Bob le Flambeur* (*Bob the Gambler* [1955]), which depicts a gambler who, it seems, enters an altered state of consciousness and bets it all. This could also describe Robert Altman.

OLIVER STONE

Oliver Stone left university study and volunteered for army infantry during the Vietnam War. He served for a year with the 25th Infantry Division in Vietnam. He has made several films about the war and war veterans, including the somewhat autobiographical *Platoon* (1986), about a company in the 25th Infantry, and a man who enlisted in the army from college (Stone had been attending Yale when he dropped out), and the aforementioned *Born on the Fourth of July*. Stone first went to Vietnam in 1965 as a civilian volunteer for the Free Pacific Institute of Taiwan and was stationed in Cholon, the Chinese section of Saigon. He also worked as a merchant seaman, pursued his desire to write, and then, in 1967, enlisted in the army and requested infantry. After the TET offensive he volunteered to join a recon unit of the First Air Cavalry. He received a Bronze Star and two Purple Hearts (Toplin, 2000, p. 72).

Stone collaborated in screenwriting with director Michael Cimino to make the *Year of the Dragon* (1985), with Micky Rourke playing an arrogant, obsessed Vietnam War veteran police captain in charge of New York's Chinatown. Unlike that unfortunate depiction, *Platoon* is an excellent example of what a veteran can do creatively with his combat experiences. His scene at the ambush could only have been made by someone who had had the experience.

Narrative in Film and War Veterans

After a gruesome gunfight in Daniel Barber's *Harry Brown* (2010), Michael Caine, playing Harry, stands over a drug and gun trafficker he has shot in the stomach, and relates with flat paradoxical humor, as only Michael Caine can, how he had watched his friend die as a British Marine in Korea. Then he states with piquant reflection, "I never told it to anyone."

Repressed memories of trauma come forward in behaviors and are recognized as familiar, because they mimic the event. In this case, as 77-year-old Harry has recalled the memory of his friend dying, when the thug he has shot in the belly is writhing on the floor. Such memories are not necessarily this dangerous, but they are usually emotional and dramatic. Under good conditions in a course of psychotherapy, repressed memories are described and discussed, establishing a system of order. It is a goal of psychotherapy, as I practiced it, to fit the traumatic experiences of combat in a proper container, in the context of the veteran's other memories, all of which, together with body sensation, form the veteran's identity. However, forming a narrative of trauma events is not easy to do for a combat veteran. By definition a traumatic event is considered outside the realm of a veteran's normal experience. The memory of that event, inaccurate though it may be, must be made to fit what has been normal for the war veteran.

In the 1989 film, *In Country*, Vietnam War veteran Emmett, wonderfully played by Bruce Willis, is drawn into telling his niece about his experience in combat, because Sam (for Samantha, played by Emily Lloyd), his niece,

In Country (1989), Norman Jewison, director. Emily Lloyd plays Sam (short for Samantha), who is trying to find information about her late father from her Vietnam War veteran uncle Emmett (Bruce Willis), who served with her father in combat. Sam's jogging becomes a rhythmic segue in the film that is based on Bobby Ann Mason's novel of the same title. (Warner Bros., Inc.)

has been reading her late father's diaries. Her father, Dwayne, was a soldier with Emmett and was killed in action. First she frightens her uncle by going into a Kentucky swamp at night to experience the "boonies" while reading her father's diary. The TV series *M*A*S*H* has been a shared experience between Emmett and Sam. Sam needles her uncle:

"Are you going to talk, Emmett? Can you tell about it? Do the way Hawkeye did when he told about that baby on the bus. His memories lied to him. But he got better when he could reach down and get the right memories." Sam was practically yelling at him. She was frantic.

Emmett said, "There ain't no way to tell it. No point. You can't tell it all. Dwayne didn't begin to tell it all."

"Just tell one thing."

"O.K. One thing."

"One thing at a time will be all right."

Emmett lit a cigarette and started slowly, but then he talked faster and faster, as though he were going to pour out everything after all. He said, "There was this patrol I was on..." [Mason, 1985, p. 222].

Here, war veterans influence each other across cultures. Second World War veteran Robert Altman's film about a past war in Korea commenting on the current war in Vietnam, which was, per his style, made with highly creative crew interactions on the set, and eventually turned into a popular TV series (which Altman had nothing to do with) and is taken up as a subject by Bobby Ann Mason writing *In Country*, a novel about a Vietnam War veteran being pried out of his shell of avoidance by his niece just graduating from high school. The theme music from *MASH* and M*A*S*H, "Suicide Is Painless," written by Altman's son, becomes their mutual communication. Sam, with her naïve persistence, has begun to free her uncle of the burden of repression.

Memories of combat are difficult to fit into ordinary life because they usually increase the veteran's feeling of alienation. Harry Brown felt compelled to lock away his combat memories when he met his wife-to-be, while Sam, a girl just out of high school, is able to begin to unlock her uncle Emmett's memories. Movies play a role in dramatically communicating this process of establishing a narrative. Theoreticians and academic researchers parse out the variables of psychotherapy for examination and often seem to leave out the ineffable key ingredient: the relationship of the therapist to the veteran that is created for the purpose of understanding and relieving the posttraumatic symptoms, chief among them being the feeling of alienation.

Building a narrative for a veteran of combat entails creating a place for combat memories. No one is to dictate how one should do that. It could be as basic as finding a way to talk about military service. Pre-Homeric oral poets built stories out of more or less discrete segments, scenes to fit the occasion, repeated phrases ("gray-eyed Athena," "city-sacking Odysseus," "dawn's rosy fingers," "sailing the wine-dark sea,") the way a modern sportscaster can, in a spirit of freshness, reel off sports clichés for every game, because by saying a phrase ("he hit a frozen rope," for example), the announcer triggers imagery that the sports fan can imagine. Nothing so glib would be appropriate for a veteran to describe combat experiences, but the idea of building a natural, honest way of talking, or at least thinking, about the really significant things that one witnessed is essential to psychological wholeness. Having a repertoire of phrases about war experiences gives one an arsenal to fall back on in a conversation that otherwise could get emotional.

The prolific writer James Hillman, referring to general life narrative, stated:

> Life review yields long-term gains that enrich character by bringing understanding to events. The patterns in your life become more discernible among the wreckage and the romance, more like a well-plotted novel that reveals characters through their actions and reactions. Life review is really nothing other than rewriting — or writing for the first time — the story of your life, or writing your

life into stories. And without stories there is no pattern, no understanding, no art, and no character — merely habits, events passing before the eyes of an aimless observer, a life unreviewed, a life lost in the living of it [1999, p. 91].

Some veterans write novels or memoirs, like "that strange coupling," Hephaestus suspending Ares and Aphrodite for everyone to see (Erich Maria Remarque's *All Quiet on the Western Front*, Ford Maddox Ford's *Parade's End*, E. B. Sledge's *With the Old Breed*, Norman Mailer's *The Naked and the Dead*, Joseph Heller's *Catch-22*, Karl Marlantes's elegiac Vietnam War novel, *Matterhorn*, and Brian Castner's memoir of an Iraq War veteran explosive ordinance expert, *The Long Walk*). Film directors like Oliver Stone, Jean-Pierre Melville, and Samuel Fuller, made movies about their time in combat — and called it fiction. A unique way to tell the story is through film animation. Filmmaker/animator, Ari Folman created a narrative of his experience in the 1982 Israeli war in Lebanon in his 2010 animated film, *Waltz with Bashir*. Kyle Hausemann-Stokes filmed the story of his own post-combat alienation in *Now, After*.

Joseph Heller gives an exemplary account in *The Paris Review* of being inspired to write *Catch-22* in 1953 by permitting a memory to take seed and sprout: "I was lying in bed in my four-room apartment on the West Side when suddenly this line came to me: 'It was love at first sight. The first time he saw the chaplain, Someone fell madly in love with him'" (Daugherty, 2011, p. 176). Daugherty adds, "The morning after the first sentence took shape, he arrived at work ... with [his] pastry and a container of coffee and a mind brimming with ideas, and immediately in longhand put down on a pad the first chapter of an intended novel."

With modes of expression like autobiography and fiction the author is then forced to find an order that works to express the event that caused trauma. If the veteran produces a work to be viewed or read by others, the narrative changes and takes on a cultural context. Iraq War veteran Brian Castner (2012) put it nicely in his "Author's Note" to *The Long Walk*: "Everything in this book feels true. It's as correct as a story can be from someone with blast-induced memory lapses. Nothing was changed to create a moral or to ease comfort. It's as real as I can make it, though reality and objectivity sometimes have little to do with one another."

A narrative for a combat veteran can also become a product of psychotherapy, or a product, as *In Country* shows, of family interaction, the passing on of experience. But the veteran risks the reality that his or her memories may not be well received. Recently it was reported in a Baltimore, Maryland, newspaper that a veteran wrote an essay about Iraq combat for an English class, which the professor liked and reprinted in the college newspaper. The essay unsettled administrators, leading to the veteran being banned from campus because he was perceived as having a violent potential (Walker, 2010). Apparently, he wrote that he liked killing and even missed it. Every veteran must face the reality that his or her memories of trauma might be something that the society is not ready to accept. A Vietnam War veteran friend told me about his shame when he realized he'd sent photographs of enemy corpses to his mother. Psychologist Paula Caplan (2011) advocates lay listeners initiate contact with war veterans and elicit their narratives, which sounds risky for some who might quail upon hearing the consciousness-darkening details of combat.

Movies show a whole variety of these approaches, often referring metaphorically to the emotional memories of combat. In John Frankenhiemer's *The Manchurian Candidate* (1962) what happened in Korea, the hypnotic brainwashing, becomes an enigma because of nightmares. The hypnotic techniques used by the evil Communist enemy, like sleeper cells planted in the unsuspecting veteran, became a metaphor for repression. In *Jacob's Ladder*, directed by Adrian Lynn in 1990, the secret experiment with drugs that caused hallucinations in the veteran also caused him to seek affiliation with fellow veterans.

Whether it is the persistent prying of *In Country*'s Sam into her uncle's combat memories, or the intrusive recollections in the form of hallucinations in *Jacob's Ladder*, or nightmares in *The Manchurian Candidate*, the narrative of combat merges with the present. In the big-budget 1956 film *The Man in the Gray Flannel Suit*, directed by Nunnally Johnson, Second World War airborne army veteran Tom Rath (Gregory Peck) meets a veteran of his outfit working an elevator operator in the building where he has just started working. This particular veteran is associated with a romantic affair Tom had in Rome, after Germany's surrender, when he thought he was about to depart for the Pacific, where he strongly believed he would die invading Japan. The elevator operator knew the Italian girl who bore Tom's child and produced a message that she needed help. This was occurring at the time of transitional crisis in Tom's career and marriage, having to do with his values and aspirations, reflecting in some ways his country's striving for material success at the expense of family. Meeting his fellow veteran triggered intrusive recollections and offered Tom a chance to piece together a narrative, not just of what happened to him in the war, but what it meant, because the only way he could convey the facts to his wife was to talk about his state of mind. And, as in *Brothers* (2010), it is the spouse who is the primary recipient, the listener, as the narrative begins.

When the issue arose in therapy that perhaps the veteran should tell his wife about what happened in the war, the common objection that I heard was that she might use it against him when they fought. No one wants traumatic memory brought up as punishment or sharp retort in a domestic dispute. In *The Man in the Gray Flannel Suit*, the spouse, Betsy (Jennifer Jones), is outraged that Tom had an affair that he kept secret. He tries but fails to give her the context of trauma and his belief in his impending death. She is not sympathetic, although eventually, after her anger dissipates, she decided to help him.

For many combat veterans, the experiences and events during the war run together. The time dimension of trauma memories is often confused. One can recall the painful death of someone who had been close, but often the memory is avoided, as if it were kept in a room that is seldom entered, because to dwell on the traumatic event evokes tears and increases one's sense of alienation. Instead, one weeps at a sappy scene on TV, and soon sappy movies are avoided, too. Much of the action in *The Dry Land* is driven by the veteran, James, seeking to find out what happened, but what he learns finally seems to worsen his sense of alienation.

Memories of trauma are sometimes presented in movies as flashbacks or intrusive recollections triggered by current events. These usually go unshared. The origin of the word *flashback* is in the context of narrative — that is, the interrupting of chronological sequence. (There is another, more poetic, use of the word having to do with the explosive flame of a gun's backfire.) The salience of the word *flashback* was enhanced with the 1980 introduction of PTSD into the nomenclature of psychopathology, inviting study by identifying expected symptoms. Flashback, in this latter context, refers to a memory that intrudes on consciousness, sometimes with such prominence that one loses sense of the present. In many ways, the DSM-III introduction of PTSD was to the field of psychological trauma what the Hubble telescope was to the study of the cosmos in the sense of opening up new vistas for examination.

It is not necessary that memories be in chronological order, or conform to anyone else's sense of correctness. The narrative need only fit the veteran's need for wholeness. If a veteran chooses to construct a formal written narrative, the task itself demands an order, even if the story is fictionalized. Karl Marlantes reproduced many of his Vietnam combat experiences as autobiography in *What It Was Like to Go to War* (2011), then converted them to fiction for his novel, *Matterhorn* (2009), which he published first. Veterans who keep journals are sometimes able to develop and elaborate a recalled memory, although verbalizing the experience with an intimate companion would probably enhance the process. The time demanded in sorting through pictures taken during the deployment, adding captions, is a process that can facilitate integration and end by fashioning a narrative. Ultimately, it is upon the veteran to find a way to construct the story, whether in the form of an Internet blog, a pictorial collage, fiction, stories told to a child, or not shared at all. However, the problem with delving into wartime memories alone is personified by the Sirens in *The Odyssey*, who lured sailors to their deaths with heroic songs of their wars — a warning that the veteran is liable to become stuck in one perspective and set of beliefs. Complex spontaneous memories of trauma can develop a pattern of circularity, if dwelled upon, that do not develop or change and often become ruminative, like a cow chewing its cud, but the salience and repetition of traumatic memories can also act as a dynamo of energy creation. Having a goal, a method of developing a narrative, helps to orient the veteran through the maze of the painful and the confusing. An excellent collection of wartime narratives, both oral and written, can be found in *Shadows of Slaughterhouse Five* (Szpek & Idzikowski, 2008).

World War II veteran James Jones spent most of his literary career struggling to finish his third volume of his war trilogy (*From Here to Eternity*, *The Thin Red Line*, and *Whistle*). *Whistle* is his dark story about surviving Guadalcanal and being returned to an army hospital in the Midwest. Jones died of a heart attack at age 55, leaving the last three chapters unfinished, to be completed by his writer-friend, Willie Morris, from Jones's notes.

Marlantes (2011) relates various scenes from his experiences in combat as a Marine platoon leader fighting on the DMZ with scenes of his childhood in Oregon and his long period of adjustment following his return after discharge. Like Castner's *The Long Walk*, he moves back and forth between memories of combat and his struggles with postwar adjustment to marriage, work, and his own soulful healing, creating, as McGilchrist put it, a "self with a narrative and a continuous flow-like existence" (2009, p. 88).

In contrast, J.D. Salinger, whose combat record in World War II was substantial, resisted talking about his war experiences. He wrote in a letter after his discharge that "he now saw the world as being divided between those who had shared the anguish of war and those who were 'too civilian'" (Salwinski, 2010, p. 142). He was clearly traumatized by his exposure to combat and the Nazi atrocities, yet he was adamant about not disclosing the details. He ends his famous novel, *Catcher in the Rye*, with the comment, "Don't ever tell anybody anything. If you do, you start missing everybody" (Slawenski, 2010, p. 139). Salinger withdrew from society at the height of his literary celebrity and fought until his death to guard his privacy.

In psychiatrist Jonathan Shay's book sequel to his *Achilles in Vietnam*, *Odysseus in America* (2002), Shay devotes the second half of his latter work to the Internet correspondence of veterans recounting their narratives, with a focus on a veterans' Internet group that reacted to the suicide of Lewis B. Puller, Jr. Puller, the author of *Fortunate Son: the Healing of a Vietnam Vet*, was the badly wounded son of the late Chesty Puller, a Marine Corps' legendary hero (Shay, 2002, pp. 179ff).

The risk, as always with the Internet, is one of reliability. It is meaningful in psychotherapy if a veteran remembers an event in combat in a distorted fashion. Time distortions are common in such recall. The overlapping stories in *Shadows of Slaughterhouse Five* gives excellent examples of distortions in veterans' memories (Szpek & Idzikowski, 2008). It may not be helpful to another veteran to try to make sense of someone else's distortions. The advantage of the Internet is that one might arrive at a consensus among other witnesses. The risk is that they all have distorted memories, and while their distortions may be meaningful to each of them, they may mislead or confuse the veteran trying to form a narrative. As Gerald Edelman writes, "Memories are necessarily associative and are never identical" (i.e., representational) (2004, p. 53).

A veteran's war memories are the subject of Ernest Hemingway's 1925 short story, "Soldier's Home," perhaps the most succinct portrayal in literature of a war veteran's alienation, which he published in his story collection, *In Our Time.*

"Soldier's Home" is a loaded title, suggesting both an institution for disabled or elderly soldiers, and the recent return of the soldier to his home. Narrated in the third person, the reader is introduced to Krebs. Hemingway's choice of using only his last name suggests impersonal objectivity and lack of connection. Krebs's mother calls him Harold and his little sister, "Hare," a sobriquet of connection. Krebs had joined the Marine Corps in 1917 and served two years, and the narrator tells the reader that Krebs had been in five major battles involving U.S. troops: Belleau Wood, Soissons, the Champagne, St. Mihiel, and "in the Argonne." A busy two years, and then he was part of the force that occupied Germany. Krebs has difficulty talking about his combat experiences. He feels he is forced to lie, describe "apocryphal incidents," because the truth would sound too mundane, but the lying left him with a bad taste.

Hemingway states that the only time Krebs let down his guard was with other veterans, when he could say that "he had been badly, sickeningly frightened all the time." And the author adds enigmatically, "In this way he lost everything." What would he lose? His pride? His pose? He was admired as "still a hero" to his two younger sisters. His mother tried to talk with him about the war, but "her attention always wandered." His father does not appear in the story, but evidently is "noncommittal," and seems distant and unfeeling. When his mother says that his father said he can drive the family car, Krebs replied (and one can almost see him smile with affection for his mother), "I bet you made him." When Krebs folds the morning paper to read at the breakfast table, his mother expresses concern that his father would find the paper "mussed."

Hemingway sets the contrast between the veteran's experience of war and his civilian status with his permission to use the family automobile. After having participated in five battles during the war, his father is going to give him permission to use the car in the evening, with the hope that Krebs will use it to socialize with girls. Krebs likes girls but finds relationships too complicated. "It wasn't worth it," he states.

Much of what we are told about Krebs suggests that he is in a situational depression without much creative energy at his disposal. He appears to have suffered consequences in battle. The use of repetition by Hemingway gives emphasis. "He did not want any consequences. He did not want any consequences ever again. He wanted to live along without consequences." Krebs doesn't have interest in world affairs and looks only at the newspaper sports section. He uses the public library, but his interest is only in reading the history of his war.

Krebs has been home only a month. The second half of the story starts with Kreb's mother pressuring him to get on with his life, to get a job and have a relationship.

This is a scene repeated in the post–World War II movie about veterans' homecoming, *Till the End of Time* (1946). It is a difference of perspective between civilian continuity of time and a veteran's need to recover time. His mother asks, "Have you decided what you are going to do yet, Harold?" She compares him to another young man his age, who has a job and is settling down and planning to get married. She states firmly, "You are going to have to settle down to work, Harold." Krebs grows angry at her needling. Hemingway only states that Krebs watched the bacon fat harden on his plate. His mother applies more pressure and asks him if he loves her. He says, bluntly, no: "I don't love anybody." His mother starts to cry. Then Hemingway articulates the alienation: "It wasn't any good. He couldn't tell her, he couldn't make her see it." See what? Krebs can only state, "I was just angry at something." Which implies that she merely tapped an anger that was already in him.

But Krebs's anger was the crux of the issue. When his mother asks him to pray, he cannot, and when he walks away finally, Hemingway states that "none of it had touched him." A month home and he was numb. He didn't have the energy to devote to relationships or creative activity. "He wanted his life to go smoothly," and be free of stress until he recovered his spirit.

Retired army psychiatrist Charles Hoge presented a nice discussion and rationale for the veteran developing his or her narrative after combat deployment (Hoge, 2010, p. 116). The safety and reliability that is essential to the psychotherapy relationship when forming a narrative is too often given short shrift in time-limited counseling programs with brief follow-up. The 1994 film, *The War*, depicted a Vietnam War veteran returning from VA alcohol treatment. The veteran, played by Kevin Costner, tells his son, Stu (Elijah Wood), that he has PTSD and describes the source of his guilt. The insight, which seemed to be a product of his treatment does not anticipate the powerful way he will re-enact the trauma.

Emotions attached to traumatic memories can be profound, particularly the sometimes not-so-subtle emotions attached to guilt. Recall the earlier example of J. D. Salinger. I do not know what Salinger's motivation to withdraw from the public was, but I have seen many combat veterans in psychotherapy who have stopped or mitigated success *probably* because of their survivor's guilt, including those who stop before the finish line, before the degree is completed, passing up a good job offer, resigning in the face of promotion, etc. It is a form of avoidance behavior akin to seeking physical isolation in the woods, like Krebs, wanting to avoid consequences. One former combat medic I knew turned down the prized opportunity to captain a fishing boat because, he said, he didn't want the responsibility. (I use the qualifier "probably" because there is really no definitive way that I know of to determine causality when cause and effect are separated in time.) Claude Lanzmann (2012, p. 108) described his own combat guilt after an ambush of German convoy after D Day as irrational: "I should have tried to help him. There was no way I could have succeeded and come out alive, but I should have tried, I should have rushed to him without thinking, like Schuster and Lheritier. I have blamed myself my whole life for not doing so. Was it cowardice?"

The combat veteran who has formed a narrative is not freed from symptoms such as guilt associated with memory of trauma, but has, hopefully at least, managed to gain enough perspective to provide a sense of conscious choice, making irrational decisions rational. By creating a narrative that encompasses the events and experiences in combat, the veteran relates to the rest of his or her life, the past and the present in a continuous, if bumpy, flow. The events may form a new chapter, but not a new story.

Joseph Heller, a veteran B-25 bombardier, at age 51, while writing *Something Happened*, is fearful of dying or having disaster strike. He confesses to his daughter, "I think I'm in trouble. I think I've committed a crime. I've always felt so. The victims have always been children" (Daugherty, 2011, p. 320).

Suicide in Veterans

In the beginning of the 1988 film *Distant Thunder* a Vietnam War veteran, Louis (Tom Bower), is walking on the Burlington Northern Railroad tracks with a freight train coming his way. Mark (John Lithgow) walks along-side trying to dissuade his friend and fellow veteran from suicide. But Louis is determined. He carries a knife to keep Mark at a distance. He has just had a fight with his wife. He shouts just before the train hits him, "It don't mean nothin', man." A double negative ironically used in that war, and with a double meaning now.

The rate of suicide for veterans is difficult to accurately calculate. In Japan, after the Second World War, suicide was a subject banned from media discussion by the American Occupation (Hirano, 1992). A suicidal act can be disguised, and without knowledge of the intent of the deceased, attribution is often ambiguous. Such acts as single vehicle accidents, accidents with firearms, drug overdoses, are labeled by the coroner as death by misadventure. The three acts of suicide by veterans in James Jones's novel *Whistle* are all called something else. One walked in front of an oncoming car (accident), one provoked a bar fight and was beaten to death, one slips over the side of a troop ship headed for Europe. It may be that the suicide rate among the current combat veterans is not much different than it was for veterans of other wars, but we are in a different age of information that broadcasts more, and psychological sophistication has also grown among veterans as well as those who treat them. According to the latest figures cited by the Centers for Disease control, the national suicide rate as of 2007 was 11.5 per 100,000. The National Center for PTSD, a VA institution, lists the rate for 2005 as 23.19 for male veterans, 5.6 for female veterans. The rate, according to the National Center for PTSD, for VA users in 2005 was 37.9 for males and 13.59 for females. CBS television, in a documentary aired in 2009, listed the law-enforcement suicide average as 20 per 100,000. In the border patrol it was 30 per 100,000. CBS, in its research, estimated that the rate for veterans of the wars in Iraq and Afghanistan in 2005 was 44.99 per 100,000, which increased the next year to 56.77, which is more than four times the national average. Citing a Defense Department survey, Hicks (2011) reported 15.8 percent of surveyed soldiers in Iraq reported suicidal ideation within the previous four weeks in 2007. A factor that seems to be at least correlated with the increases above the national average in the professions of law enforcement, border patrol, and soldiering is the involvement of long periods of watchfulness, participation in violence, and firearms. And, of course, veterans who were involved in combat are often intermixed in surveys with veterans who were never deployed and may not have had the prospect of ever being deployed to a combat zone.

A VA News Briefing (11/12/2010) quotes Veterans Affairs secretary Eric Shinseki's Veterans Day interview on National Public Radio in an effort to explain why "veterans died at a more rapid rate after returning from Iraq and Afghanistan than died in Iraq and Afghanistan." In the interview, General

Shinseki said, "I don't know that I have enough insights, but it parallels a little bit of my experience when I was still serving in uniform, where you take a unit on a very, very difficult operation, you come back, there is a tendency for these kinds of things to occur, the motorcycle accidents, the driving long hours, trying to get as much living in on a weekend and trying to make it back on a Sunday night, early Monday morning, to the first work day formation. But the suicides always get our attention, because they tie back very clearly to some of the exposures to stress that go on in an operation." William Styron's story, "Suicide Run," is about two Marines trying to pack in a weekend with their girlfriends and nearly dying on the road. One of the Marines is reminded by the scare of his near death in Okinawa under mortar fire (Styron, 2009).

Seminars and workshops that attempt to address the issue of suicide too often resort to presenting statistics and the immediate causal situations, such as the presence of chronic pain, debilitating illness, significant loss, lack of social support, etc. The overriding question is often lost in the analysis: Why do veterans opt to suicide more than non-veterans? The issue is missed, perhaps because it confronts the involvement of the nation in combat, the circumstances and meaningfulness of policy, custom that makes firearms an easy and common access, and (perhaps) the emptiness of a society that has lost its social closeness to electronic media.

The Presence of Death

> We had Death too long for a companion; he was a swift player and every second the stakes touched the limit. — Erich Maria Remarque, *The Road Back*

Marleen Gorris's excellent 1992 production of Virginia Woolf's novel *Mrs. Dalloway* takes place two years after the 1918 Armistice. A veteran, Septimus, who his wife says had done well for two years, begins obsessing about his friend Evans, who was killed by an explosion while walking toward him in the trenches. Septimus is wrenched by feelings of guilt because he did not feel anything at the time. The doctor states that he has "delayed shell shock" and wants to incarcerate him because the veteran wants to commit suicide. When he comes to take Septimus to the hospital, the veteran jumps out the window and impales himself on the spikes of the iron railing a floor below.

Clarissa's concern is expressed in a line that succinctly sums the core of the problem of alienation in war veterans: "Don't talk about death in the middle of my party."

An important factor that is present in the professions of law enforcement, border patrol, and soldiering, but is more common in combat trauma, is the presence of death. Some in combat witness deaths regularly for months and grow numb in reaction. It is one of the things that separates war veterans from civilians and fosters alienation in the veteran. The federal government is complicit in the separation of death from war when it tries its best to keep the civilian public from viewing the funerary process of those killed in action. Movies like *The Messenger, Taking Chance,* and *Gardens of Stone* deal directly with the process of the impact of battlefield casualties on the military and the civilian cultures. (See also Caplan, 2011.) In the 1990 Argentine film *Blessed by Fire,* the narrator remarks that more veterans of their war against the British in the Falkland Islands died from suicide than were killed in action. The 2001 British film, *Last Orders,* directed by Fred Schepisi, depicts aged war veterans ceremoniously distributing the ashes of their comrade. The OIF veteran's death in the film *In the Valley of Elah* seems to have been brought about by his comrades who had become numb to the consequences of killing. We saw in the film *Jacknife* that the death in combat of a friend stays with the veterans as undigested guilt. In *Gods and Monsters,* the aged veteran, after a stroke, is overwhelmed by the memory of his friend's death in the trench-protecting barbed wire. In *Missing in America* and *Distant Thunder* the deaths experienced in combat are attributed with driving the veteran into exiled isolation. In *Key Largo* and *Bad Day at Black Rock* the plots are driven by Second World War veterans seeking out the families of their comrades who were killed while engaged in combat.

Death became so common during the U.S. Civil War that specialty retail stores catering to the aggrieved sold appropriate mourning apparel in both Northern and Southern cities (Faust, 2008). The Japanese army officer in Kurosawa's "The Tunnel" (a segment of the 1990 film *Akira Kurosawa's Dreams*) returning home after his release from being a prisoner of war, is hounded by the ghosts of the dead soldiers under his command. John Dower (1999, p. 57) writes of the Japanese veteran: "It was commonplace to see demobilized soldiers returning from abroad with the ashes of deceased comrades, which they had undertaken to return to surviving kin."

Death separates the war veteran, often, from those at home in the U.S., because death has entered the veteran's symbol system, becoming a frame of reference, while the general public is protected from the deaths caused by wars. One strong argument against suicide is that it then opens the possibility for other veterans, friends, and family members (Ernest Hemingway's family being a prime example). Death is simply not as remarkable to the veteran of combat as it is to the civilian at home.

Death sets the plots of the noir films about World War II veterans, leading to mysteries to be solved adventurously in *Crossfire, The Blue Dahlia, Dead Reckoning,* and *Ride the Pink Horse.* Coming home and having to deal with criminals can be a lively and marketable metaphor for the alienation that war veterans feel. Mark Halprin, in his 2012 novel *In Sunlight and in Shadow,* asserts that underworld criminality thrived during the war and the criminals greeted the returning veterans with mayhem.

The most infamous form of Death appeared in Swedish director Ingmar Bergman's 1957 classic, *The Seventh Seal.* The figure of Death (Bengt Ekerot), pallid and gaunt, dressed in a hooded black robe, is challenged by the Knight (Max von Sydow) to a game of chess. The Knight has just returned from the Holy Land Crusade and is brooding. Death is everywhere in the land, in the form of the Plague and the self-flagellating, tormented peasants carrying processional images of the suffering Christ. Death tricks the Knight into revealing his chess strategy by posing as a priest hearing the Knight's confession. In the confessional, the Knight reveals his doubt that seems meaningful for summarizing the alienation of veterans returning from foreign wars. "Through my indifference to my fellow men, I have isolated myself from their company. Now I live in a world of phantoms. I am imprisoned in my dreams and fantasies" (Bergman, 1960, p. 149). Just outside the church a witch, who is to be burned to death, is portrayed as a teenaged girl who is delusional, believing that she can see the Devil everywhere and is surprised the Knight cannot. The Devil and Death are quite similar as chthonic deities that are aspects of the same archetype that veterans were exposed to in combat. The Knight and his squire seem to feel akin to the witch: "She sees what we see."

The innocents in *The Seventh Seal* are traveling minstrels. The juggler, Joff, is apparently also delusional, for he sees visions and spirits who travel by. His opposite is the war-weary Knight's Squire, the worldly wise Jons, who knows how to get on in any society. Jons is the earthy sidekick to the Knight's hero of legend. The innocents, in the end, are the only ones spared from Death's scythe. They were the ones who were spared from war and its consequences.

In the 1956 film *Man in the Gray Flannel Suit,* the veteran's children seem to be obsessed with melodramatic fascination with death assisted by gunfights on television and leading indirectly to his flashback of killing in combat.

Films depict the veteran making suicidal gestures and attempts: *The Dry Land, Forrest Gump, Distant Thunder, Brothers, Lethal Weapon,* or engineering an "assisted" suicide as *Gran Torino, Cutter's Way,* and, arguably, *Dead Presidents.* In *Stop-Loss,* the veteran, who has wrecked his own wedding after returning from combat, eventually commits suicide over his loss, and in *The Deer Hunter* the trauma-induced suicidal "Russian" roulette game becomes compulsive ritual and a brutal symbol of the war.

Death is present for the veterans who were severely wounded in combat. In the 2010 British film, *Made in Dagenham*, World War II veteran George (Roger Lloyd Pack) is dependent on his wife for her constant support. He becomes distraught, therefore, when she becomes involved in a labor strike for equal pay for women. So distraught, in fact, that he commits suicide. The severely wounded veteran Prell, in Jones's *Whistle*, candidly tells his doctors that if they amputate his legs he will commit suicide. In *Oliver Sherman*, the severely wounded Iraq War veteran gives no clue that he is planning suicide, but his impulsivity is facilitated by brain injury and alcohol when he experiences the rejection of his veteran rescuer.

In what may have been a veiled reference to suicidal thoughts, J.D. Salinger, in a letter to a friend, describes sitting on his bunk on VE day in Germany, with a pistol in his hand, with an urge to shoot himself in his other hand (Slawenski, 2010, p. 156). This was after fighting from Normandy through the Hürtgen Forest and participating in the liberation of the Dachau concentration camps. Salinger was of Austrian Jewish heritage. He checked himself into a hospital "in a constant state of despondency" (Slawenski, 2010, p. 135).

Feeling as Memory

"The past is never dead," Faulkner once said. "It's not even past." Paul Fussell, World War II infantry veteran and commentator on veterans' culture, quotes Faulkner in relation to Studs Terkel's oral history of the Second World War, *The Good War* (Fussell, 1988, p. 138). Fussell continues: "Many of Terkel's informants broke down in sobs forty years back. Of course, war trauma being one of our dirty little secrets, always there beneath the surface, seldom showing except on occasions like this."

In addition to the problems caused by mood disorders, PTSD, and substance abuse, death is a larger option for the combatant in the field because of fatigue, emotional numbing, and the proximity of lethal weapons; and, for the combat veteran at home, because of memory and alienation. Jakupcak and Varra (2010) point out that a war veteran handling a firearm can in itself be a trigger for depressed mood. In memory, feeling states may accompany imagery, but often memory can manifest solely, and often subtly, as an imageless feeling state, such as a sense of jeopardy, dysphoria, or anger. They are the emotional memories of trauma. The memory, in such cases, consists of emotions that were experienced at the time of the traumatic event. Such states as a feeling of helplessness, anger, rage, grief, loss, horror, alarm, fear, guilt, humiliation, embarrassment; feelings that were appropriate and understandable in battlefield conditions, yet occur seemingly out of context, triggered by an evocative reminiscent cue. However, the veteran who is unaware that memory has been cued, is liable to misattribute the feeling as applying solely to the present, putting the veteran at risk for making inappropriate decisions, such as Harry Brown's vigilante vendetta that he waged against the thugs, or the deadly armored car raid conducted by veterans of two wars in *Dead Presidents*. In *Oliver Sherman*, the traumatic memory of abandonment was death, and abuse of alcohol combined with the concrete impulsivity of brain injury, resulting in suicide.

Grief recalls grief, and sometimes cumulative grief leads to feelings of desperation. The veteran who has underreacted on the battlefield to encounters with death, overreacts when confronted with a loss at home and is saddled with a flashback of accumulated grief. Such reactions to current events can lead to confusion and miscalculation. For example, when a situation evoking a feeling of helplessness occurs naturally, such as witnessing the 9/11 Twin Towers terrorist attack on television evokes memories of combat in which helplessness led to a heightened state of vigilance, as in Wim Wender's *Land of Plenty*. If the natural feeling evokes traumatic memory, the veteran is vulnerable, especially if unaware that memory has been triggered, to misattribute the *feeling* and react inappropriately to the here-and-now situation. For example, a veteran who was a Marine radio operator/wireman in Vietnam was 20 years later repairing a broken wire in his stereo system. It was twilight and he was crouching behind the cabinet, clenching one wire in his teeth while he attached another, when he felt a wave of anger of such intensity that he had to get away. His wife asked him if he was ready for dinner and he snapped at her as he left the house. He made the mistake of driving to a gas station and was standing in line to pay when the man in front was arguing with the cashier. The veteran raged at the man and challenged him to a fistfight. The customer cooled down and left apologetically. What the veteran realized, finally, was that he had been flooded with a feeling-toned memory of being sent to repair telephone wire during a firefight at twilight and had been pinned down and became enraged that he had been sent out. He was wise enough to get away from his wife when in this angry state (he had learned that in therapy), but was caught and triggered by the argumentative customer.

Veterans who have engaged in prolonged combat are vulnerable to memory that is inured to the fear of death. Death becomes, if you will, a viable option. In *Lethal Weapon*, Mel Gibson's character, Martin Riggs, a Vietnam War veteran of the Phoenix Program grieving over the death of his wife, puts his pistol barrel in his mouth in a suicidal gesture. In *The Dry Land*, the OIF veteran, James, behaves similarly, in reaction to grief from the combined losses of his mother and wife. Neither pulls the trigger. Martin goes on to fight crime, teaming up with another Vietnam War veteran, while James, more realistically in *The Dry Land*, is taken to the VA hospital accompanied by his estranged wife. (Can anyone guess which film grossed more at the box office?)

The process of psychological numbing relates to the suppression of emotional responses. Combatants, after prolonged fighting, grow numb to the threat of death as they grow familiar with the use of firearms and are comfortable with having them close. They take risks that might be deemed suicidal in another context, actions that may, in fact, be recognized by the military with awards for valor. Fate becomes a player on the field. Combatants make decisions knowing they are going to die, if not now, then soon. Feeling states evoked from such memory can make one feel desperate, feel as if something terrible is about to happen. So when the veteran's spouse does not come home as expected, a small feeling of frustration in the veteran evokes the memory of waiting for a combat team that never shows up, leading him to blow the situation emotionally out of proportion (it becomes, in his mind, a life-or-death situation), when she returns after merely having stopped to talk to a neighbor. She can't understand why he is furious and trembling when she is only a half an hour late.

In *The Hurt Locker*, discussed earlier, there is a strong sense that the bomb disposal sergeant, played by Jeremy Renner, is returning to his very dangerous job for his third deployment, knowing he will die, for we have seen his recklessness that seemed to defiantly invite death. He has stated flatly that he does not expect to survive. Brian Castner, a genuine Iraq War explosives expert, characterized his homecoming with this state of mind: "I simply exist from moment to moment. There is no meaning in my past. My present is intolerable. I don't expect my future to exist" (p. 148). The veteran who does not expect to survive combat, and then returns home, is in his or her mind living on borrowed time, and life thereafter is a huge anticlimax. Such a feeling may spark a number of decisions with positive or negative outcomes, but a constant variable for most such veterans is that Death, like Ingmar Bergman's character in *The Seventh Seal*, is still waiting, perseverant, grinning, hiding the chess pieces behind his back.

The Sense of Having a Foreshortened Future

DSM-IV gives us the formula for arriving at a diagnosis of PTSD. It lists as the seventh example of Criterion C, concerning avoidance symptoms, a symptom that is often overlooked because of its subtlety: "sense of a foreshortened future (e.g., does not expect to have a career, marriage, children, or a normal life span)" (APA, 2005, p. 428). It is a subtle symptom response to a cue because it operates unobtrusively as an influence on the veteran's decisions. Over the long run, however, if the symptom's influence is not detected, it can leave the veteran with a lonely life with no retirement benefits and unpaid taxes. Early after combat this symptom can have a disinhibiting influence on decisions, as General Shinseki observed, like whether or not to engage in dangerous activities, whether or not to sign up for long-term training, or make a commitment to a relationship. If a veteran, who does not feel he or she should be alive anyway, grows depressed over a loss, the normal inhibiting thought that things will be better tomorrow does not occur, or is not convincing if it does, if the veteran does not believe in a tomorrow. Combine this symptom with the numb familiarity with death and add the lethal means, the firearms, and the decision to commit suicide is something to be considered without much fuss.

One of the consequences of the symptom of having a sense of a foreshortened future lies in having no plans. The veteran doesn't file for disability compensation, doesn't register for school, drinks and uses drugs excessively, gambles in various ways testing fate, because, what difference does it make? One would hope this symptom would dissipate the longer one is away from the combat zone, although alcohol, drug abuse, and other forms of avoidance can perpetuate the maladjustment. Alcohol, and (more subtly) marijuana, can induce disinhibition, so that the veteran acts in the present with diminished regard to consequences. One can suggest to a suicidal veteran that things may get better, but if one has no sense of future, it is like telling a colorblind person about red. The other side of that expression is that things for a well-adjusted veteran may get worse and the feeling of futurelessness may return as memory.

Charles Hoge (2010, p. 123) states that traumatic memories are stored in the limbic system for quicker access and that is why they are experienced as independent of time. "Stored" may not be the correct term. Rather, one could say that traumatic memories are "reassembled." Neurobiologist Gerald Edelman (2004) elaborates on this important issue regarding memory:

> Thus, each event of memory is dynamic and context-sensitive — it yields a repetition of a mental or physical act that is similar but not identical to previous acts. It is recategorial: it does not replicate an original experience exactly. There is no reason to assume that such a memory is representational in the sense that it stores a static registered code for some act. Instead, it is more fruitfully looked on as a property of degenerate nonlinear interactions in a multidimensional network of neuronal groups. Such interactions allow a non-identical "reliving" of a set of prior acts and events, yet there is often the illusion that one is recalling an event exactly as it happened [p. 52].

One can hear the older veterans say that the long-term combat memory is as fresh as yesterday, but the "freshness" may have more to do with the memory's salience and the narrative that contains it than with its recall of exact detail.

This kind of memory keeps the associations to the present compelling when death is forefront because of some current loss. In civilian life, barring catastrophe, deaths rarely bunch many over the course of a year, as frequently happens in combat. Having memories of death stay fresh makes the veteran vulnerable to a sense of being overwhelmed. It takes a concentrated effort on the part of the veteran to keep the feelings for the present separate from the memories of combat, which feel immediate. The Coen Brothers' 1998 comedy, *The Big Lebowski*, played this for laughs when the Vietnam War veteran, Walter (John Goodman), with his friend Dude (Jeff Bridges), are at the seashore scattering the ashes of their bowling partner who has died of a heart condition. Walter, sincere but bombastic, cannot resist, as he speaks about his bowling friend who died so young, recalling the dead of Khe Sahn and other Vietnam battle sites, as the wind blows the ashes back in their faces. Dude is furious and asks, "Why does everything have to do with Vietnam?"

Having deaths accumulate in a veteran's life creates a sense often characterized as anticipating yet another deadly event will soon occur. More subtly, the feeling of loss is linked by association to feelings of grief. Losing a friend, a favored object, a chance at a job, etc., is a feeling in itself that is logical, but its association to more serious loss, such as the loss of fellow combatants, the loss of innocence caused by combat conditions, steps into the irrational and can make the current loss seem far more serious than it need be.

One of the most strikingly memorable events in cinema was the suicidal gambling in which Nick (Christopher Walken) engaged in Michael Cimino's 1978 epic, *The Deer Hunter*. Nick never left South Vietnam after he was wounded and hospitalized. He had been forced as a POW to engage in "Russian Roulette" as a contestant on whom his jailers bet. A guard loaded a .38 revolver with one round and ceremoniously twirled the cylinder, forcing Nick on threat of death to point it at his head and pull the trigger. When he escaped the prison with his comrades he was wounded. After his hospitalization, Nick disappeared into Saigon and became addicted to the reenactment of the suicidal gamble, assisted by the use of heroin, and, finally, lost the bet. (See my review in Early, 2003, pp. 212–216.) *The Deer Hunter* addresses in a sensational and profound way the phenomenon for persons who survive psychological traumas in combat and are unable to conceive of themselves as returning to civilian life and conforming to order.

Anger and Reckless Behavior

I once knew a Vietnam War veteran who was terribly traumatized in the war, and carried with him significant guilt. He had a major struggle adjusting to civilian life, with bursts of ambition and hard work mixed with bursts of wild behavior, including high-stakes gambling. But then he met a woman with whom he wanted to have a relationship. She was successful, classy, and dedicated to her profession. A week before they were to marry, they went on an overnight camping trip in the Cascades in which they got a bit off course and had a hard trek getting back before dark. While their lives were not really in danger, the veteran was aware of his associations to long-range recons that he had been on in North Vietnam as a high risk of casualties. The evening after the hike, after he dropped his fiancée off at her apartment, he was driving home when he was cut off by a man in a pickup truck. Startled, he angrily honked his horn and the man responded by flipping him off. The veteran became enraged and drove his heavy sedan aggressively, smashing into the pickup, backing off and smashing into it again. No one was hurt, and the veteran was immediately ashamed. The pickup driver was an astonished, frightened young man with his ball cap turned backwards on his head. The veteran was arrested and pled guilty to a felony, refusing to use his veteran's status in his defense. (He did manage to follow through on his marriage.)

When I heard his story I was reminded of Humphrey Bogart's character Dixon Steel, in Nicholas Ray's 1954 movie, *In a Lonely Place*. Dixon, I thought, had what psychologists call "trait anger," perhaps even a personality disorder. Trait anger is found significantly more often in combat veterans compared to veterans who did not see active duty. A research group led by Janice Williams (2010) examined a very large sample of 4,620 men who participated in a health study of atherosclerosis. In their study of the aging men, they found that veterans of the Vietnam and the Korean wars had significantly more trait anger than their noncombat peers. Similarly, Kuhn, Drescher, Ruzek, and Rosen (2010) found that combat exposure was significantly related to aggressive driving in a group of WOT veterans, a sample of 474 patients in a day treatment PTSD program. The researchers concluded that their findings suggest that risky driving is common in male war veterans, at least those attending a VA treatment program for PTSD. They also suggested that there was a link between PTSD avoidance and arousal symptoms and aggressive driving.

The aggressive channeling of anger is taught in every infantry training. If it is practiced (i.e., over-learned) in actual combat, it is contained in salient, often traumatic memory. When the warrior becomes a civilian the aggressive anger is expected to be suppressed. Fortunately for civilization, it usually is. But the great danger is there in potential when the combat veteran becomes depressed and channels the anger into self-destructive behaviors. One of the great films inspired by the Vietnam War era was Ivan Passer's 1981 *Cutter's Way*, which featured a veteran named Cutter (John Heard), a traumatized, severely wounded veteran, who engages in reckless, self-destructive behavior, accompanied by alcohol abuse. When he is presented with a real-life murder mystery by his friend, Bone (Jeff Bridges), who witnessed a man dumping the body of a victim into a trashcan, Cutter channels his undifferentiated anger (he did, in a drunken fit, crash his car into his neighbor's that was blocking his driveway) into the task of solving the murder. Cutter accomplishes the task with such intensity that he seems fearless, and ends up sacrificing his life for the cause. His aggressive, furious anger is presented in sharp contrast with his mellow, anxious childhood friend who had avoided the war.

The Advantage of Psychotherapy

"You may say that everyone who had taken physical part in the war was then mad. No one could have come through that shattering experience and still view life and mankind with any normal vision" (Saunders, 1996, p. 90). Ford Madox Ford took part in the Battle of the Somme, was shell shocked and concussed, went through a period of rehabilitation, and returned to trench combat. His biographer, Max Saunders, writes that he never hid the effect the war had on his postwar adjustment.

Anger and self-destructive or aggressive behavior are not necessarily symptoms of a behavior disorder, and may not even be abnormal, if we skew our norm to accommodate a recent history of combat. All the problems that arise from coping with combat memories (and reflexes are memories, too) need to be taken for what they are: driving infractions, assault, domestic violence, etc., and dealt with in the courts, with or without addressing the defendant's combat history. As the U.S. adjusts to accommodate a war veteran culture, Veterans Courts become a formal way of taking into consideration the veteran's wartime past and guiding him or her, if possible, into treatment.

The greatest advantage of psychotherapy is that it alerts the veteran as to where his or her vulnerabilities are, so that crises can be avoided. Out of a therapeutic discussion can come the details of the veteran's personal traumas and the major combat experiences, along with the veteran's narrative perspective on who was there and what they were doing at the time, allowing the veteran to discover his or her own feelings about the events. Importantly, in psychotherapy, the veteran's narrative is being presented during parallel consideration of here-and-now events in the veteran's civilian life that are included in the therapeutic discussion, so that opportunities arise to make the connections of events in the present to the relevant past.

Psychotherapy is not necessarily just for those with behavior problems, although it is often such a problem that brings the veteran in into a therapist's office: poor concentration on the job or in the classroom; conflict in relationships; persistent sleep disturbance; etc. The advantage of psychotherapy is that it fosters a relationship with a listening therapist and the therapist's knowledge of how PTSD manifests in human behavior. PTSD is a diagnostic category, but its symptoms can manifest in veterans who do not satisfy criteria for a full diagnosis. Focusing on the symptom (for instance, anger) is not to exaggerate its importance, but to understand how it operates in this particular veteran. Hyperarousal as a symptom can be very specifically triggered by what happened during a period of trauma — anger, frustration, overreaction to loud noises — whatever leads that unique experience to take up a prominent place in the veteran's personality as memory, one that was not part of the recruit's personality upon his/her entrance into service.

Psychotherapy may ameliorate suicidal symptoms (Jakupcak & Varra, 2010), and a good therapeutic relationship can give the veteran self knowledge to better cope with persisting symptoms. Jakupcak & Vara advise the therapist: "In general, the patient's subjective appraisal of distressing symptoms should be used to guide treatment." Psychotherapy for amputees consists of helping the amputee adapt to the new handicap. Psychotherapy for veterans with mild traumatic brain injury consists (in part) of teaching the veteran to adapt to new limitations, some of which, emotionally, may be secondary to the physical injury. Psychotherapy for PTSD symptoms is also designed to help the veteran adapt. The above example of the symptom of having lost a sense of future might well be one that manifests as a topic only in couples therapy, when the spouse complains about the veteran not wanting to have a pet because it will just get sick, run up vet bills, and die.

Individualized psychotherapy can lead the veteran to a better understanding of what is unique about the trauma experience that presents a trigger for memory and arouses the over-reactive affect that Henry Krystal described in 1978. This can be a significant advantage to the veteran who manages to stay undiagnosed because memory of trauma is mostly suppressed, so that the veteran remains largely unconscious of how the memories manifest. Subtle avoidance symptoms can divert one's career into directions that may not be beneficial. For example, the memories may manifest as the wariness of the veteran to make a commitment, the avoidance of responsibility, sensitivity to anniversary reactions, having a sense of foreshortened future, etc. Abstract descriptions of how therapy works can be derived from books (Hoge, 2010; Briere and Scott, 2006), but the application of specific aspects of unconsciousness about the effects of psychological trauma cannot always be grasped by the individual veteran alone. Castner (2012) gives a colorful description of his own psychotherapy. One of his symptoms, being suppression of emotion, he labeled metaphorically as "Crazy." In a pleasant exchange with his therapist, Castner is told that didn't have PTSD (pp. 218–219), but that his symptoms were normal; that is, normal for a combat veteran. And, of course, "normal" doesn't mean the symptoms are not problematic and worthy of discussion in psychotherapy.

A major argument for a therapeutic discussion of the veteran's wartime experiences comes from the fact that the give-and-take of discussion, along with the added point of view, changes the recollection of traumatic events. This was illustrated nicely, if indirectly, by Israel Rosenfield (1992) discussing the neurology of brain injury. He quotes a man's report of his blindness: "It is three years now since I have seen anybody. Strangely enough, I have fairly clear pictures of many people whom I have not met during those three years, but the pictures of the people I have met everyday are becoming blurred" (p. 136. Quoting J. M. Hull, 1990, *Touching the Rock: An experience of blindness*). This, I think, relates to traumatic as well as visual images. Such images are not stored intact, but are reassembled (or "recatagorized," as Edelman put it) to be experienced as memory. Rosenfield (1992, p. 85) writes: "Conscious images are dynamic relations among a flow of constantly evolving coherent responses, at once different and yet derives from previous responses that are part of an individual's past." When a psychological trauma is experienced, Rosenfield asserts, "It is isolated, not as a memory, but rather the ability to *organize* the memory is impaired" (p. 134). Like the blind man's last images, the images associated with trauma will change when reconsidered with new information and the added perspective of others as well as the changed perspective of the enlightened veteran. The very process of verbally articulating something that is personally profound in its influence has the potential to change the narrator's perception. Being able, then, to integrate the periods of trauma into the war veteran's civilian conscious identity is a major step toward wholeness.

Stigma and Posttraumatic Growth

"Somewhere along the way, what we thought would serve to de-stigmatize a trauma survivor [the diagnosis of PTSD in DSM-III] has in effect re-stigmatized him or her" (Scurfield, 2004, p. 206). When J.D. Salinger was hospitalized after prolonged combat, he wrote to Ernest Hemingway that he hoped having combat exhaustion (depression) would not impair his reputation and the sale of his novel (*Catcher in the Rye*) (Slawenski, 2010, p. 136).

The avoidance of stigma keeps many in the military from disclosing symptoms of PTSD. Charles Hoge (2010) cites evidence that less than half the deployed soldiers who have symptoms of PTSD seek treatment. We in the mental health professions, by contrast, grow numb to the onus of the disorder. PTSD is as common in our profession as astigmatism is to an eye doctor.

Perceptions of stigma persist in veterans, even after they finally come forth to seek treatment, after the symptoms become problematic. Tedeschi and McNally (2011, p. 21) discuss how they intend to address the issue: "Combat veterans should be taught that basic physiological and psychological responses are *normal* reactions to the experience of combat. Such reactions do not indicate a defect in one's character or identity as a soldier." The issue of whether the reactions are normal may be missing the point, however, when the "normal" reactions become symptoms, and, left untreated, become life management problems. A probably unintended example of the source of stigma comes from the writings of positive psychologist, Martin Seligman, while discussing posttraumatic growth.

> Post-traumatic stress disorder surely increases in likelihood because of the self-fulfilling nature of the downward spiral that catastrophizing and believing that you have PTSD engenders. Individuals who are catastrophizers to begin with are much more susceptible to PTSD. One study followed 5,410 soldiers through their army careers from 2002–2006. Over this five-year period, 395 were diagnosed with PTSD. More than half of them were in the bottom 15 percent of mental and physical health to begin with.... People who are in bad shape to begin with are at much greater risk for PTSD than psychologically fit people [Seligman, 2011, p. 158].

Dr. Seligman writes of his attempt to reduce stigma by testing all 1.1 million soldiers, pointing out their strengths and giving training modules to those who are motivated to improve. It is his wish, along with the wish cited by Tedeschi and McNally, to train soldiers in resilience that will strengthen their resistance to developing PTSD from combat conditions. Yet his example, correct as he is in citing scientific research (in a 2009 British medical journal), is an excellent one for why stigma persists; that is, that people who develop PTSD must be in bad shape to begin with. Seligman (2011, pp. 158–9) contends that disability compensation for PTSD, which is granted by the federal Department of Veterans Affairs, serves to prolong and exaggerate the disorder. Ben Shephard (2001, p. 151) traces these arguments across Europe's 20th century wars — that compensating trauma disorders leads to chronicity, and that soldiers who become shell shocked or combat fatigued were constitutionally compromised to begin with.

Webster's dictionary renders two uses of the word stigma. The first refers to a scar left by a wound, a mark of shame or discredit, and a diagnostic sign of a wound. The military would like to tackle this use of the word with the idea that post-combat reactions are normal. The psychiatric diagnostic manual

Jacknife (1989), David Jones, director. Robert De Niro plays a Vietnam War veteran truck driver, nicknamed Jacknife, here flirting with his buddy's sister, Martha, played by Kathy Baker, who is somewhat skeptical. Their relationship eventually becomes an example of posttraumatic gain. (Cineplex-Odeon Films; Kings Road Entertainment; Sandollar-Schaffel Productions. Photo credit: Steve Sands.)

agrees that there has to be a passage of one month posttrauma before a diagnosis of PTSD can be made. The shame or discredit is not from the sense of the physical wound, however, but from the ineffable sense that one did not have the emotional strength to endure the traumatic event without symptoms, coupled with the fear that others will have the same value. The dark side of the bonding that takes place in combat is in the consensus of such values.

The army's idea is that the values of positive psychology will both reduce the posttraumatic stress and allow those with symptoms to be regarded positively — that draws attention to the *Webster New College Dictionary*'s second definition of stigma: "The part of the pistil of a flower which receives pollen grains and on which they germinate." The value change would have to take place here, with the idea that symptoms of PTSD, *because* they cause problems, stimulate creative solutions. Stigma then signifies an opportunity for growth.

The problem with changing attitudes toward PTSD is that there aren't many examples of posttraumatic growth in the popular media. It is not because there aren't any examples in life, because there are plenty in the annals of psychotherapy; it is that they are not the stuff of drama. One way posttraumatic growth is dramatized is in the disguise of romance. The 1989 movie *Jacknife*, directed by David Jones, is about Vietnam War veterans dealing with post-traumatic symptoms that were generated by witnessing the death of their mutual friend. Robert De Niro plays the truck driver veteran (Jacknife) who, with the help he attributes to a veterans' group, endeavors to follow through on a promise to his buddy, Dave (Ed Harris), to go fishing together. His buddy, however, has taken up dysfunctional avoidance — i.e., alcohol abuse. The positive note comes in the form of Dave's sister, Martha (Kathy Baker), who is attracted to Jacknife, and Jacknife has enough strength of identity to reciprocate her attraction. One could argue that romance is the motion picture's way of portraying posttraumatic growth that comes unexpectedly following the attention given to symptoms.

The potential for gain from symptoms of PTSD is derived from the meaning that is attributed to or gleaned from the traumatic experience, from the rigor of discipline that is sometimes required to cope. Functional avoidance, keeping busy, might be a product of creative ways to make life interesting enough to distract the veteran's attention from symptomatic memories. Many psychotherapists these days are suggesting to veterans that they create a narrative of their military experiences, including the traumatic event. In the electronic age, veterans can go online to connect with other veterans who were present in the same combat, which can help the veteran gain organizing perspective of the often fragmentary aspect of such memories.

Stigma then leaves one with an option of staying with the first definition, the sign of a wound, shame, etc., or the second definition, an opening for germination. The trick that psychotherapists know is that memories of combat are not fixed in the brain, but are re-collected, as it were, with each recall. So that discussing and examining troubling memories involved in symptoms of repetition changes the associations to the memories, allowing an opportunity for the veteran to turn the negative on its ear. Obsessional thinking usually implies repetitious scrutiny of the same memories, whereas a more creative approach is the obsessional, if you will, organizing of the memories, giving them structure. They are the same memories, the difference being in what the veteran attributes to the recall: that is, is the memory an intrusive, unwanted sign of psychopathology ("crazy") or a sign of healing and growth stimulated by discussion and review.

The discussion of stigma associated with PTSD cannot ignore the reality that there is bias in hiring and promotions, just as there is gender, ethnic, or racial bias. One cannot imagine a politician with combat-generated PTSD running for president — although several may have who kept it in the closet, the way FDR conspired with journalists to overlook his paralyzed legs. It would be helpful in changing the stigma of PTSD if people in public life and high office did come forward and declare that they have dealt with the disorder, that even though the symptoms may be considered normal, they can cause problems, and that coping with the problems can lead to gain.

Much of the stigma comes from examples of violence perpetrated by veterans who apparently have PTSD, which often makes the news identifying the perpetrator as a war veteran as opposed to a psychopath who went to war. This coverage is never balanced by the news that a veteran accomplishes something positive: "Vet with PTSD writes and publishes a novel!"

Part of the alienation that veterans experience returning from a combat deployment is the loss of the common culture of shared experiences. The army is hoping that it can inculcate its soldiers with enough positive psychology that they can carry into civilian life the attitude that PTSD symptoms present an opportunity for growth. It is also realistic, however, for the veteran to be able to assess the biases and prejudices of the civilian world into which they enter. It has to do with being worldly wise: Having posttraumatic symptoms is a normal process that can lead to problems if not given attention.

The positive side of the war veteran alienation is represented in *Made in Dagenham*, in which Albert (Bob Hoskins), a World War II veteran and union official, declared that he is not afraid to become involved in the controversial labor strife involving women factory workers' struggle for equal pay, because he fought Rommel in North Africa, which was far worse. The positive side of stigma is the war veteran as a symbol of strength, courage, and devotion to duty, as shown in my *War Veteran in Film*, a symbol long cherished and exploited by filmmakers.

The current war veterans who saw combat in Iraq and Afghanistan are serving notice that they do not want to be judged by the medical model of the disorder attached to posttraumatic stress. They stress that it is normal, in keeping with Tedeschi & McNally (2011), to come out of a combat zone with symptoms of posttraumatic stress, and would probably prefer the more normal term "reactions" rather than "symptoms." I can imagine veterans of past wars having the same reaction after returning from combat. There is a wish imbedded in the sentiment that the posttraumatic reactions will dissipate and the veteran will return to some ideal pre-war normal or at least achieve a new postwar sense of normality. The Vet Center movement that made outreach contact with Vietnam War veterans did not begin until 1979, which for many veterans was five to 15 years after their exposure to combat. What counselors found in those veterans were conditions that had become chronic: alienation composed of anger, guardedness, dysfunctional avoidance, domestic distress, and physical symptoms of chronic stress.

Of course, this is overstating the condition of any one veteran. It matters to the self-esteem of the veteran that his or her condition is described as either a disorder or as normal. The reaction to prolonged combat is a disturbance like the rings created from a rock thrown into a pond. The more turbulence there is in the pond, the less noticeable the rings. The more at peace the community is, the more the veteran's stress appears abnormal. Judging the evolution of the psychiatric diagnostic manuals and treatment of psychological trauma, there appears to be a kind of pendulum swing from psychologizing trauma to calling it normal to the point that it disappears from awareness. Psychologist Paula Caplan (2011, p. 102) refers to the "psychiatrizing of society" and sees drug-prescribing psychiatrists as a major source of harm to veterans. She finds fault with the erratic, flawed nature of the national mental health system and sees the only relief coming from the reduction of the efforts of the nation to pursue war. She discourages the value of a veteran having a good psychotherapeutic relationship and seems to find it a rare occurrence. Marcia Angell (2011) shares Caplan's view that there is an over-reach in psychiatry and its Diagnostic and Statistical Manual that leads to over-diagnosis. It makes sense that if PTSD were regarded as a psychological — as opposed to a psychiatric — problem not necessarily requiring medication of symptoms, veterans might be more amenable to counseling and psychotherapy. It is also upon non-medical mental health practitioners, as Carl Rogers urged in 1946 (Rogers & Whalen, 1946), to detach from dependence on the medical model in defining problems. Angell points out that there is also a problem from the insurance companies, as well as many other healthcare-related institutions, which requires medical diagnoses to reimburse for treatment.

Medical model aside, however, the veteran would be wise to seek the advantage of an additional perspective, some kind of counseling or a valued non-professional relationship along the way, to avoid the unhappy stories of normal war veterans grown old and alone. (See the films *Made in Dagenham, Gran Torino, Ulee's Gold, In Country, Desert Bloom,* for a sample of the problems created by chronic stress over the long term that are generated by combat.)

CHAPTER 8

Movies and the
Alienation of War Veterans

He's alive. He's coming back to us. — Nora Temple (Lauren Bacall),
in the final scene of John Huston's 1948 film adaptation of Maxwell
Anderson's play *Key Largo*

We are accustomed to seeing in movies the alienation that is found in
veterans returning from a war portrayed in such a way that his alienation is
not without reason. The veterans come back to their homeland and no longer
practice their warrior skills; they may even have developed a distaste for the
military identity. But the warrior identity is forced upon them again, and it
is that identity that gives them strength.

Two films illustrate this theme well for us, both of which depict the veteran seeking out the family of a dead comrade to whom he credits life-saving
heroism. The visits are seen as obligatory, as if to fulfill a promise made on
the battlefield. In both circumstances hostility occurs which the veteran did
not cause, but to which he must respond. The World War II veterans appear
in John Huston's *Key Largo* (1948) and John Sturges's *Bad Day at Black Rock*
(1955), and they encounter forces as hostile as Penelope's suitors. Both films
were reviewed in *The War Veteran in Film*, but here it is worthwhile to examine
their common theme, because alienation is often projected as being a force
in the veteran's environment, as well as originating in the veteran, and to this
end, in both films, the veteran enters a world populated by hostile men. Both
stories manage to dramatically isolate the veteran so that he can rely only
upon his wiles to survive.

In *Key Largo*, returning veteran Frank McCloud (Humphrey Bogart)
travels to Key Largo on a bus that is stopped on route by cops looking for two
Seminole Natives who have escaped from jail. Frank is seeking the family of

his buddy who was killed in Italy directing artillery fire from a forward position and died while talking to Frank on the field telephone. His late buddy's widow, Nora (Lauren Bacall), and her wheelchair-bound father-in-law, James Temple (Lionel Barrymore), manage the Hotel Largo in the Florida Keys. Johnny Rocko (Edward G. Robinson) is alienation personified, a vain, arrogant, cruel gangster who was deported to Cuba and has secretly returned to the mainland with his mob to make a crooked deal selling counterfeit money to another gangster. They have commandeered the Hotel Largo, and made prisoners of Mr. Temple and Nora. McCloud's predicament is made worse by the fact that he has sworn to himself not to fight "other peoples' battles" anymore.

Bad Day at Black Rock (an adaptation of Howard Breslin's story "Bad Time at Hondo") has the veteran John J. McCreedy (Spencer Tracy) arriving on a Southern Pacific railroad train at the isolated Arizona town of Black Rock. McCreedy has come to Black Rock to visit the father of a soldier who

Bad Day at Black Rock (1955), John Sturges, director. Spencer Tracy (left) played World War II veteran John J. McCreedy, visiting the Arizona desert town of Black Rock, dressed as an alien in black suit, shown here shaking hands with a Black Rock resident, the nefarious racist Reno Smith, played by Robert Ryan (right). McCreedy is trying to locate the father of the soldier who was killed saving his life. (Metro-Goldwyn-Mayer.)

fought in a Japanese-American company that McCreedy commanded in Italy. The Nisei soldier died saving McCreedy's life. He is met by townspeople who are wary of the stranger and view him suspiciously. They meet his requests for information with passive hostility and outright lies.

In both films the veterans were wounded, in a manner of speaking. McCreedy lost the use of his left arm, and McCloud lost the will to fight. Both veterans express displeasure with the world and a desire to retire from human interaction. They both have one last duty to perform in obligation to the dead, and both are obstructed by criminals with whom they must fight, and, to a certain extent, they each acquire a new sense of human participation by caring enough to fight.

The topic of racial prejudice is strong in both films. The Seminole Natives in *Key Largo* have been driven off their land. They come to the Hotel Largo to escape a hurricane, but are denied shelter by the ruthless Johnny Rocko. Tracy's McCreedy finds in Black Rock that a Japanese-American, Komoko, has been murdered in his house by a fire set by the townspeople in an expression of anti–Japanese hatred early in the war. The righteous townspeople covered up the death under the leadership of the bigoted Reno Smith (Robert Ryan), who claimed that the fire was accidental. The opposition to racial injustice serves to highlight the cause for alienation in the war veteran. This topic of anti–Japanese prejudice was picked up poignantly by *Snow Falling on Cedars* (1999), which depicts a Nisei veteran who returns from the war to find his family's Northwest island farm land sold to a German-American family under coercive conditions.

Race is not the issue, per se, as in *Devil in a Blue Dress* (1995) and *Dead Presidents* (1945), in which racial prejudice combines with combat-induced alienation to push the veteran into a fight to survive. McCreedy and McCloud are disgusted witnesses of the prejudice and I think, like the 1947 noir *Crossfire*, express Hollywood's fear that ethnic and racial prejudice would link up with fascism in America as it did in Europe. Hollywood movie-making was, by the end of the war, a city of artistic refugees. We can see this also expressed as fear of a recurrence of fascism in the post–World War II homecoming films, *Best Years of Our Lives* and *Till the End of Time*, when the veterans fight with racial bigots.

In both *Key Largo* and *Bad Day at Black Rock* the hostile opposition to the veteran is perpetrated by bad guys who did not serve in the military. They are thugs: Johnny Rocko and his mob, Curly (Thomas Gomez) and Toots (Harry Lewis), in *Key Largo*, and a lineup of tough characters in *Black Rock*: the menacing Reno Smith whom, he said, was rejected by recruiters; Coley Trimble (Ernest Borgnine); and Hector David (Lee Marvin). The veterans are portrayed, by contrast, as righteous but disillusioned men who did their duty and incurred obligations as the result of combat. McCreedy says that he has one last duty to perform before he "resigns from the human race." Both veterans have to be rallied out of their cynicism by the blunt forces of oppression. McCreedy says, "I guess I was looking for someplace to get lost because I was afraid I couldn't function any longer." Frank McCloud says, "One Rocko more or less isn't worth dying for." Rocko mocks him, "A live war hero — now I know how you did it." Hector mocks McCreedy as he starts up the hotel stairs toting his bag with his only good arm: "You look like you need a hand."

Another parallel in the two films that is worth observing is the complex roles of women: Nora, the widow of the dead soldier in *Key Largo*; the helpful Liz Wirth (Anne Francis) in *Black Rock*; Gaye Dawn (Claire Trevor, in an Academy Award-winning performance) an alcoholic chanteuse and Johnny Rocko's humiliated girlfriend, who finally lands on the side of right. While Liz Wirth is helpful, she, in the end, knowingly leads McCreedy into an ambush, only to be shot down herself by the treacherous Reno Smith. When Frank McCloud wrestles with his desire to fight the criminals, the two women, Nora and Gaye, speak in chorus like muses, one in each ear, as Frank holds the dead veteran's medal and decides what to do. Each film ends in a final shootout that puts and end to thugs who threaten goodness. McCreedy gives the medal he'd brought to the townspeople of Black Rock for having the courage to turn on the murderers.

The war veterans' alienation is usually personified as "out there" in the movies for the sake of drama. Film critic David Desser put it well:

> Yet it is possible, despite all these implications of crime and the public's apathy to it, to see crime as only an index of Frank's alienation, symbolic of the general malaise into which he has fallen. Or crime, perhaps more strongly, is only the *dramatic* sign of postwar disillusionment.... After all, Frank *begins* the film alienated, out of step, drifting. His confrontation with the gangsters is not responsible for his crisis of faith and his loss of values. Yet, it is only by resisting the gangsters and the inner angst and disillusionment they represent that Frank can be reintegrated into society [Desser, 1993, p. 30].

Inner struggles are more difficult to portray to an audience paying for entertainment. Rocko mocks Frank McCloud, calling him "Soldier" with derision. McCreedy says, "Everybody's been needling me since I got off the train." McCreedy throughout *Bad Day at Black Rock* is clad in a dark suit, which is, in this rustic setting, a symbol of alienation, because it places him quite in contrast to the casual western garb of the townspeople. The mocking scorn of civilians is heightened when personified in the talents of such great character actors as Ernest Borgnine, Lee Marvin, and Edward G. Robinson. The veteran is led into the confrontation with outlaws by his sense of obligation to the dead. Once ensnared by the complications, he persists in seeing the challenges through. He has to fight against odds, one man against many who would do him harm. Eventually, he wins over the confederates. In *Key Largo*, Gaye Dawn is converted and helps the veteran by sneaking him a gun that he uses in the final shootout. In *Bad Day*, Doc (Walter Brennan), and Liz's brother, the hotel clerk, Pete (John Ericson), are won over to help the veteran McCreedy win the day.

The tension between war veterans and civilians seems like a perpetual feeling of alienation for some, particularly the discomfort of civilians with the wounded veterans. McCreedy makes a statement for war veterans in general about civilians in his homeland, when he says to Pete, the hotel clerk, "You'd like me to die quickly without wasting too much of your time, so I won't embarrass you too much."

Key Largo has Nora Temple wait for Frank McCloud to return. They will surely have a good relationship because they have been impressed with each other all through the film. Nora has the last words in the movie after Frank telephones her from the boat that he is coming back: "He's alive. He's coming back to us." McCreedy, however, boards the train leaving Black Rock, alone and still cynical, although he's been given a new life to live. The comparison of the two outcomes is a statement of the role of affiliation in the healing of the war veteran's alienation. As Reno Smith says of Black Rock after the veteran came to town: "Since he's arrived this town has a fever, an infection, and it's spreading."

Racial and ethnic prejudices continue to be a source of alienation for minority groups in the modern United States. Returning from combat has only served to increase alienation and heighten the sense of injustice among African American, Asian, and Native American war veterans. One African American veteran, wounded as a combat engineer in the Korean War, described his fury at being turned away from a restaurant in Washington State outside his army base while his white friend was offered service. This, in the decade of the 1950s, for minority American veterans was not an uncommon experience. Melinda Pash (2012) chronicles many other incidents of this prejudice toward Korean War veterans. Three films, reviewed by this writer (Early, 2003) that capture this collective problem of the prejudicial treatment of minority veterans are *Dead Presidents* (1995), directed by Alan and Albert Hughes, *Snow Falling on Cedars* (1999), directed by Scott Hicks, and *Powwow Highway* (1989), directed by Jonathan Wacks. Other films capture this prejudice toward minority veterans, such as Clint Eastwood's *Flags of Our Fathers* (2007), and the excellent 1995 detective drama, *Devil in a Blue Dress*, directed by Carl Franklin.

Dead Presidents features African American veterans of the Vietnam War, and another from the Korean War, who struggle with unemployment and poverty in urban America. They finally opt to apply their skills learned in combat by robbing an armored car. This film is especially striking because it shows dramatically the evolution of the idealistic boy who declines a chance to go to college in order to experience "something different." He enters combat in Vietnam as a Marine in Force Recon and returns with his values changed. *Dead Presidents* contains one of the most striking cinematic images of war veteran films, one that succinctly captures extreme alienation, showing the black robbers in white-face makeup as they ambush the armored car and engage in a fire fight with the guards. The film offers a complex alternative in showing a black cop who happens on the scene as the robbery is about to happen. He stops to help the lookout, who seems to be waiting for a bus. The cop is attracted to the man's Marine Corps field jacket with a Force Recon insignia. The helpful cop was also a Marine, he says, just before he is shot dead by the robber.

Snow Falling on Cedars, mentioned above in relation to *Bad Day at Black Rock*, is a courtroom drama that takes place in the gray atmosphere of the Pacific Northwest islands, featuring Japanese-American farmers who are forcibly interned at the start of World War II. The primary focus is on one veteran who served in the army, fighting with a Nisei regiment in Italy. He is accused of murder, after he returns from the war, when he tries to claim his family farmland that has been illegally sold. The film is based on a novel by David Guterson and sets the war veteran mystery nicely by juxtaposing a Caucasian veteran and local newspaper editor, Ishmael (Ethan Hawke), and Japanese-American fisherman veteran, Kazuo Miyamoto (Rick Yune), who were childhood friends. *Snow Falling on Cedars* captures the racial and ethnic prejudice that swept the country after the Japanese attack on Pearl Harbor. The Roosevelt administration capitulated to a grossly unjust policy to assuage the fears of the Asian threat, policy that led to the internment of Japanese-American citizens.

Louis Malle's *Alamo Bay* (1985) renders a version of this racist rage by showing a Vietnam War veteran (Ed Harris) who is losing his fishing boat and caught up in the projected hatred of immigrant Vietnamese fishermen on the Texas Gulf coast, who seem to be more successful because of their communal family enterprise.

Powwow Highway concerns a Native American veteran of the Vietnam War (A Martinez), who is discouraged about Native tradition and is brought back to his heritage by a friend, Philbert (Gary Farmer), who plays something of a foolish trickster guide during their road trip to Santa Fe, New Mexico, to rescue the veteran's sister from jail. This film offers a view of the important aspect of Native American culture that welcomes, with ritual, the warrior back to his community, providing meaning and community respect to the impact of war on the veteran. *Powwow Highway* also illustrates the isolation of the Native tribal lands from the dominant culture of the United States that makes it difficult for the Native American war veteran to integrate into the general American culture, and, ironically, makes it difficult for veterans from the diverse culture to integrate back into society without ceremony or ritual. Tom Holm (1996) gives a broad overview of the Native American attitude toward warriors, war veterans, and the ceremonies that protect and cleanse. He also shows combat training and skills being utilized in defense of tribal rights in the AIM (American Indian Movement) activism at Wounded Knee (Holm, 1996, p. 176). Ray Scurfield (2004, pp. 104–6) discusses the awkward interface between the VA system and Native American rituals.

The common theme in these movies about war veterans who are members of minority groups is that alienation, which is part of being a minority citizen in the United States, is enhanced by the war veteran status. Those who grow up feeling alienated have to contend with the burden of added alienation as the result of experiences in foreign combat. As a counselor, over the years, I deduced that it was the white Vietnam War veteran who was surprised by the rejection and negative labeling that was awaiting him in the society to which he returned. The minority veteran had already had the experience of playing the shadow role; he had been conditioned not to expect gratitude and reward from American society without overcoming obstacles of bias, and was consequently less indignant when the reality of his reception was what he expected.

Alienation in the veteran is influenced by his culture. In *Lonely Are the Brave*, the main character's cowboy heritage, resistant as it is to modern civilization, is spurred to the radical by his Korean War experience. In *Who'll Stop the Rain*, when a Vietnam War Marine Corps and Merchant Marine veteran is saddled with a smuggler's stash of heroin, he becomes a fugitive, leading him to the same exotic high desert of New Mexico ridden by the cowboy in *Lonely Are the Brave*. The Vietnam veteran overtly shows his anger, but the cowboy's anger is disguised behind a charming mask of civility. In the end, however, both war veterans are destroyed for their failure to conform.

I Am a Fugitive from a Chain Gang (1932) presents the returning World War I veteran as too restless and ambitious to settle back into his old job, but his timing is bad, as it was for veterans then, in having the Great Depression over-shadowing his adjustment. The 1931 film *The Last Flight* casts a deadly undertone to the wounded World War I American pilots who party in Paris instead of returning home. Another film featuring a World War II veteran as a main character is *The Blue Dahlia* (1946). Returning to a hostile society, he is blamed for his wife's murder, and must act on his own as a fugitive to identify the killer. A series of films from the 1980s feature the Vietnam War veteran

John Rambo (Sylvester Stallone). In the initial installment, *First Blood*, Rambo seeks out a fellow veteran only to discover from his widow that he's died of cancer. And then, when he's harassed by a cop in a manner that speaks of prejudice against Vietnam War veterans, Rambo is forced into outlawry à la Robin Hood. Another film, less well known, is *The Ballad of Andy Crocker* (1969). Andy (Lee Majors) returns from Vietnam to find that his business partner (Jimmy Dean) has cheated him out of his motorcycle business, and his girlfriend (Joey Heatherton) has married. Andy finally assaults and beats his business partner, and then rides his motorcycle across the country to re-enlist in the army to return to Vietnam.

The mundane lives of everyday war veterans are usually far less dramatic than their screen depictions. They struggle with conformity in school or the workplace and try to fit into family life. The recent film of an OIF veteran, *The Dry Land*, is an example of a more mundane drama of a veteran returning from a combat deployment to find his friends asking him insensitive questions, a co-worker who taunts him, and his wife becoming afraid of his sleep disturbance and his moody volatility. Ordinary life, married or not, is usually complicated by emotions that the veteran may not know how to share.

The obligations harbored by survivors of combat are myriad and diverse, much of it traditional. They served with comrades who became casualties. They witnessed the cruelty and brutality of combat conditions. They witnessed and participated in archetypal suffering. What circumstances surrounded crushed ideals, disillusionment, shock, betrayal, faulty leaders, injustice, prolonged apprehensiveness, mistakes made under awful conditions? These are the memories of the veterans returning to live with civilians. They are of conflict too often repeated. Karl Marlantes's thoughtful discussion of his own experience in *What It Is Like to Go to War*, states that he "felt had." He writes in a footnote (p. 27): "Feeling had is one of the predominant feelings of my whole Vietnam experience."

It follows that the veterans of each era see themselves differently, as distinct from the past, and, as such, they become a cultural statement. The veterans of the current wars in Iraq and Afghanistan are challenged with news of wars that are ongoing and without borders. Psychological trauma is identified now as a stressor that can cause a disorder with which the society grapples, but the war veteran remains isolated and oppressed by memories that seemingly cannot be shared, or shared only with great difficulty. The successful completion of psychotherapy, the successful integration of the traumas of combat into a narrative of a whole person, sounds like a movie plot that won't sell.

The mask of civility does not necessarily hide a dark persona, but it does conceal the memories of combat and the knowledge of the dark side of humanity.

CHAPTER 9

Movies Reviewed

The synopses and commentary that follow are of the movies mentioned with more than passing emphasis and are presented here more or less in the order that they are mentioned. Additional synopses and commentary can be found in my *The War Veteran in Film*.

Seven Samurai, 1954

Seven Samurai takes place in the throes of civil wars in Japan, set in the early 16th century. In Japan, as in Europe in the Middle Ages, the distinction between soldiers raiding and pillaging and independent roving gangs of bandits was not clear. The film opens with bandits raiding a rural village and threatening to raid again at the time of the next harvest. The frightened farmers of the village confer with their elder, an old man at the water mill. He advises them to hire samurai for protection. The villagers abide by his sage advice, pool their meager resources and set out on an improbable quest to hire samurai to protect their interests. They have very little to offer in compensation. Director Akira Kurosawa emphasizes their poverty and humble circumstances when gambling rogues mock them at a wayfarer's hostel. The farmers' search delegation finally finds a samurai who has a sense of integrity, Kambei (Takashi Shimura). They watch Kambei pose as a monk with shaved head in order to rescue a child from a thief, while asking for no compensation. The farmers' delegation approaches Kambei, who listens to them and consents to help the village defend itself against attack. He is actually swayed to their side by the bandits ridicule of the farmers' poverty.

With a sense of bemusement about his task, Kambei, in turn, searches out five other samurai, and finally, on the road to the village they add a seventh, when Kikuchiyo (Toshirô Mifune) joins them. Kikuchiyo is an inarticulate, rough country person who aspires to the samurai code and, finally, is invited to join the six in their mission to protect the villagers. He is a rude bumpkin who vulgarly mocks the action, creating a nice balance for the deadly serious contest that is looming, and provides to the samurai a crucial knowledge of village life.

Each of the chosen samurai is defined as a unique individual with warrior skills. They are Katsushiro (Ko Kimura), a young aristocrat and also an aspiring samurai; Shichiroji (Daisuke Kato); Gorobei (Yoshio Inaba); Heihachi, the "woodcutter samurai" (Minoru Chiaki); and Kyuzo (Seiji Miyaguchi), the master swordsman. They have a sense of familiarity with each other that is characteristic of many veterans. The seven travel to the village and assess the situation. Throughout the film, the earthy, passionate Kikuchiyo provides comic relief and a cultural bridge between the villagers and the samurai. (He plays a role that we see repeating through sagas about heroes, illustrated by the Knight's squire in *The Seventh Seal* and Tonto in the Lone Ranger series. Kirosawa's genius was to later combine the earthy one with the warrior and create a solid heroic character in *Yojimbo* and *Sanjuro*.)

The samurai prepare defenses and drill the farmers, and finally there are a series of skirmishes with the anonymous bandits. Bandit scouts are captured. A raid is made on the bandits' camp, which the samurai set afire, resulting in a conflagration and the death of the bandits' prisoner, the spouse of a villager, and the first death of a samurai, Heihachi.

The samurai and villagers finally defeat the bandits after reducing the raiders' number in a fierce rain-drenched battle (one of the most memorable in all of international cinema) by using superior strategy. The fighting cost the lives of three more samurai, Gorobei, Kyuzo, and Kikuchyo. When the combat is ended and the villagers are safe, the surviving three samurai have no further function in the village at peace. It is a tradition in many cultures that the warrior is unwelcome in the town when there is no war. At the end of the fighting, as the farmers return to the fields for planting, Kambei says to another surviving samurai, Shichiroji, "Again we've survived." And later, "Again we're defeated. The winners are those farmers. Not us." The villagers are planting their rice, moving in harmony to the accompaniment of traditional drum and flute, while on a knoll above, four samurai swords mark the graves of those who are buried, having given their lives defending the village.

Yojimbo, 1961

The time is 1860; the setting is the Japanese countryside. *Yojimbo* opens with a wandering samurai (Toshirô Mifune), traveling without a destination, which is shown when he approaches a "Y" in the road and tosses a stick up into the air. He takes the road it points to on landing. The text introduces the theme: "A samurai, once a dedicated warrior in the employ of royalty, now finds himself with no master to serve other than his own will to survive and no devices other than his wit and sword."

An older man crosses the road in front of the samurai chasing a younger one, scolding him. They argue in front of the samurai because the young man, the son, is leaving home to make his living among the town's merchants. After the fracas, when the samurai stops at the angry father's hut for water, he hears the man complaining to his wife, discussing the rival factions of merchants in town who have turned to violence. A humorous aspect of this scene shows the man's wife placidly weaving cloth, apparently enjoying her work, while her husband seethes with anger.

The samurai then enters the deserted town and it is here that the inspiration of American Western films becomes obvious, for the vacant street is wind swept with blowing dust, while people peek with fearful curiosity from windows and doors. The scene could be transferred to the American West of the 1870s with a Civil War veteran riding into a frontier town. The samurai, walking warily in the wide empty street, is startled when he sees a dog trotting along toward him, carrying a severed human hand in its mouth. (American film director Sam Peckinpah featured that same scene in *The Wild Bunch*, 1969, as a tribute to Kurosawa. Sergio Leone is said to have fashioned his Westerns *Fistful of Dollars* and *The Good, the Bad, and the Ugly*, featuring the gunfighter with no name, after *Yojimbo* [Prince, 1991, p. 16].)

A townsperson approaches the samurai obsequiously and says, "Samurai, want to be a body guard? I can fix it up for you." The samurai learns from a merchant who runs a little shop selling sake and rice that the two groups of merchants are really rival gangs of outlaws led by Seibei and Ushi-Tora, respectively. The truculent proprietor (Eijiro Tono) relates the circumstances in the town very cleverly, by opening various window shutters in his little shop, revealing a view of the various town characters. The proprietor angrily urges the samurai to leave instead of selling his services, but the samurai replies bluntly: "Listen to me. I get paid for killing. Better if all these men are dead. Think about it."

The samurai, when asked, gives his name as Sanjuro, which means 30-year-old man, although it seems to be an arbitrary choice.

The samurai then proceeds to offer his services to each side as a bodyguard. Each gang is stocked with rough characters who brag about being outlaws and seem to take killing as a matter of routine. When the two factions are stirred into action by vying for the samurai, he opts out and watches from the town bell tower as the gangs comically confront each other.

As in *Seven Samurai*, the samurai has no strong interest in profit and only manages to eek little gain from the conflict. In the end, he must move on, because he doesn't belong. He takes a vicious beating, is imprisoned by one gang, risks his life in combat with multiple adversaries, killing most, sparing some, showing extraordinary skills. After he escapes his imprisonment, half dead, the sake shop proprietor and the undertaker manage to smuggle the samurai out of town hidden in a coffin. He recovers over time, sheltered in a shrine, and finally returns in full strength to finish off the two gangs. When he kills the last villain, a cocky, pistol-toting bandit (Ikio Sawamura), the unrepentant dying man croaks, "Samurai trash. I'll be waiting in hell for you."

The samurai, in the tradition of the hero, must move on and leave town after the fighting is done. He has no place to make his home.

Sanjuro, 1962

Sanjuro is an odd film, especially in relation to *Yojimbo*. Kurosawa had written the screenplay for *Sanjuro*, which he adapted from a story by Shugoto Yamaoto, but then, for various reasons, made *Yojimbo* first. With *Yojimbo*'s success, Kurosawa rewrote *Sanjuro* to make the samurai character more skillful. Toshirô Mifune again plays the masterless samurai who calls himself Sanjuro, a name that stands for a 30-year-old, though he adds that he's closer to 40. He appears walking out of the inner room of a shrine, into a meeting of young samurai. He had been sleeping there and overheard the nine gentlemen talking about corruption in government and their attempts to bring it to the attention of officials. Sanjuro's appearance and demeanor presents a studied contrast to the young samurai. They are stylishly attired and carefully groomed. He is yawning, stretching, poorly groomed, and scratching inside his rumpled clothing. He essentially takes over the group's concern by observing that, as he overheard it, they are being set up to be killed by agents of the corrupt official, and he offers to help them. Sanjuro violates samurai code by asking for money for his efforts. When the young samurai who has been the vocal leader of the group takes out his purse, Sanjuro takes only a few coins. This contrast, with the poverty and wear of the masterless samurai and the wealth of the younger noblemen, is characteristic of the Western hero who abjures wealth and material gain, settling instead for a solitary, minimalist life.

Sanjuro leads the young samurai through a series of intrigues, rescuing the chamberlain, who has been held prisoner because he is the uncorrupt official, and the chamberlain's family, while Sanjuro single-handedly manages to kill or capture all the corrupt official's sword-wielding agents. Sanjuro then walks off, avoiding further affiliation with the young men.

Sanjuro says something interesting for this study of masterless samurai as war veteran. When he is first introduced in the film, Sanjuro swaggers in from a dark inner chamber of the shrine, which was his free sleeping place, and states: "They say outsiders can be good judges." It is interesting because the war veteran tends to adopt the role of an outsider in the community in which he or she resides. That the veteran disdains involvement or practices emotional detachment in the event that he or she must be involved, indicates the war veteran's altered frame of reference. Possessing an outsider's point of view, as in Sanjuro's case, comes in handy.

Sanjuro engineers the rescue of the chamberlain's wife (Takako Irie) and daughter (Reiko Dan), who are comically delicate ladies. The wife, however, adds a serious bit of wisdom when Sanjuro acknowledges that he had to kill guards to save her. Pursing her lips, she says, "I'm sorry to say this ... particularly since you were so very good to have saved us, but (shaking her head with gentle emphasis) killing people upon the slightest excuse is really a bad habit, you know." She then admonishes him to keep his sword in his scabbard. "Swords," she adds, "the really good ones, should be kept in their scabbards and not used at all" (Richie, 1998, p. 158). This delicate lady might be speaking for civilians all over the world who feel simultaneously protected and threatened by the presence of war veterans.

In the pattern of the samurai who has no master, Sanjuro has taken on a cause for little compensation, and departs without having made a lasting attachment.

Stray Dog, 1949

Akira Kurosawa made *Stray Dog* in 1948 during the American Occupation of Japan. Filmed in Tokyo, it is a story of two war veterans who faced similar depressing circumstances upon their return from the war. Both had their knapsacks stolen, which itself is a statement about the poverty of the time. One veteran, Yuro (Ko Kimura) becomes a thief, a stray dog, one of the alternatives offered to returning veterans with a raging black market created by profiteers of war surplus and the breakdown of Japanese industry. The other veteran, Murakami (Toshirô Mifune), felt like he was at a crossroads of his life and decided to find a job, eventually becoming a cop.

On a very hot day in Tokyo, Murakami, who is a new homicide detective, is on the police firing range. Returning to his office on a crowded bus, Murakami's gun is stolen by a pickpocket. With the help of the crime library files he identifies the woman who stood next to him on the bus, and, following her through the streets, Kurosawa introduces us to postwar Tokyo. Americans

are nowhere to be seen (their images were subject to censorship by the Occupation), although the Western influence is apparent as kimonos change to
Western dress and greetings are made with American slang.

Detective Murakami is assigned to search for his weapon by posing as
an impoverished, desperate man wandering the black-market area by the train
station. He dresses as a destitute demobilized soldier, a sight that was common
at the time. Kurosawa gives us a very long montage, lasting eight and a half
minutes, of scenes from the black markets of postwar reconstruction. The
teeming activity in the market is a testament to the desperate time when 66
Japanese cities had been virtually destroyed by American bombs.

Finally, Murakami is approached and makes contact with a gun trafficker,
who, in turn, identifies a gangster who deals in firearms. The detective is given
help on the case in the person of Detective Sato (Takashi Shimura). While
Murakami is intense and anxious about recovering his gun and his pride, Sato
is a cop of long experience and guides the young detective in his work. They
are led to a delicious scene for baseball fans, to a stadium where a crowd of
50,000 are watching the Giants play the Hawks. Baseball was popular in
Japan before the war and encouraged by the American Occupation. (See the
remarkable film by Masahiro Shinoda in 1985, *MacArthur's Children*, for a
sense of baseball's influence in postwar Occupied Japan.) It was also a favorite
sport of Kurosawa's and he devotes some loving moments to the scenes on
the field, while at the same time following the detectives as they search for
and eventually catch the gangster, who gives them a lead on the thief who
possesses the detective's gun.

The symbolism of the gun, a small caliber semiautomatic pistol which
is in the possession of the veteran who has gone bad, is significant for Japan,
whose warlike culture has just recently gone underground. Murakami identifies
with the war veteran thief because they experienced similar setbacks after
returning from overseas. He sees the thief, Yuro, as made bad by circumstances
and poor choices.

Murakami says, "All those years in the war so many men became beasts
at slightest provocation, over and over."

Sato, replies, "What do they call it?"

"You mean, *après guerre?*"

"That's it," Sato says. "You're part of that postwar generation. Maybe
Yuro is, too. You identify with Yuro too much."

Murakami tells Sato that he also had his knapsack stolen: "I was half out
of my mind with rage. I could have pulled off a robbery back then. But I
realized I'd hit a dangerous crossroads. I deliberately chose another way, and
got myself a job."

"I see," Sato replies. "There are two *après guerre* types: like you or like

Yuro." (The French term, which means "after war," was used as an adjective after the First World War, when one was said to be *après guerre* as a state of being.)

Kurosawa, like all Japanese filmmakers at the time, had to submit his script for American censorship, which restricted all criticism of the Occupation. Films depicting suicide, samurai, and devotion to feudal society were similarly banned. Kurosawa solved this by never once showing an American, even at the baseball game, while at the same time documenting in a wonderful way the culture of the immediate postwar society.

Yuro, the veteran who went bad, is repeatedly referred to as sad and despairing, being driven to desperation by poor choices. With those problems he represents a large swatch of the postwar Japanese population. There were in Japan at that time 6–10 million unemployed, with many forced to deal with crime one way or the other to survive crippling poverty.

Stray Dog documents the life on the streets at the time when cultural traditions had been turned topsy-turvy. Women now had rights. When Murakami is following the woman who is the pickpocket, she asserts her individual rights and waves off the cop with an American "Bye Bye." We learn earlier when the detective identifies her from the files that she wore traditional kimonos. Now she sports a Western hairdo and dress, and a newfound sense of independence.

To a 21st century American audience, the fuss over a small caliber semi-automatic pistol that is stolen seems quaint. Detective Murakami counts the number of bullets in the clip and watches the news of robberies, going to the crime lab to identify the shells. In the final chase scene, in which the detective runs down the killer and tackles him in the mud, he is shot at with the final three bullets, the last two missing their target. There is a sense that the bad veteran does not want to kill him. During the struggle in the mud, a middle-class woman in a nearby house is playing a Mozart piece at the piano. The playing pauses at the sound of the gunshots, and then starts again. There is a sense that she represents a prosperous segment of Japanese society that not only survived the war but seems to be thriving.

Stray Dog begins with a voice-over statement: "It was an unbearably hot day." Credits are introduced over a panting dog. The only censorship criticism that Kurosawa received, it is reported, was from an American member of the censorship board who belonged to the SPCA. Kurosawa had to testify that the dog was not tormented, but was filmed after the dog had run with its owner riding a bicycle. Kurosawa was peeved and said it was the only time he ever regretted that Japan had lost the war (Kurosawa, 1982). The film gives a lasting impression of a profound but transitory time of postwar readjustment of a defeated nation.

The Messenger, 2007

The Messenger opens with Iraq war veteran Sgt. Will Montgomery (Ben Foster) receiving eye drops as part of an optical exam. The opening shot gives a close-up of his tearing eye. Sgt. Montgomery was wounded in the eye as the result of an IED explosion. He is serving out his last few months of enlistment at an unnamed stateside army base, supervising Humvee mechanics, and is given an additional assignment of assisting Capt. Tony Stone (Woody Harrelson) in the job of informing next of kin of the deaths of soldiers in Iraq. Capt. Stone goes over the details of the work, emphasizing the detached, rigid nature of the protocol. They are to stick to a set script, speak only to the designated kin, remain emotionally detached, and under no circumstances are they to touch the "NOK" (next of kin), or they, as Capt. Stone warns, will "surf a fuckin' ocean of grief." During the course of the film the messengers, dressed in their Class A uniforms, make seven such notifications.

The Messenger was the directorial debut of Oren Moverman. It was written by Moverman and Allesandro Camon. Sgt. Montgomery is recovering from multiple wounds and has a short temper, which he shows when he remonstrates a mechanic he's supervising. He is emotionally isolated and needy. His girlfriend, Kelly (Jena Malone), informs him after a sexual encounter that she is engaged to be married. He is identified as a hero by others, including the admiring Capt. Stone, who was himself in Desert Storm, though not in combat. Both men perform with rigid physical discipline and both at various times experience emotions that finally break their composure. Sgt. Montgomery smashes the wall of his apartment when Kelly calls to apologize to him because her father mistakenly sent him a wedding invitation. Capt. Stone is overwhelmed by emotion after breaking his abstinence from alcohol in a drunken binge that culminates with Montgomery relating his traumatic experience trying to rescue another soldier in Iraq and accidentally causing his death by placing the wounded soldier next to an undetected IED.

The somber plot is saved by Harrelson's intense performance as Capt. Stone, and also by the recipient of the team's third messenger mission. Sgt. Montgomery is fascinated by a young widow named Olivia (Samantha Morton), the soulful mother of a small boy. After several intense yet restrained encounters, Olivia seems just as fascinated by Capt. Stone as he is with her.

Each of the team's notification missions present a unique and complex family. The first is a pregnant African American woman (Yaya DaCosta), engaged to the deceased soldier, whom the team cannot address directly, because she is not NOK. The scene erupts with screams of grief. Another mission gives notice to a father, Dale Martin (Steve Buscemi), who accuses the messengers of being cowards because they're not in combat; he then spits on Montgomery, who remains rigidly stoic. The repentant father later appears at night at Montgomery's residence to ask forgiveness. Another mission presents an Hispanic father of a female soldier; we see her toddler on the floor in the apartment. Another father vomits in a store upon hearing the news.

The Roman poet Ovid, in his *Metamorphosis* (Melville, 1985, pp. 40–43), relates a story of how the raven became black. It seems the raven was originally white, but was turned black when he brought the god Apollo the news that his mortal lover, Coronis, had trysted with a human. The god immediately killed Coronis, and then regretted his rage. He then rescued his unborn child from Coronis's womb just as she was to be consumed in the flames of her funeral pyre. The child grew up to become Asclepius, the Greek demigod of healing. Apollo was angry at the raven for bringing him the bad news, and turned the raven black. Northwest Native Americans have a parallel myth of a raven turning black after bringing light to the world, showing that the raising of consciousness is not always appreciated (Reid & Bringhurst, 1984).

The Messenger delivers the worst kind of war news when it illustrates the grief of each of the individual family members whom they notify. Dale Martin, the father of the deceased soldier, best illustrates the rage of Apollo. *The Messenger* also presents a beautiful elaboration of the raven myth, when turning black becomes a symbol for a coming to consciousness. In this case, the wounded war veteran, who has expressed his guilt about being decorated when he feels he caused the death of another soldier, is able to follow his fascination with the soulful widow, Olivia, and, through her, breaks out of his emotional isolation. To do this he disobeys the messengers' protocol. Olivia explains that she no longer loved her husband who went to Iraq, but now that she has learned of his death, she loves him again.

A remarkable note on the progress of U.S. culture is that the widow, Olivia, is Caucasian. Her departed husband was African American, and their child, therefore, is of mixed race. This is amply illustrated in a scene when both families are gathered at the military funeral. *The Messenger* does not choose to comment on the racial differences, which is itself a comment that amounts to a metaphor for the racial integration that has become part of U.S. society (especially the U.S. military), and suggests that the right kind of leadership can bring harmony to racial integration. Melinda Pash (2012, p. 86) illustrates that necessity played a large role in facilitating racial integration at the beginning of the Korean War.

Sgt. Montgomery compares the return home after a tour in a combat zone to traveling to another planet. As he says, in a reference to fighting in a combat zone: "You can't unsee the shit anymore." His magnetic attraction to Olivia is kept tense by the protocol of grief, but is also a vehicle for his emotional reentry. His vision improves through the course of the film.

The Messenger is another of the movies about the Wars on Terror that brings the effects of prolonged overseas combat home. It erupts with corporal effluvia when the messages are delivered: vomit, spit, tears of grief. The movie harkens to an excellent Vietnam War film, *Gardens of Stone* (1987), directed by Francis Coppola, which told the story of the strict army funeral details at Arlington National Cemetery and the defined, rigid protocol connected with mourning. They are the Honor Guard elite who salute their departed comrades. It is a ritual as ancient as the funeral pyres of Troy.

Brothers, 2010

Brothers takes up the issue of PTSD in a veteran of multiple combat tours in Afghanistan. Sam Cahill (Tobey Maguire), a Marine Corps captain who returns for another tour of combat and is traumatized as a prisoner of the Taliban. Publicists for the movie like to portray *Brothers* as a film about family relationships, but the fact is, films about the veterans of the Wars on Terror have not been popular. *Brothers*, as the title suggests, is about a family coping with deployment and readjustment; it is also a dramatic depiction of PTSD.

Sam's brother, Tommy (Jake Gyllenhaal), is released from prison just before Sam leaves for Afghanistan. Sam and Tommy's father (Sam Shepherd) is a Vietnam War veteran of the Marine Corps who favors Sam, nagging Tommy in a mean-spirited fashion. Sam and his wife, Grace (Natalie Portman) have two little girls; before the deployment, the core family seems to be harmonious.

Brothers, in many respects, parallels the plot of *Indian Runner* (1991), which was Sean Penn's directorial attempt, about two brothers, one a rural sheriff's deputy, and the other, just returning from Vietnam, drifts into criminal life. Both films have the brothers' father as a veteran of a previous war. *Brothers* departs from the parallel when the helicopter in which Sam is riding is shot down and he and another Marine survive. They are captured by insurgents and tortured. In the meantime, the family is informed that Sam was killed in action. Initially, Tommy is depicted as an impulsive young man who has not matured with adulthood, however, when Sam is reported as dead, Tommy helps Grace and the children. The more he endears himself to them, the more he seems to gain emotional depth.

After enduring torture and the death of his fellow POW, Sam is rescued and returns home, but he has been transformed into a numb and rigid man who struggles with emotional expression and grows increasingly hostile. When Sam finally loses control, he is taken to a military hospital after a suicidal/homicidal confrontation with police.

Brothers was helmed by Irish director Jim Sheridan, with a screenplay by David Benioff, based on a Danish film, *Brødre*. In *Brothers*, viewers are not given much insight into military culture. Very little time is devoted to the war, although what we see of the Taliban insurgents is impressive. The focus instead is on family, each of whom is challenged by heart-wrenching grief, estrangement, and accommodation. Tommy is drawn into the role vacated by Sam's departure. Appearing at first to be hard drinking and irresponsible, in trying to help his brother's family his loving character gradually manifests, until the girls grow to prefer him to their father when Sam finally returns. Sam's and Tommy's characters reverse, in that Sam's emotional range, because of his traumas, has narrowed to inflexibility. This is illustrated nicely at the dinner table when one of the girls compares a dog with big ears to an elephant. Sam is unable to make the abstraction, even after it is explained to him, and grows angry at his befuddlement, which is a probable symptom of traumatic brain injury. One commentator introduced his negative review of *Brothers*, calling it dismissively as "the new home-from-the-war film" and Maguire as "playing crazy" (Denby, 2009). In my opinion, the critic failed to appreciate the confusion that brain injury and PTSD can cause.

Many stories and films about war veterans address what seems like a universal theme about the man who is changed so profoundly by the war experience that he no longer fits in his pre-war roles. After trying to fit into family life, Sam requests to return to the war zone to be with his men.

Estrangement caused by the traumas of combat are sometimes depicted in film as externalized, with the veteran dealing with social forces, economic challenges, drug and alcohol abuse, criminal activity, preoccupation with work, rehab, or revenge. Films showing the traumas of POW torture have the burden of portraying the severe traumatic sequelae. *The Manchurian Candidate* sensationally showed the veteran as a victim of hypnotic trance. *The Deer Hunter* depicted the veteran as a suicidal compulsive gambler. *Rolling Thunder* has the veteran fighting criminals in a border town. Fitting the returning POW back into a harmonious family life proves to be, at best, awkward and difficult.

Brothers manages to show depth of character by allowing the family to change with events. The war veteran father softens toward his wayward son when Tommy helps his sister-in-law and remodels the family kitchen. Ironically, when Sam returns, it is the kitchen remodel that causes him to become suspicious that Tommy might have made love to Grace.

There is a political statement in *Brothers*, but it is very subtle and humanitarian in nature. It looks at the intergenerational transmission of trauma from war veteran father to son. The father cannot convey to his sons the problems caused by the traumas of combat. His preference for one son demeans the other. It is not a coincidence that his favored son joins the Marine Corps as an officer, while his other son goes to prison.

There is an interesting comparison to be made between the Vietnam-era *Indian Runner* and the current day *Brothers*. It has to do with the mood of the people in America. In the former film, Joe (David Morse) is a blond-haired deputy sheriff with a caring demeanor; in other words, a good cop to have in the community. He even tries to rehabilitate his dark-haired brother, Frank (Viggo Mortensen), who has just returned from Vietnam, wearing a patch on his army uniform of the First Air Cavalry. He is dark and moody. When he gets out of jail, where he was sentenced for domestic violence, his torso is covered with tattoos and he seems to be on a one-way path to nowhere. He is abusive to his girlfriend and avoidant of responsibilities, and eventually murders a man during one of his rages. In *Brothers*, Sam is the one who loses control of his emotions. *Indian Runner* had a sense of profound fate. The veteran, Frank, probably had an anti-social personality disorder before he went to war, and after the war was unredeemable, while Joe, the sheriff, remained steadfast and loyal. Twenty years later, when *Brothers* was released, everyone seems to have hope for improvement and positive change. The dark brother, Tommy, grows light, whereas the wounded veteran, while clearly damaged, is confronting his combat trauma. At least he tells his wife a bit about his worst trauma and begins forming a narrative. The generational difference between the two films has to do with the emotional acceptance of foreign war, even the ambiguous protean Wars on Terror.

The Hurt Locker, 2010

The Hurt Locker is probably the best of the fiction films so far that have to do with the Wars on Terror. It concerns a bomb demolition squad, and virtually the entire film is composed of harrowing action. Some veterans criticize it for not showing accurate procedures. Castner (2012) gives another, more mundane perspective of the work. In the beginning of *The Hurt Locker* the EOD expert is killed trying to disarm a bomb that is remotely detonated by cell phone. He is replaced by Staff Sergeant William James (Jeremy Renner), who we quickly learn is reckless with regard to his own safety. He has been similarly involved during other deployments and mentions Afghanistan as his most recent. He has pockmarks on his body that someone identifies as shrapnel wounds. His only comment is to claim that his mother dropped him as a baby. He admits that he expects to die doing his job.

Sgt. James's method of going about his work exasperates others in his squad, particularly his second in command, Sgt. Sanborn (Anthony Mackie), because his actions place them in increased danger. Much of the squad's work is viewed by the local Iraqis, ominously peeking out of doorways and down from balconies and windows. The onlookers pose a constant potential for danger, and occasionally someone gets shot. Sgt. James's squad is forced to stand guard as backup while their leader dons his protective suit. The ritual is like the armoring of a medieval knight; at the same time, it looks like a spacesuit in which the wearer must work with tools in an alien environment.

The Hurt Locker is directed by Kathryn Bigelow, who made her reputation directing action films such as *Point Break* and *Blue Steel* and, more recently, a film about the killing of Osama bin Laden. The film was written by Mark Boal, who last gave us the script for the quality war veteran film *In the Valley of Elah*. *The Hurt Locker* mainly concerns the squad and its principals, but diverts to action subplots as James takes off impetuously into the city at night to locate the family of a boy whom he befriended and who was killed when his body was rigged with explosives. There is another subplot in which the squad, while detonating explosives in the desert, come across a group of armed civilians with headscarves hiding their faces. They turn out to be agents of some kind, apparently mercenaries, for they have two hooded prisoners they were transporting before their Humvee broke down. (One of the agents is played by Ralph Fiennes, and when he exposes his face and speaks to the squad who have him at gunpoint, there is a moment when T.E. Lawrence is recalled in *Lawrence of Arabia*. Fiennes did, in fact, play Lawrence in a biographical picture.) This scene deals with an ambush by snipers and is the only scene of prolonged combat, which proves to be as gripping as the city bomb sites.

Renner's Sgt. James does not have heroic movie star stature. He has a round face and a lumpy body, but when he and his squad mate fall into a drunken male contest for dominance to see who can hit the other in the stomach the hardest, he shows himself to be physically tough. He is portrayed as someone who has been repeatedly traumatized and considers himself to be fated to die while doing his job. In the very brief domestic scene when he is between tours, James is shown to be alienated from his wife and child.

The enemy is often ambiguous and hard to identify. When we see him, it is an anonymous profile, a figure with scarf obscuring the face, peering from a distant viewing space. Bigelow never lets us grow familiar with anyone but the bomb squad members. The pathetic, tense scene that occurs when a suicide bomber tries to surrender presents the only enemy figure with personality, and he is, so to speak, locked up in his work.

There is a mental health officer who visits Sgt. James, and when James challenges the officer to see combat, he rides along with the squad. The officer proves to be a feckless innocent who seems to have only some mental health provider social skills that are not useful when delivered in a combat zone.

Sgt. James is not a war lover. He keeps returning to combat because he no longer fits in anywhere else. He is not fearless, but rather reckless, and he is resigned to dying on the job. He is inured to the hardship and suffering around him, although he has cracks in his armor. When the boy who was selling DVDs is killed and his body rigged with explosives, James is anguished with grief and for a while puts his life in jeopardy in an ill-conceived one-man hunt. There is a touching moment during the desert battle with the snipers when he manages to get a fluid package containing a straw and generously offers it first to Sanborn, who is concentrating on spotting to kill, and, unaware of the scarcity of water, drinks it as James watches.

Some veterans of combat are afflicted with a terrible sense of unfinished business when they leave the combat zone, fully believing that they would die there. These are veterans who have participated in multiple situations that were potentially traumatic, and although they may not qualify for the DSM-IV 309.81, they are influenced by the belief that they will die and should have died in the combat zone. They might not file a VA claim for PTSD disability because they don't see themselves as having a future. Guilt is in the memory of the people — the soldiers, innocents, and the enemies who died. Once having surrendered to the idea of death, the veterans fail to live fully in a peaceful environment, although recklessness and impulsivity may cause their lives to fill with demanding challenges. They make troublesome, if colorful, civilians. And they don't take very good care of their health.

The Hurt Locker never makes an overt political statement, such as was made in *In the Valley of Elah*. We see callused, battle-hardened soldiers and officers. We see the destruction. In one scene, when James is searching for the killers of the boy, he is misdirected to an apartment where he confronts the residents with a drawn pistol. The man greets him with courtesy and offers his hospitality. The woman, however, howls with rage when she is confronted by the alien in her own kitchen and attacks James with kitchenware, driving him away. That, in a symbolic way, captures the problem of fighting the Wars on Terror in foreign lands. The U.S. may have its way and prevail over the terrorists, but many indigenous lives are lost and homes and livelihoods disrupted and destroyed in the process. Consider, too, the lives of the combatants, many of whom are left with troublesome symptoms, which for some cynics in the civilian community are valid only if not expressed and probably a lie if a disability claim is filed.

A real-life EOD Iraq War veteran, Brian Caster, described his experiences as an air force bomb disposal technician for two deployments in a well-written memoir, *The Long Walk: A Story of War and the Life that Follows* (2012). He gives a different, but no less dangerous, take on the explosives ordinance work, and the post-deployment adjustment that is demanded: "I simply exist from moment to moment. There is no meaning in my past. My present is intolerable. I don't expect my future to exist" (p. 148).

In the Valley of Elah, 2007

In the Valley of Elah is a creation of writer, producer, director Paul Haggis, but it will probably be remembered as Tommy Lee Jones's *tour de force* as he plays Vietnam War veteran, retired career army MP, Hank Deerfield. Hank and his wife, Joan (Susan Sarandon), have already lost one son to an army training accident, when he learns his only other son is AWOL after his return from deployment in Iraq. Hank figures his son must have a good reason for being AWOL and drives to Fort Rudd in New Mexico from his home in Tennessee with the intention of finding him. The movie then becomes a police murder investigation with jurisdictional disputes between the local law enforcement and the army CID.

A local police detective, Emily Sanders (Charlize Theron), a tough, single mother who is harassed on the job by her fellow detectives for being cozy with the chief. The grizzly murder of Hank's son, Mike, involves his buddies with whom he served in Iraq and who were with him drinking the night he was killed. In talking to the men and merchants who encountered his son that night, Hank discovers that his son had changed into an angry, mean-spirited man.

Jones presents Hank as a character who is aged and grim to the point of being dour. He has been out of the army so long that he no longer has any contacts. When he is presented the awful news about his son, he is emotionally contained behind a stoic but very sad face.

Elah was co-written by Haggis from a story by Mark Boal about an actual death of an army specialist in 2003. Haggis has fictionalized the character and situation, turning it into a powerful murder-mystery drama. The director of photography was Roger Deakins, who uses muted, washed-out colors in exploring the tawdry commercial world that surrounds a military base, with strip clubs, fast-food joints, and drinking establishments. Hank is not alienated by this environment of camp followers and there is no judgment in his eyes.

The movie's title comes from a biblical story that Hank relates to Emily's son, David, who is fearful of the dark. It is the story of David and Goliath, who meet in the Valley. For the purposes of the movie, the story is somewhat ironic, if we think of the U.S. influence as Goliath.

Haggis manages to make this murder mystery become a criticism of U.S. policy in Iraq without a single political speech. The film powerfully shows the impact of the war on the veterans, hardening them and making them both angry and numb to emotion. Haggis uses a narrative technique that has a mysterious allure. Hank steals his son's cell phone when he is allowed to look at his barracks room. Mike carried this device in Iraq and took videos of his activities, although the pixels have scrambled because of the heat. Hank takes it to a technician who gradually sends him images and sounds that are somewhat unscrambled. (I was reminded of Michelangelo Antonioni's 1966 *Blowup*, as it seems the unscrambling only leads to tantalizing ambiguity.)

For all the sadness and grimness in *Elah*, we are not left feeling sorry for the characters. They are struggling with the same heavy blows that strike us all. In his *New Yorker* review, David Denby recalls the 1956 John Ford film, *The Searchers*, in which John Wayne plays a Civil War veteran in search of his lost relative, an innocent captured by Comanche warriors. In *Elah*, Hank encounters the damage done by the war, not inconsistent with other wars, but the current war, causing current damage to its warriors returning to *our* contemporary society. The war veterans return as changed men, hardened and brutal. When Mike's buddies are interviewed, they gradually reveal their anger, as if they have been contaminated by the age-old hatreds of the land they occupied.

The police detective, Emily, is confronted early in the film with a woman who wants her boyfriend arrested for drowning her dog. Emily dismisses the woman, saying that it is not a crime for the police. Later, the woman herself is found drowned in the bathtub by the same brute she was complaining about. Emily weeps when she views the corpse. Similarly, Joan is stunned with anguish when she views her son's grizzly remains. Hank, however, has been in combat. He does not weep. He absorbs emotion like a black hole draws in light.

Stop-Loss, 2007

Stop-Loss is a movie about those who fight in the Wars on Terror and the families to whom they return. It is a highly political movie that has not become a commercial success. *Stop-Loss* manages to capture what is a not-uncommon dream for veterans, sometimes a nightmare, that they find themselves back in the military and stuck in a war zone.

Stop-Loss is directed by Kimberly Peirce, who also co-wrote with Mark Richard, and stars Ryan Phillippe as Sergeant Brandon King. The movie begins in *cinema verité* style shot as video by GIs frolicking, singing, and then at a check point where they are attacked and chase terrorists into side streets, where they are ambushed. Sgt. King is the leader of a platoon and ends up with a large number of casualties, leaving many civilians and terrorists dead as well. The film then segues to their Brazos, Texas, homecoming, where they are honored. We see Brandon and his friends Tommy Burgess (Joseph Gordon-Levitt) and Steve Shriver (Channing Tatum) honored in a parade and reception. The men are greeted by family and friends, they drink too much, and are beset by intrusive memories and nightmares. Tommy is engaged to be married and gets so drunk and rowdy that his bride throws him out. The veterans end up on a ranch, using his wedding presents as shooting targets. Steve is also engaged to be married to Michelle (Abbie Cornish). Brandon's father is a Vietnam War veteran. Tommy eventually commits suicide off camera.

Brandon and Steve believe that they are going to be discharged, but Brandon finds out that he has been stop-lossed, the title now a verb. He objects: "I'm done with killing and I ain't leading any more men into slaughter!" He decides to go AWOL and travel to Washington, D.C., where he believes he will get help from his senator. Steve's fiancée agrees to travel with him. The film now becomes a road movie as Brandon and Michelle have adventures, including an alleyway brawl after toughs break into their car. Brandon confronts the robbers who are improbably dividing up the booty in an alley and calls them "Hajiis." (Abbie Cornish's Michelle here bears a spooky resemblance to Ali McGraw in Sam Peckinpah's famous 1972 road movie, *The Getaway*.) Steve pursues his friend in an effort to get Brandon to return to the army and reveals that he has made a bargain with the army to reenlist and become a sniper if they will take Brandon back without court martialing him.

During their sojourn to the United States capital, they stop at an Army hospital to visit a wounded comrade, Rico Rodrigues (Victor Rasuk). He was severely wounded in the alley ambush that began the film and has lost three limbs and his eyesight. The scene is reminiscent of the visit to the VA hospital in *The Deer Hunter*. We have the added involvement here of Rico's family, who are not yet U.S. citizens. "If I got killed," he said, "my family would get Green Cards."

Brandon has a significant flashback when they stop at a motel and he is sitting fully dressed on the motel swimming pool diving board. Staring into the water, he sees an object submerged near the pool drain and hallucinates that it is the body of a wounded comrade in desert battle fatigues. He dives into the water and "saves" a discarded garment. These kinds of flashbacks are a terrible burden, usually suffered less dramatically in silence by the war veterans, like the panicky feeling when buckling one's seatbelt after a combat tour in a Humvee.

Brandon connects with another veteran who has been stop-lossed and is on the run with his family. He is given the phone number of a liberal New

York lawyer who will help him get across the border into Canada. Brandon, however, cannot go through with leaving his country. The final scene enacts that repeating war veteran's dream of the return to the battlefield.

The scenes of drunken reverie among the war veterans are as wild as similar scenes in *Born on the Fourth of July*. In one scene, Steve, in his skivvies in a drunken flashback, digs a grave/foxhole and passes out with his .45 clutched to his breast, waiting for the Hajiis. *Stop-Loss* has been compared to the classic post–World War II film *The Best Years of Our Lives*, but there are very significant differences, the biggest difference being that that war was over and the U.S. victorious when the film was made. *Best Years* was about three men from different walks of life. *Stop-Loss* is profound for keeping the veterans together who served in the same combat unit. *Best Years*, while featuring excessive drinking and emotional readjustment, was decidedly upbeat, in keeping with the era. Even the maimed sailor with prostheses for hands is married to his sweetheart in a touching final scene. What makes *Stop-Loss* significant and political is that the war continues, and the veterans are *forced* to return to combat. In stark black-and-white letters at the end of the film we are informed that, at the time the film was made, 81,000 veterans had been stop-lossed. Historian Melinda Pash (2012, p. 34) writes of veterans being prevented from leaving the service, having their enlistments extended at the beginning of the Korean War.

The implication of sending war veterans back to a war zone is controversial. Brandon, for instance, will be taking with him a profound sense of guilt for having led his troops into an ambush. He already feels responsible for their deaths, and one wonders how his guilt will affect his future decisions. Steve, who will become a sniper, also has PTSD symptoms that will not be improved by further killing.

Director Kimberly Peirce's previous film, *Boys Don't Cry*, was well received. Here she casts her characters in a romantic light, with handsome men and attractive girlfriends. When they party at a Texas honky-tonk (the film was shot in Austin) they are all a part of the culture, and when a fight breaks out, it all seems like good fun with no hard feelings. In the end, the men return to Iraq, already afflicted by PTSD, for another round of fighting for ideals no less romantic than those depicted in the film.

Jarhead, 2006

Jarhead plays with war movie clichés set in the contrasting traditions of old-fashioned Marines in a high-tech war that is fought without them. Director Sam Mendes lets the clichés play on themselves: the boot camp obscenities, initiation into a new outfit (in this case, the second platoon, Golf Company), the fear and taunting about the infamous fabled Jody. We know that Marines are branded by their military experience, and Mendes takes the branding literally, as a USMC iron is heated with a blowtorch. The party in the barracks, circa 1990, also has rappers and break dancing.

Consistent with the theme of war movie clichés, *Jarhead* features the two most prominent movies about the Vietnam War. It has the Marines robustly cheering the Wagnerian helicopter assault on a Vietnamese village in *Apocalypse Now*. And when the Marines are in Saudi, one Marine's wife sends him a video of *The Deer Hunter*, which might be a switch on a Dear John letter. The video turns out to be a home movie of his girlfriend in coitus with her neighbor. She taunts the poor Marine as he watches aghast, while his comrades cheer.

Jarhead is about Marines who train for combat, go off to a real war in the desert, Desert Storm, and never get to fire a shot. They are fired on, by their own "friendly" Warthog anti-tank aircraft. They get to see the detritus of war, the blackened, smoking wreckages of vehicles and corpses that were trying to escape from Kuwait back to Iraq. Sam Mendes manages to create a truly surreal scene as the Marines on the march encounter the grisly scenes of carnage, after those same Warthogs and their ilk have attacked the crowded highway of escape. Blackened corpses look at once like victims of volcanic explosions, splattered and emulsified as if by alien spaceships or the A-Bomb victims of Hiroshima. If these Marines didn't get into the fighting, they will still have plenty to dream about.

The same technology that kills the enemy before the Marines arrive cannot make their radios work. They march into fields of burning oil wells. Reddened by fire, the blackened sky rains oil. In a spooky scene, a horse approaches a Marine, a symbol of bollixed nature, covered slick with oil. The horse seems to be on his last legs, snorting desperately. (We are assured in the ending credits that SPCA certified that no animal was harmed making the movie, although we know from the news at the time that the whole Kuwait zoo was slaughtered by vengeful Iraqis.)

Jarhead has some excellent casting. The screenplay is by William Broyles, Jr., and is based on a book by Anthony Swofford. Swofford is the name of the protagonist, played by Jake Gyllenhaal. We follow him as he completes boot camp, maligned and harassed by the DI (Scott MacDonald) in classically sadistic tradition. The embedded star of the show is Staff Sergeant Sykes (Jamie Foxx). The movie definitely picks up pace when Sykes struts in. In one surrealistic scene, as the Marines are dug in watching the oil wells blazing in the night, Sykes tells Swofford, in a moment of sentimental revelation, how much he loves his job. Swofford could be a Marine in any war walking through the aftermath of an artillery or air strike. He stares at the charred corpses, human road kill, and vomits. "Hoorah!"

Jarhead, which is about the war in the desert of the Middle East, was filmed in Mexico, California, and Arizona. It is a hypermasculine "Hoorah!" that lusts for battle. The song at the very end of the credits sums up the theme: the lifelong dream of being "a bad motherfuckin'" Marine. The only line in the film spoken by a woman on screen is delivered deliciously by a TWA flight attendant as a rejoinder to a Marine on board, mocking his masculinity.

The Marines in *Jarhead* fire each other into Dionysian revelry. They mimic having a homosexual orgy before a visiting female reporter. This follows a prolonged football game performed in desert heat in full haz-mat protective gear. During a bombastic Christmas party an almost naked Santa cavorts as liquor is poured down the throats of the revelers from a jerry can. The Christmas tree becomes a Dionysian ceremonial tree around which the revelers dance.

Perhaps the spookiest scene in the film comes as Staff Sergeant Sykes insists that the Marines quaff a pill, having them first sign a liability waiver for the pharmaceutical company. Sykes insists that the pill is necessary as an antidote for the type of nerve gas that Iraqis used on the Kurds. This theme develops as one chemical threat follows another until the war turns into an ecological disaster, as it seems all wars have. The same Marines who are urged to "hydrate" with bottles of water, who are obviously at the peak of their physical prowess, become the enemies' prey. They are told by a briefing officer when they arrive in country to maintain a "constant state of suspicious alertness."

Jarhead ends with a brief look at the Marines returning home. One is dead, one has long hair, and Swofford is viewed sitting home alone in a room. They all had their breakdowns in the face of combat that never really happened, the prey of forces that make wars happen. As they ride on a bus together in a victory parade, a haggard Vietnam War veteran, bedecked with insignia, boards the bus and shouts a hollow cry that falls absolutely flat, "*Semper Fi!*" The he follows it with, "Mind if I sit down?"

The Dry Land, 2010

The Dry Land, a film about an OIF veteran's difficult first days home after deployment, was shown at the 2010 Seattle International Film Festival. It was written and directed by Ryan Piers Williams, with Ryan O'Nan as the army veteran, James, and America Ferrera as his wife, Sarah. Ferrera was also executive producer of *The Dry Land*. The description of the film in the festival brochure, by critic Tom Keogh, yawned that the film had "generic echoes of every stress disordered vet movie in history." Hardly a promotion, and sad to say, for *The Dry Land* was made with great sincerity, with, according to the director, much processing with veterans and approval of the army, which cooperated with filming at Walter Reed Hospital.

The Dry Land is a grim film that shows the sad-eyed veteran, James, returning to his mobile home outside El Paso, Texas. The homecoming party is awkward, with his long-time friend, Michael (Jason Ritter), plying him with questions about killing. James does not remember a traumatic event when his Humvee was blown up by a rocket-propelled grenade. Three of the five crew survived, but one survivor was badly wounded.

James has a bad first night home in bed, clutching his wife in a strangle-hold during a nightmare in a vividly real dark scene that conveyed the involuntary nature of PTSD arousal.

James visits his mother, who is disabled with emphysema. His Vietnam War veteran father had died of an alcohol-related disease. ("Your daddy was a real mess when he came back.") His mother is played by Melissa Rio with convincing charm and pathos. She blithely smokes with an oxygen tube in her nose, dismissing her son's scolding warning.

James gets a job at a cattle slaughtering yard and is shown on his first day of grizzly work as a cow is slaughtered, scenes which drove a few folks from their theater seats. *The Dry Land* had excellent casting. One gross co-worker at the slaughter house is as obscene as the work, taunting James: "The war fuck you up, or what?" When James's friends coax him into an after work drunk, they end up in the desert fighting and James gets smacked, blind-sided, in the head with a rifle butt.

Sarah tries to get James to talk about his deployment, but he is flummoxed by the inadequacy of his memories. When he receives a letter from a veteran who was with him in the Humvee, James goes abruptly to visit him.

James's friend refuses to talk about the traumatic event, but rides with James to Walter Reed to visit their wounded comrade, also with sad eyes, a double amputee who is humiliated by an episode of incontinence during their visit, but who does relate the missing facts of the trauma. These relate to the "Hajiis" using a civilian family as bait, wounding a woman whom James insists that they stop and help, making their vehicle an easy target for the rocket.

James falls into a crisis when his mother dies in the hospital. In a scene reminiscent of *Brothers*, James, drunk, having fought with Michael, drives off followed by police, and makes a suicidal gesture with a pistol in his mouth in a standoff before he surrenders to police, who, it seems, are going to take him to the VA hospital.

The Dry Land director, Ryan Piers Williams, told the audience at the 2010 Seattle International Film Festival screening that he made *The Dry Land* "for less than a million dollars." Despite the tight budget, the film was loaded with well-cast supporting roles, including one shepherd dog that commanded attention in every scene he was in. Despite these strengths, *The Dry Land* lacked the ingredient that made so many post–World War II films work: an entertaining plot. *The Dry Land* rubs the viewers noses in torment and suffering: nightmares, vulgar taunts, a mother dying, cattle slaughtered on camera, a double amputee in agony. All this seems too real. If a war veteran movie is to be successful, in terms of box office, there needs to be a dramatic lure for the audience.

Restrepo, 2010

Restrepo is a documentary about an infantry platoon (Second Platoon, Battle Company, Second of the 503rd Infantry Regiment, 173rd Airborne Brigade Combat Team) who are sent to build and defend a remote outpost in the Korengal Valley of Eastern Afghanistan. They name the outpost Restrepo after Doc Restrepo, their medic who was recently killed. The film follows them into the Valley, patrols with them up the mountain ridge, and is with them as they fight off daily enemy assaults. As the captain explains, beyond Restrepo the enemy, the Taliban, are in control.

What is remarkable about this documentary is its juxtaposition of scenes of intense combat action with periods of intimate reflection. There is no sense that these infantrymen are numbed by constant combat. They are lively, expressive, playful, and willing to grieve over their losses.

Restrepo was produced, directed, and photographed by Sebastian Junger and Tim Hetherington. The filmmakers demonstrated their talents with courageous action cinematography, spending enough time with the platoon to elicit their acceptance and familiarity. The purpose of the American combat action in the Valley was to provide security for road-building. The job of Captain Dan Kearney was to influence the local tribesmen living in primitive conditions on the side of cliffs without electricity or running water. Unfortunately, they visit a village that has been recently hit by an air strike, killing and wounding both Taliban and villagers. The camera captures the bodies of children with fresh wounds to their faces. The captain says, at a meeting with the village elders, "Let's put it behind us."

Part of the documentary, the close-up interviews with several members of the platoon, took place after they returned to their base in Italy (photographed by Jake Clannell). Much credit should be given to the editor, Michael

Levine, for the fluid counterpoint of combat action with the personnel reflecting on their reactions. The documentary exploits several unique characters as commentators. Specialist Miguel Cortez has a soft smiling countenance, even when he is expressing sadness and grief. Specialist Misha Pemble-Belkin is a benign-looking young man with rosy cheeks who speaks of his childhood with hippie parents who did not allow violence to enter his life. He describes how they would not let him have a plastic frog toy because it was a squirt gun, and then we see him confidently firing his machinegun. It is reported at the end of the film that Misha re-enlisted and is scheduled to return to Afghanistan as an infantry sergeant. The gentleness in his face, a gifted rapport with the camera marking a talent for relatedness, he reports that his parents, while they did not want him to re-enlist, supported him in his decision.

Mental health practitioners will recognize several scenes that spell trouble for adjustment to civilian life. In one almost comical scene after an exciting firefight, one of the young men, Steiner, his eyes glittering with adrenalin, talks about his reaction: "You can't get a better high. Better than crack. Once you've been shot at you really can't come down."

A voice off-camera asks, "How are you going to go back into the civilian world then?"

Steiner, entrenched in the present, replies, "I have no idea."

Restrepo interposes scenes of the platoon relaxing in the close, dark confines of their bunker, or bare-chested in the sunshine. They taunt each other, wrestle, dance like rockers in a mosh pit, clean weapons, play guitar, play hand-held video games. They are shown on sick call, being given IVs after period of diarrhea and nausea which they had nicknamed "Kornegal Crud."

The filmmakers go on patrol with the platoon and chase after them under fire. When a cargo helicopter comes in with sling nets of supplies, the camera is right under the ship as it hovers dangerously low while the soldiers unhook the slings and hook up another sling of material to send off.

Among the more subtle elements of humor in *Restrepo* are several references to a cow that was killed, apparently when it got tangled in Outpost concertina wire. Eventually the village men come to complain and present a claim for damages. One soldier in the platoon would later refer to the unfortunate bovine as a "same-day cow." I was reminded of a cartoon from Bill Mauldin's *Up Front*, documenting the World War II Italian Campaign, which depicts the war-weary grunts, Willie and Joe, staring out of a machine gun emplacement with the barrel smoking. The caption reads: "I coulda swore a coupla krauts was usin' that cow for cover, Joe. Go wake up th' cooks" (Mauldin, 1945, p. 174).

Restrepo draws a sharp contrast between the harsh conditions and poverty of the villagers with the high-tech abundance of the platoon. Their dental work alone is contrast enough. One can appreciate why it is reported that musculo-skeletal injuries are the most common medical complaints of veterans returning from combat deployments. When the platoon starts out on patrol, they must load up with huge backpacks and belts of heavy gear. The camera and microphone picks up the grunts and gasps of the men moving out.

One of the high-tech differences with this era of soldiers is their ease of personal communication. One sergeant, before departing on patrol, reports that he has just talked to his parents on the phone, and will soon call his wife before he "takes off." Captain Kearney refers to all his men as being "really like a big family." Gottman, Gottman, and Atkins (2011, p. 53) comment insightfully on the problems this ease of communication entail, which results in the "sense of the soldier's being psychologically present with the family while deployed yet physically absent for long periods of time. The result of this dynamic is a strong sense of ambiguous loss."

The camera follows the men on a long patrol called "Rock Avalanche" ("They wasn't coming to you — sometime you had to reach out to them.") in which there are casualties, including the death of a sergeant who was deemed to be the best warrior of the platoon. They observe how they are all threatened when their best fighter dies.

The success of *Restrepo* lies in the vividness of the combat action that is conducted by troops that we grow to know through their words and close-up expressions. When the sergeant dies, one man sobs in grief, yet seems to stay alert and aware of his situation. Some men who handled the casualties continue on with bloody hands and utilities. Smiling Specialist Cortez sums up the action in an interview back in Italy: "I can't even sleep — I dream about it pretty bad."

I have included *Restrepo* in my review of fiction films about war veterans, mainly because the filmmakers follow the soldiers after they leave their unit and become veterans. Recalling the controversy of the war photographer Robert Capa as to whether he set up some of his famous action shots (Capa, 2001), some scenes in *Restrepo* could well have been staged or at least initiated by the filmmakers, but they were consistent and, if staged, set up to replicate spontaneous scenes, as when the photographer was in the bunker when the men were wrestling or dancing.

Restrepo ranks with the best of American war documentaries, including John Huston's *Battle of San Pietro* and John Ford's war service as a documentary filmmaker. Ford was blown off a bunker while filming an attack by Japanese aircraft during the battle of Midway (McBride, 2001, p. 360). He was wounded (probably concussed) and received a Purple Heart. Robert Capa was killed in 1954 while documenting the French fighting in Indochina. The dangers that war documentary filmmakers experience was most recently demonstrated by the death of Tim Hetherington, killed in action by a mortar blast in Misrata, Libya, on April 20, 2011. His work partner, Junger, constructed a moving documentary of Hetherington, *Which Way to the Front Line?* showing his career that came to be devoted to filming wars.

The Jacket, 2004

The Jacket, released in 2004, is a confusing movie about a soldier in the 1991 Gulf War who is shot in the head by a child he stops to help. The sequences are presented in surrealistic fragments. At the field hospital it is declared that he is alive, because he blinks, although he has been given up for dead. The nurse says that he has no family. Then, in a scene in Vermont 12 months later, the veteran is seen hitchhiking on a winter highway with a backpack. It is declared that he has won the Bronze Star and has retrograde amnesia and psychological depression. His name is Jack Stark (Adrien Brody).

The veteran comes upon a pickup truck stalled on the road. A woman is retching in the snow with a child standing beside her. Apparently the woman is high on some substance. The child, as is sometimes the case with the off-spring of substance abusers, speaks with precocious maturity. Jack sets about to get the truck started. The girl sees his dog tags dangling on a chain from his backpack and asks if she can have them. Jack assents. The mother, who has seemed disoriented, becomes alarmed and wildly accuses Jack of being a child molester, pushes the kid into the truck, which Jack has managed to start, and drives off, leaving the veteran on the highway.

He returns to hitchhiking and, unfortunately, his next ride is with a man who is soon pursued by a police car. When the cop approaches the driver, the driver shoots him. The wounded cop shoots back, hitting Jack, who has stepped out of the car, knocking him out. The cop dies and the criminal wipes the prints from his pistol and drops it in the snow beside Jack's unconscious body. Jack cannot recall what has happened or even who he is. The film doesn't deal with the fact that the veteran would have had a VA hospital ID card. He cannot explain how he got into the predicament, but since he is the only one on the scene, he is tried and convicted of killing the cop and committed to a hospital for the criminally insane — and, believe it or not, things go downhill from there.

The Jacket is directed by John Maybury and has a group of high-level producers, including George Clooney and Steven Soderbergh. The movie is well cast and well acted, but the editing and plot leaves the viewer as confused as the poor brain-injured veteran. Jack is given pills and injections at the mental hospital and subjected to a bizarre treatment in which he is bound in a straight jacket and stuffed into a locker as if he were a corpse. The hospital director is Dr. Becker (Kris Kristofferson) who, it seems, is conducting an illegal treatment that has caused the deaths of other patients. When Jack is stuffed into the locker, he has flashbacks and also flash-forwards, and apparently he dies, but doesn't die.

There is a good doctor at the hospital, Dr. Lawrenson (Jennifer Jason Leigh), but she is unable to confront the powerful Dr. Becker, who bullies the staff in a forceful, authoritarian manner. The viewer may recall the film *Jacob's Ladder*, which also featured the confusing flash-forward and horrific treatment at the VA hospital. This may have been a hallucination of the veteran who was in an infantry unit given hallucinogenic drugs in Vietnam.

An interesting feature of *The Jacket* is that the veteran encounters the child who took his dog tags, now an adult (Keira Knightly), and she assists him in trying to figure out what happened to him at the hospital. It seems that he is able to prevent the death of her mother, who, in one version of reality, died in a fire when she fell asleep with a lit cigarette.

Mental health treatment is presented in *The Jacket* as horrific and torturous, contributing to the fears some veterans express about seeking medical care or psychotherapy for PTSD. Fears are expressed that the treatment itself will make the veteran psychotic. Recall the horrible treatment that was featured at the VA hospital in Oliver Stone's *Born on the Fourth of July*, which professed to be a factual, autobiographical account of a paralyzed Marine veteran of the Vietnam War. Compare that account with the hospital scenes of the treatment of paralyzed World War II veterans in *The Men* (1950). In the latter film, the paraplegic veterans are suffering, but the medical treatment is delivered by caring and competent doctors and technicians. In 1950, at least, medical treatment was considered benign. What has happened in the interim to cause such a change in regard for veterans' medical care? It appears that the respect for medical authority has deteriorated, at least as far as the movie industry is concerned, and I believe that the movies reflect, in some respect, public opinion.

Feature films dramatize psychological situations with action. In the film, *Oliver Sherman*, in which a brain-injured Iraq War veteran seeks out the veteran who had saved his life on the battlefield, we see through the eyes of the veteran the confusion that goes along with recovery, particularly when the veteran leaves rehabilitation and supportive psychotherapy. Memory for facts are fragmented and behavior is impaired in terms of reading the expectations of the public. Alienation in the veteran returning from service in a foreign war is normal and to be expected. The veteran has just left a closed culture in which traumas have occurred and horrible scenes are lurking in memory. Add to the veteran's situation the fact that he or she has experienced brain injury and has to learn compensatory behaviors and develop new neuronal pathways to function in society. *The Jacket* dramatizes this alienation and presents the veteran's dilemma as a succession of horrors perpetrated in the criminal treatment of a brutal doctor practicing illegal treatments designed to "create a womblike environment." At one point, Jack is told by the doctor, "Just because you suffer from a delusional disorder, it doesn't mean you're crazy."

Oliver Sherman, 2011

Oliver Sherman is a difficult and moving film about a veteran of the Iraq War who, seven years after serving in combat, visits the man who saved his life in a firefight. The film's title is the reverse of the veteran's name, Sherman Oliver. Sherman is played by Garret Dillahunt. He is first seen on a bus, photographed from behind; clearly visible is a white scar beneath his hair. Sherman explains to his rescuer, Franklin Page (Donal Logue), that when he recovered consciousness after his head injury he could not remember his name. Upon reading the bed chart, which identified him as Oliver Sherman, he thought it was his correct name.

Franklin Page works at a mill, has a wife, Irene (Molly Parker), and two young children. He is surprised to see his former colleague and invites him into his house. Sherman has symptoms of brain injury, most notably a flat, restricted range of affect, an awkward, socially inappropriate bluntness, rigidity, and concrete thinking, which makes for difficult dinner conversation. When Irene asks him what kind of work he does, he replies succinctly, "Just a vet. Nothin' much."

The problem develops as Sherman stays on in the Page household. The family has a custom that if anyone uses foul language he or she has to deposit money into a kitchen jar. When, at a birthday party for one of the kids, Sherman walks into a chandelier, he collapses to the ground in shocked surprise and curses with uninhibited gross GI language, casting a pall over the party and making the baby cry. He finishes his meal alone in a bedroom and deposits $10 into the jar.

Franklin and Irene soon feel the tension as Sherman stays on in their house. He visits the local library during the day and Franklin picks him up after work and drives him back to their country house. Sherman drinks beer and whiskey steadily. Irene becomes irritated about the effect the visitor is having on her husband and becomes nervous having him around her children.

Sherman seems to be an example of war veteran alienation when he says, "I feel like I'm on the outside of everything, looking in." When Franklin asks him about his plans, Sherman reveals that he has no plans and doesn't think about the future.

Mixing the name in the title, *Oliver Sherman* is a statement that Sherman's injury has affected his identity. It is as if Sherman wants to be rescued again and helped to make an adjustment to civilian life, but isn't able to articulate his need.

Oliver Sherman is directed by Ryan Redford, with a screenplay from a story by Rachel Ingals. It is a modest, low-budget film that is loaded with a sense of peril because of Sherman's social awkwardness. For instance, he at one point shows a four-year-old child his combat knife, which he carries with him. The child holds it, fascinated, as his father walks in. The knife begins to loom large as an instrument of peril in this gloomy film that will likely be a commercial failure, although it is well acted and directed, with excellent photography by Antonio Calvache. Credits at the end of the film suggest that it was shot in Canada. I attended a screening on a sunny Sunday morning and estimate that there were more film festival volunteers than patrons in the audience.

Wars have a way of unexpectedly surfacing in a veteran's life. Sherman Oliver seeks out the man who saved his life in hopes of belonging again. Franklin Page remarks to his wife that he's not sure: "Did I really help him or curse him?" Sherman considers Franklin a hero and cajoles him into digging his Bronze Star out of a trunk in the attic and showing it. Sherman taps his head and says, "I got some metal here."

Several films in recent years have taken their plots from the theme of the war veteran reappearing unexpectedly in the life of the protagonist. The most controversial is the 1972 anti–Vietnam War film directed by Elia Kazan, *The Visitors*. The storyline has two veterans seeking out the man who testified against them at a trial which convicted them of raping and murdering a Vietnamese girl. They show up at his remote country house after being released from federal prison on a technicality and torment the peace-loving veteran.

Another example of this theme — although a vastly more positive one — is the 1989 film, *Jacknife*, in which a veteran visits his Vietnam War buddy after completing a life-changing therapy group for veterans. His buddy is still in the throes of alcoholism. The visit is marked by strife and tension, but ends with a positive note of one veteran helping another to adjust to civilian life.

There is tension also in *Missing in America* (2005), in which a veteran seeks out his former platoon leader who is living in an isolated Northwest cabin. The visitor brings his nine-year-old Vietnamese-American daughter and imposes on the protagonist to take care of her after the visiting veteran goes off to die of cancer.

In *Oliver Sherman*, the veteran's wife fails to understand why Sherman cannot put the war behind him the way her husband did. The film focuses on the peril of the threat of violence, which becomes a metaphor for the violence of combat in foreign lands that comes back to haunt American society. The veteran may have made a good adjustment to civilian life, but the memories of combat traumas become real in the form of a visiting veteran.

The sense of peril generated in *Oliver Sherman* is also reflected in the title character's anger when he realizes that he is no longer a welcomed guest. He vents some of his anger at Irene, which only makes matters worse. He tries to ingratiate himself and change their attitude toward him, but his ineffectual attempts only serve to increase everyone's alienation.

The brain-injured combat veteran would not necessarily be a subject for insight therapy. He desperately needs a helping relationship but hasn't the social tools to make a relationship last. The man who saved his life, in the end, has to ask Sherman to leave on the next bus. To Sherman, this seems like an act of betrayal. He keeps the deadly combat knife in his belt behind his back, and the sense of peril increases right up to the last unhappy moment.

An earlier Seattle Film Festival war veteran offering, *The Dry Land* (2010) went directly to video. Chances are very good that *Oliver Sherman* will follow the same route. It is a realistic film that could happen to any veteran who may otherwise have made a good adjustment after a period of foreign combat.

The Lucky Ones, 2008

The Lucky Ones features three veterans of the Iraq War, two of whom are wounded and on furlough, and one who is injured and a discharged army reservist, who travel together across the U.S. What sets it apart from other films is that one of the veterans is a woman. *The Lucky Ones* was released briefly to theaters in 2008 and received lukewarm reviews.

One veteran, T.K. Pool (Michael Peña) is shown in the opening scene wounded in the groin while riding in a Humvee that is hit by a blast from an IED. He is released from the hospital and we learn that he is temporarily impotent as a result of the wound. (Perhaps it is significant that, just before the blast, T.K. was joking with his fellow travelers about raunchy sex.) Processing for furlough, he teams up with Ed Cheever (Tim Robbins), and Colee Dunn (Rachel McAdams). Cheever is an army reservist who is heading home to St. Louis at the end of his deployment after injuring his back. Colee is on furlough, recovering from a gunshot leg wound. They team up to rent a car at the stateside airport when an electrical blackout has canceled all flights. A nice touch occurs when the rental clerk gives them a car when he finds out they are vets just back from Iraq, after telling all the other customers that there are no more available.

The Lucky Ones is directed by Neil Burger, who manages to capture the natural camaraderie of the three veterans. Colee exudes Southern charm and is as comfortable with the men as if they were her brothers. She is heading for Las Vegas to return a guitar to the parents of her buddy who was killed in action. Cheever is a middle-aged sergeant in the reserves who is looking forward to returning to married life and his civilian job. TK is also heading for Las Vegas, the land of professional sex workers, to seek a cure for his impotence before he meets his girlfriend. On the way there is a roadhouse bar fight when Colee is mocked by other women for her awkward limp. It is apparent that she is quick to anger. Her buddies have to extricate her from the resulting melee. All three veterans have a winning harmony, even when they clash and disagree. In one scene, Colee splashes TK with a soft drink when he insults the integrity of her departed buddy.

The trio first travels, accompanying Cheever to St. Louis, where he is expecting to be reunited with his wife and son. He calls ahead, but when they arrive no one is home and he has no key. His wife, when she returns, greets him coldly and tells him that she wants a divorce. A poignant moment occurs when their son arrives home and breaks the big news to his dad that he has been accepted at Stanford, and only needs $20,000 to supplement his scholarship. Cheever, who is expecting his son to be reacting to the impending divorce, is again caught unprepared. He does not have $20,000 and finds out that he has no assets, because his house has been mortgaged and there are no savings. He promises his son that he will get the money, but leaves in despair with his comrades. His vague plan is to travel with them to Las Vegas, where he hopes to score at the roulette table. To facilitate his unrealistic plan, he quaffs pain pills and finally passes out in the back seat of their van. Because he has voiced suicidal tendencies, his friends panic when he doesn't respond. In their panic, TK diverts his attention from driving and crashes into the rear of a truck, sending a lumber beam through their windshield. No one is hurt, and they drive on.

While the car's windshield is being repaired, Colee is diverted to a church revival where the preacher invites worshipers to come forward and be healed. Colee volunteers her friends, to their embarrassment: TK for his wound to "his privates," and Cheever for his back injury and his suicidal feelings. Although they are not healed directly, a worshiper invites them to his birthday party, and they discover he is a wealthy man who resides in a mansion. At the party, Cheever is picked up by a lustful woman who takes him up to one of the many bedrooms. When Cheever finally flees, pulling on his pants in the hallway after the husband arrives, he tells his friends that he is not feeling suicidal, at least "not at the moment."

When they arrive in Las Vegas, Colee finds that her dead buddy had been lying to her with his stories of his checkered past. The guitar she intended to return to his parents is quite valuable and she takes it with her when she leaves. TK discovers that his impotence is cured by a tornado, during which he hugs Colee in a desert culvert. Colee is the remarkable figure in this film. She is a character who sought the army life after a troubled childhood and parental rejection. She is a spark in her friendship with men, casual and uninhibited. She obviously likes being with men and they accept her as a comrade, a signature tribute to the modern U.S. Army as it has been deployed to Iraq. There are only a few residuals of posttraumatic stress symptoms. TK shouts in a hotel room, erupting from a nightmare. Cheever virtually jumps out of his skin when a van door slams shut. But the residual effect of combat is positive here, with the easy affiliation of soldiers who have trained and worked together as a common frame of reference. Unfortunately, as the attention passes between the individual veterans' stories, each with its own interest, the tension does not build to a climax and the stories remain shallow in terms of revealing much of their past or individual psychologies. T.K.'s personal background is left unexplored. In the end, they all return to Iraq and are absorbed in a long line of uniformed troops.

The Invisible War, 2012

Again the Seattle International Film Festival introduced a film that is relevant to military veterans. *The Invisible War* is a documentary, directed by Kirby Dick, that examines the painful subject of rape, sexual assault, and harassment in all the branches of the military, and reveals what is equally as disturbing: the consistent pattern of command failure to investigate and prosecute these crimes. *The Invisible War* cuts between women veterans from all branches of the military, including the Coast Guard, as well as a male veteran, who describes his experience of being assaulted and raped.

The pattern that these veterans describe is not far removed from what has been exposed in recent years in other institutions, including religious, sports, and youth organizations. Consistently, it seems that those who seem to be otherwise professional, opt to protect the institution instead of reporting sexual crimes. *The Invisible War* notes, by cutting between interviews, that as many as 80 percent of women in the military who are sexually assaulted do not report the crimes because they view the institutional system as unsupportive.

The Invisible War is successful in lending sympathetic human faces to the reports of experiences with the sexual assaults and the aftermath, sometimes being blamed for the crime, often having to deal with perpetrators or their friends as next in command. At the end of the film the director reported that the documentary was shown to then-secretary of defense, Leon Panetta. After viewing the film, Secretary Panetta acted to take authority for investigation of alleged sexual assaults away from unit commanders, handing it over to an independent investigative authority.

The documentary was effective in showing the long-term impact of the sexual assaults, made worse by the fact that no justice followed the crime. As one veteran said so poignantly, "Never does it not run through my head." *The Invisible War* documents repeated examples of perpetrators being given awards (e.g., "Airman of the Year") or being promoted after being accused. The veterans describe their suicidal feelings and attempts. The documentary camera is on hand when one veteran goes to the mailbox to retrieve her notification from the VA of her disability claims. This scene seems staged, perhaps after the real mail delivery. She sits on the couch with her husband and child to read the judgment that she has been denied claims of injuries resulting from her assault.

One veteran demonstrates her frustration, visiting a VA hospital, then displaying the horde of medications that she has been prescribed to deal with all the medical sequelae related to the sexual assault: pain meds, anxiety meds, anti-depressants, etc. One commentator in the film observed that sexual assault in the military has the impact of incest, both on the victim and for those investigating the crime. The reaction is so consistent that it seems to reflect a pattern: a reflexive protection of the collective, whether it be family, or company, or sect. As another veteran said in the film, "They're going to punish me because of what they did."

The Invisible War presents the issue of failure of leadership. It is true that the bonding in military units mimics family bonds of brother, sister, father, mother. However strong, military bonding is still less than familial bonding, because it is not genetic and does not develop from birth and childhood. In the military family there are characters of various backgrounds and customs, some of whom may be psychopaths, at times disinhibited by alcohol, or struggling with adolescent immaturity (hardly from the same family), who can only be controlled by strong, commanding leadership. In a twist of irony it seems that reporting a sexual crime is a bad mark against the unit commander.

The disability claims that follow sexual assault and the secondary injuries are so often charged with a veteran's history of career, social, and emotional disruption. It is not like an injury that follows an accident or an illness that develops while on active duty. *The Invisible War* captures a bit of the long-term impact. One veteran developed a disorder of the jaw (TMJ) when she was hit in the face during the assault. Treating the disorder is a matter of medical care, but the veteran has emotional associations that make the problem more complex. The disability claim may be addressed objectively in the VA system, but that misses the emotional load that the veteran applies to it. There is a history of veterans' claims being discounted by the public and politicians as fabrication and exaggeration. The speakers in the documentary observe that most sexual crimes in the military are not reported, and often, when they are reported, cannot be independently verified. The fact that there are usually no corroborating witnesses leaves the charge of fabrication wide open. And just as often, when investigation follows, the claim proves to be valid.

The Invisible War won the 2012 Sundance Film Festival documentary award. It is a film that will prove to be educational for therapists and other health care providers, those who chance to encounter veterans, to be alert to the issue of sexual trauma in the military. It is part of veteran's culture. Communication has changed so dramatically in recent decades that there now exists networks of like-minded persons who constitute a virtual village. Veterans can keep in touch across different networks, and veterans with histories of sexual trauma can find support and guidance in furthering their claims.

The counter-pull in this case lies in the shibboleths that accompany sexuality in many societies and cultures. Take, for example, the ancient view of women as property as influencing the ongoing public debate about issues in women's health care. This cries out for leaders to try much harder to make sexual assault, harassment, and cover-up, crimes that are not tolerated. Until that time arrives, it is a sad truth that reporting a sexual crime in the military may be a career-ending decision for the victim.

The Veteran, 2011

The Veteran is a traditional depiction of a war veteran who experiences alienation when he returns home and is caught up in the violence of his community. Toby Kebbell plays Robert Miller, who lives in a violent, ethnically mixed public-housing community in England, known as The Estate, where his friends are caught up in drug and gang violence. When he is discharged from the army he is recruited by a fellow veteran to join a clandestine quasi-government operation that is fighting terrorism, which is being imported from Pakistan by Muslim extremists.

The Veteran was directed by Matthew Hope, a name that carries an ironic connotation, because his film is a cynical dose of nihilism. The movie shows the influence of violent electronic game technology as the veteran seeks out terrorist operatives, follows them through streets and corridors of homes and the maze-like housing projects. There is a tradition here that dates back to the Vietnam era in American film history.

Robert Miller has the cool, disciplined persona of Charles Bronson. The story exploits the veteran's training and courage. "We need men with your particular skill set," he is told. He doesn't shy away from taking on a dangerous task. He trusts a fellow veteran he had served with, although in the end, he learns that the credential of "we served together," doesn't guarantee righteousness.

The Veteran also exploits the racial and social inequality of the United Kingdom. There is a feeling that Great Britain is bogged down in disorder, and the Muslim extremists are merely exploiting the malaise that already exists to their advantage. "We're the enemy at war with ourselves," says one character who seems to be on the right side. Films made after the Vietnam era did no credit to the returning veteran, but merely exploited the combat scenes for ticket sales. The addition of electronic media adds to this exploitation with the rapid fire of automatic weapons and the cell phone gimmickry that facilitates segues from scene to scene.

In the U.S., the World War I veteran returned to face the gangland violence fueled by the misguided policy of Prohibition (see, for instance, the HBO TV series, *Boardwalk Empire*). Many World War II and Korean War-era movies portrayed the veteran as unjustly accused, setting him up for the task of clearing his name by finding the real enemy. The closer we get to the present age, the more technology takes over the plot with rapid fire and instantaneous communication, but morality seems to stumble from beating to firefight, desperately clinging to the simple veteran's struggle to survive.

No Country for Old Men, 2009

The Wars on Terror take another form with *No Country for Old Men*, which was directed by the Coen brothers, returning to the tradition of their first suspense film riddled with dark humor, *Blood Simple* (1984). The terrorism involves the bloody clashes of the drug-smuggling gangs across the U.S.-Mexico border. After their opening scene, the Coens cut to a hunter stalking a herd of antelope on the South Texas desert. He wounds one animal from a great distance, and, in tracking the herd, he happens upon another blood trail, one which leads him to a scene of human carnage. It is the site of a drug deal gone deadly, with bodies and vehicles shot up in a standoff. One survivor, wounded but still alive in his truck, begs for water. The hunter replies with a grunt, "I got no water." One blood trail leads off to the bush and the hunter follows to find yet another corpse, this one with a satchel full of hundred dollar bills.

Josh Brolin plays the hunter, Llewelyn Moss, who takes the money back and hides it under his mobile home. There he has a brilliant comic exchange, a much-welcomed relief, with his wife, Carla Jean (Kelly Macdonald). At night he cannot resist the call of the dying man and returns to the scene of the carnage with a plastic bottle of water. His compassion is his downfall. He is shot at and chased by gunmen and their pit bull. Although he manages to escape, his pursuers have his truck, and therefore, his identity. Moss has to hurriedly gather up his wife, his money, and flee. He sends his wife to her mother and he hits the road, with Anton Chigurh (Javier Bardem), the morbid professional killer, close behind. Chigurh (Moss mockingly calls him "sugar") is a relentless demon who uses a cattle-slaughtering stun gun to blow out door locks. He has an unstoppable, unfeeling remorselessness of a supernatural being.

There are two exchanges that tell us that Moss is a Vietnam War veteran. In one exchange, a second killer, Carson Wells (Woody Harrelson), is on his trail, this one a friendly fellow veteran, seeking to help Moss by taking his money and sparing his life. Later, Moss, after crossing the border into Mexico, is quizzed by the officious border agent on his return in hospital gown and cowboy boots, and is admitted back into the U.S. only after he identifies himself as a two-tour infantry veteran of the Vietnam War.

The war veteran quality of Llewelyn Moss gives his character a ready believability. Consider, for example, his wary, stalking approach to the crime scene in the beginning, his unemotional survey of the corpses, and his rough response to the dying man. Later he displays his dogged compassion and perhaps a sense of duty, when he returns with water for the dying man. The ruthless killer and the wry old Sheriff Bell (Tommy Lee Jones) both track Moss through his wife, who has left Llewelyn to live with her mother.

The number of innocent victims in this two-hour film is astounding; it seems as though the town's population is living amidst terrorism. Sheriff Bell, seemingly disenchanted with humanity, decides that the time has come for him to retire.

The title of the film comes from the W.B. Yeats (1983, pp. 193–4) 1926 poem, "Sailing to Byzantium." Yeats's poem has been interpreted as the definitive statement about the agony of old age and the imaginative and spiritual work required to remain a vital individual even when the heart is "fastened to a dying animal" (the body). The film was faithfully adapted by the Coens from a novel by Cormac McCarthy. Exchanges of dialogue were lifted whole from the novel into the movie. However, two important elements were missing in the screenplay, although they seem not to have impaired the movie version by their absence. In the novel, the sheriff is also a war veteran, and apparently has been a sheriff for 38 years *because* of what happened in his war. He had been a squad leader in France in World War II. He had won a Bronze Star: "I was supposed to be a war hero and I lost a whole squad of men," he admits sadly. In the closing pages of the novel, Sheriff Bell visits his invalid uncle and relates — for the first time to *anybody*— how he had won the Bronze Star, holding off Germans after a mortar blast. His squad was buried under rubble, and some were crying out. He held off the Germans with a .30 caliber machine gun and then fled at night because he knew they would creep up and lob hand grenades. When his uncle heard this, he said: "Well, in all honesty I can't see it being all that bad. Maybe you ought to ease up on yourself some" (McCarthy, 2005, p.278).

The Coen brothers' adaptation also left out a sequence of scenes in which Moss picks up a teenaged runaway girl who enjoys the fact that he is a wounded fugitive. She is drawn to the folly and becomes, in the end, just another example of the film's collateral damage.

McCarthy refers to Anton Chigurh as a ghost, illustrating that his archetypal power of insatiable Death becomes the summary of the war veteran motif.

The Last Flight, 1931

The Last Flight is about a group of American combat aviators, all of whom have been wounded and released from a hospital in France after the war ended. In the beginning of this extraordinary film, released in 1931, we see them all in the air in a dog fight. One plane is shot down, the pilot pulling his gunner out of the burning wreckage. Then they are seen being released from the hospital and deciding, impetuously, to go to Paris instead of home. Two officers, apparently doctors, watch the two airmen descending the stairs of the hospital joined by two other wounded airmen. "Well, there they go, out to face life and their whole training was in preparation for death," says one doctor, and adds that their plane fell 6,000 meters, and they were "shattered, both of them, like dropping a fine Swiss watch on the pavement. They're deranged, disorganized...."

The other doctor interjects, "Spent bullets, shaped for war, hurled at the enemy, cooled off, useless." Then he wonders aloud, "Perhaps they'll take care of themselves."

The first doctor responds, "Even if they do take care of themselves, what good are they?"

We next see the four veterans jauntily clad, walking on a sidewalk in

Paris. They are Cary (Richard Barthelmess), who pulled his gunner out in the crash and burned his hands; Shep (David Manners), the gunner who has a tic, and we later learn, loses track of things; Bill (Johnny Mack Brown), an American cowboy in Paris; and Francis (Elliot Nugent), a gunner whose nickname was "Sudden Death." They enter a nightclub bar and all order martinis. Cary spies a willowy blond who is standing against the wall, still as a manikin, holding a glass containing false teeth, and introduces himself. She is Nikki (Helen Chandler) and she becomes the near-sighted muse for the carousing veterans who continue to drink steadily.

The Last Flight was directed by William Dieterle and was the German director's English-language debut. He went on to make films for 35 years in Hollywood; probably his most memorable was *The Hunchback of Notre Dame*, in 1939. The dialogue for *The Last Flight* sounds stiff and staged, perhaps a product of the primitive sound equipment, but giving some odd emphasis to statements, which seem intended to be profound but instead fall flat. The characters have no depth and the plot is shallow, but the film itself is baldly revealing in terms of attitudes at the time toward veterans' posttraumatic symptoms.

Nikki, the slinky woman in the nightclub, has an odd, stoned countenance. She accepts the antics of the four veterans with passive equanimity and they follow her to her apartment. A fifth male joins them at the nightclub. He is Frink (Walter Byron), a journalist who becomes a fifth wheel, tagging along and making inappropriate advances toward Nikki. The four veterans are asexual. Nikki seems unconcerned about her vulnerability and even invites one of them to scrub her back. Bill, the cowboy, relishes the opportunity, making leering adolescent comments, but it is Cary who has captured Nikki's interest. She is given a difficult task that many associated with veterans have in dealing with the veterans' wounds. Nikki is inclined to exclaim about how sad it is that Cary's hands have been burned, but the other veterans tell her to not comment, for "he's as brittle as a breadstick."

"Why doesn't he go home?" she asks. "Why is he in Paris?"

Shep answers, "What we are all doing in Paris ... what could he do if he went home?"

"Isn't he wasting himself?" she asks.

"On the contrary," says Shep. "He's trying to get control of himself."

Shep has to stay "tight" in order to control his tic. Nikki is told that Shep "nearly lost his mind and will not ever go home." Shep reveals that he himself is often disoriented as to time and place and has difficulty remembering things. All the veterans seem driven to excessive drinking of alcohol. They all spontaneously take a train to Lisbon, Portugal. There, while drinking heavily, they attend a bullfight. Bill, who has earlier in a folly of drunken abandon tackled a horse in the Paris street, scoffs at the bull-fighters' prowess and jumps into the ring to challenge the bull himself. He is immediately gored. He comments weakly while on a hospital gurney that "the bull certainly was hostile." Bill is the first of the veterans to die, although we don't know his fate for certain. Cary leaves the hospital room with the expectation that they will not see Bill again.

The Last Flight has an oddly staged finale. At an amusement park, they fire rifles at a shooting gallery. Frink, the offensive writer, pulls out his own small caliber revolver. The veterans have been at odds because Frink had made an offensive pass at Nikki, causing Cary to sock him in the jaw. Cary struggles with Frink over the pistol, which goes off, shooting Shep. Francis, the gunner, shoots Frink with one of the amusement booth rifles. Perhaps in those days real bullets were used. Francis shoots Frink three times and the obnoxious journalist dies. Francis then walks off quickly and disappears into the dark (a dramatic statement that is common to the other war veteran movies of the 1930s). Nikki exclaims that she never saw him look so happy. In most of the preceding scenes Francis had seemed sleepy or bored. It is not until they are in a taxi that they discover that Shep had been wounded in the stomach by the stray bullet. As he dies, he dispels Nikki's concern, saying, "It's the best thing that ever happened to me." Cary stated that Shep had died a long time ago on the battlefield and was ready to die again: "Shep had nothing more to give." Without his friends, he tells Nikki, "Nothing matters. Comradeship was all we had left."

The Last Flight has been released on DVD and is a fine example of an early war veteran film that has echoes of Ernest Hemingway's Paris after that war and the lost generation of expatriate veterans, although this film doesn't give the journalist any positive characteristics. Awkwardly produced early talkie, The Last Flight presents a story of wounded war veterans who can't go home, and apparently nobody, not even the doctors, believe they can lead useful lives. Nevertheless, the film ends on a positive note as Cary ends up with Nikki. She wants to be with him and he, who has been sad through most of the movie, and, as Shep said, "brittle as a breadstick," tells Nikki in a remarkable healing statement: "You've become very dear to me. Can't *I* do something for *you*?"

The Blue Dahlia, 1945

George Marshall directed *The Blue Dahlia* from a screenplay by mystery writer Raymond Chandler. Alan Ladd plays Johnny, a discharged navy pilot who arrives on a bus in Los Angeles. He is with two of his former crew mates. They flew Liberators in the Pacific war. With him are George (Hugh Beaumont) and Buzz (William Bendix). They decide to go into the first nearby bar for whiskey. Buzz reacts negatively to a soldier playing jazz on the jukebox. Buzz has a head injury and sports a metal plate over his brain. A scuffle ensues. It is 1945. Veterans are everywhere.

Johnny separates from his buddies, who are going to get an apartment together, and goes to his wife's apartment in a garden complex, where a party is in progress. Johnny wants to speak to her alone and finds her hostile. Johnny's wife is Helen (Doris Dowling), who wants to work in a nightclub called The Blue Dahlia. The owner of the nightclub, Eddie Harwood (Howard Da Silva), appears to be sweet on Helen. Johnny and Helen argue. She unapologetically tells him that their son was killed in a car accident when she was drunk at the wheel.

Johnny takes out a large caliber semiautomatic pistol and pauses for a menacing moment, and then drops it on the couch and leaves. In the night Helen is murdered with Johnny's pistol and the police are looking for him. He walks in the rain to the Blue Dahlia nightclub and there on the street by chance meets Eddie Harwood's estranged wife, Joyce (Veronica Lake) driving a car. She picks him up and they hit it off. He manages to clear himself of the crime and the apartment complex detective finally admits to the murder.

Chandler originally had brain-injured Buzz, who had rages and black-outs, be the murderer, but that version was censored. The false accusation of Johnny as his wife's murderer follows from her abrasive behavior. She never even read his letters from overseas. The veteran becomes implicated and flees to avoid arrest until he can find the real killer.

As the estranged wife of the nightclub boss, Veronica Lake plays a sultry soulmate to Johnny. It seems so improbable that she would pick him up as a stranger walking in the rain that we think she must have other motives. Along with his two veteran buddies, Joyce helps Johnny clear his name.

Till the End of Time, 1946

Till the End of Time got short shrift at the Academy Awards for 1946, upstaged by *The Best Years of Our Lives*. The B-movie version of the returning World War II veterans was directed by Edward Dmytryk, one of the masters of film noir. This movie, however, suffered as a drama. The screenplay was by Allen Rivkin from a novel, *They Dream of Home*, by Niven Busch. The plot quickly establishes that the two leading male characters, Cliff (Guy Madison) and Bill (Robert Mitchum) are heroes of the Marine Corps. They are, in fact, veterans of four memorable Pacific campaigns. Bill, we soon learn, has a plate in his head, for which he gallantly declines compensation.

After his return to his California home, Cliff meets Pat (Dorothy McGuire), whose husband was killed on his third combat mission with the air corps. "They ought to give Purple Hearts to war widows," says Cliff.

Cliff's mother discourages her son from talking about his war experiences. "Don't talk about it, Cliff," she says repeatedly. "I know you don't want to talk about it." At a party given by his parents, Cliff's father and a friend jocularly compare their past war experiences with the younger man.

In a significant scene, Cliff and Pat are in a coffee shop and come to the aid of an army veteran who has a bad case of the shakes. "Getting the shakes, dogface?" asks Cliff sympathetically. The dogface says he has just got out of the veterans hospital and is on his way home to Boise. He says that the doc said "they'd wear off in time." The GI decides that perhaps he wasn't going home to Boise after all and, instead, would go back to the hospital.

Cliff meets with his Marine buddy, Bill, the one with the plate in his head. Together they go visit Perry (Bill Williams), a former boxer who lost his legs in the war. He is training another boxer from his wheelchair; he refuses to wear prostheses.

Cliff's mother and father are "disappointed" that Cliff doesn't want to look for a job. He finally takes a job making furniture but abruptly quits. "What's burning me up?" he asks himself. "I'm edgy. Somebody stole my time."

Meanwhile, Bill is suffering from headaches, but refuses to go to the VA hospital. A brawl occurs in a tavern where many veterans are gathered. In an interesting subtext, veterans' organizers, calling themselves "American War Patriots," attempt to recruit Cliff and Bill, who are angered when they discover that the "Patriots" allow no Jews or Negroes, and a rousing fistfight ensues. Bill gets hit in the head and has to be hospitalized, although it is indicated that he will recover. Bill and Cliff decide that they are going to start a ranch and hire other war veterans.

Till the End of Time suffers from a predominance of Guy Madison and presages the popular screen charisma of Robert Mitchum. Cliff's passive avoidance, in this case, is his lack of activity, a difficult symptom to display on film, for there's nothing to show. The brief scenes of the dogface with the shakes appeals to the need to visually show the audience difficulty of war veteran adjustment. Bill's plate in the head causing him pain is another concrete way of representing intractable pain in war veterans.

It is worthwhile to compare this 1946 version of a war veterans' homecoming with *The Dry Land* (2010). What stands out about the contrast is the candid dwelling on specific traumas encountered by the veteran in *The Dry Land*, while the 1946 *Till the End of Time* only alludes to fighting with romantic nostalgia. The worst thing that Cliff could say about the war was to complain about the stench, and even this made his mother uncomfortable.

Ride the Pink Horse, 1947

This deceptively titled film noir was adapted from a Dorothy B. Hughes novel by Ben Hecht and Charles Lederer. It was directed by and starred Robert Montgomery as Lucky Gagin, a tough, dogged, confident, bigoted war hero of the New Guinea campaign. Arriving by bus in the southwestern town of San Pablo (filmed in Santa Fe, New Mexico), he has come to avenge the murder of his pal, Shorty. Gagin tricks the desk clerk into revealing the room number of Frank Hugo (Fred Clark), the gangster who murdered Shorty. He goes directly to Hugo's suite, rousts the secretary and draws the admiration of Hugo's girlfriend, Marjorie Lundeen (Andrea King). But Hugo is not there. Unable to get a hotel room in the town because of a fiesta, Gagin is directed to *De Las Tres Violetas* and meets Pancho (Thomas Gomez), who runs the local carousel with the titular pink horse. Pancho offers Gagin his own open-air bed. Pila (Wanda Hendrix, an Anglo actress with dark make-up), the Native girl he derisively refers to as Sitting Bull, persists, for some reason, in helping him. When he asks directions, Pila wants to know if he's looking for a friend. Gagin responds, "I'm nobody's friend." A federal cop, Bill Retz (Art Smith), who has been investigating Hugo, tries to collaborate with Gagin. Gagin refers to him derisively as "Uncle Sam." The cop is amused and responds to the veteran, "All cussed up because you fought a war for three years and got nothin' but ribbons." Hugo, it turns out, was a dishonest war profiteer.

Gagin gets attacked by two thugs with knives. He kills one, wounds the other, and is badly wounded himself. Pila, of course, helps him and nurses him back to health. He grows delirious from his wounds and talks about the jungle "where it gets so hot, when it rains, it turns to steam."

Gagin is victorious against the gangster, but cannot bring himself to say he cares for Pila. At the end of the film, he walks away with the cop to get a cup of coffee.

Ride the Pink Horse has several elements of PTSD in war veterans: anger, social alienation, and reckless aggression. His loyalty is a fierce, nostalgic bond. Everything Gagin does seems to have a hard edge, even when he's being friendly. His racial slurs are expressed in a way that seems both ignorant and defensive. He seems to relate best behind a well-defended position through which no positive sentiment passes unchallenged. His admirable traits are the combat veteran's values of loyalty and courage. The cop, in another of his retorts, tells the veteran, "You sound like a disillusioned patriot."

The Third Man, 1949

There are certain art forms that can only be produced by the collaboration of a group. Cinema has always been a group effort directed at a popular audience and, therefore, reflects more accurately the collective consciousness. Carol Reed's 1949 noir classic *The Third Man* fills that bill. Reed worked closely with writer Graham Greene, who actually wrote the story, not for direct publication, but as a foundation for the creation of a screenplay. Together, Reed and Greene had to collaborate with such diverse producers as Hungarian Alexander Korda and Hollywood's David O. Selznick. Then there was the movie production crew, including three directors of photography (one for day, one for night, and one for the sewer). And, finally, there was the filming, which took place amid the rubble of postwar Vienna.

Graham Greene, who had the idea for *The Third Man*, was a veteran of sorts of World War II. He was a writer who was involved as a British intelligence operative in international intrigue (mainly in sub–Saharan Africa) and was directly involved as an emergency worker during the London Blitz. His story concerns a naïve American writer of pulp fiction westerns, Holly Martins (Joseph Cotten), who arrives in Vienna at the invitation of his childhood friend, Harry Lime. He arrives during the ravages of winter to discover that Lime has just been killed in an auto-pedestrian collision and is being buried. At the graveside he finds himself attracted to a beautiful woman, who turns out to be Lime's bereaved girlfriend, and is, in turn, studied by a British army policeman, Major Callahan (Trevor Howard).

Martins discovers that there is much to be suspicious about his friend's so-called accidental death. For one thing, the porter in Lime's building saw three men helping Lime, whereas only two testified at the inquest. The policeman, Callahan, tries to enlist Martins's assistance, presenting evidence that Lime was involved in the black market trafficking in penicillin. Postwar conditions in the rubble of the bombed-out city of Vienna lead to an active black market. (The same was true in postwar Japan, where the most vibrant trade was war surplus.) "Everybody was involved in the rackets," the voice-over introduction declares, "whether it was cigarettes, wrist watches, or medicine." Callahan insists that Lime was involved in the worst, the watering down of penicillin, such that victims died and children with meningitis were rendered brain injured and mad.

Holly Martins is indignant, first that his friend is accused, and then, when he is confronted with evidence, that his friend could sink so low. But the force of the atmosphere of the war-ravaged city convinces us that Harry Lime is representative of what war does to everyone. The telling scene takes place when Martins meets Lime at the landmark Prater Wheel, a great Ferris wheel that was miraculously left undamaged by Allied bombing, and a huge symbol for the film. Lime has been, to this point, a shadow in the movie. He appears, walking around a merry-go-round, smiling sardonically. When Martins confronts him, Lime states in a manner that summarizes wartime cynicism: "Victims? Don't be melodramatic." Looking down from the giant wheel to the crowd below he continues, "Would you feel any pity if one of those dots stopped moving forever?" Such a lofty statement made in the midst of the rubble produced by Allied wartime aerial bombardment directly alludes to what happens when nations engage in combat.

One of the landmarks of collaboration in cinema is when an actor like Orson Welles, who plays Harry Lime, adlibs or writes his own lines. In this case, Greene (1977), in his preface, credits Welles with his famous cynical wit as Lime and Martins leave the Prater Wheel.

> In Italy for thirty years under the Borgias they had warfare, terror, murder, bloodshed — but they produced Michelangelo, Leonardo da Vinci and the Renaissance. In Switzerland they had brotherly love, they had five hundred years of democracy and peace, and what did that produce? The cuckoo clock. So long, Holly.

Welles, in his glibness, forgets to mention C.G. Jung and chocolate as Swiss products, but the point is made, that warfare stirs the pot of civilization and creates greatness at great cost. The scene that is created in *The Third Man* is a statement about the emotional numbing that comes from warfare: numbing that filters out emotions such as empathy. We can see in the accounts of people in combat in every war that civilians and enemy combatants become toughened as suffering becomes common. *The Third Man* is clear, though, that the numbing does not stop with the end of the war, but carries on as a calloused inertia.

The beautiful woman who was at the gravesite is Anna Schmidt (Alida Valli), a Hungarian actress living illegally in Vienna on forged papers. She appears to be in grief over her lover's staged death. Throughout the film she is reacting with sadness and fear. Her love for Harry Lime seems to transcend morality. She remains loyal to him even after learning of his heinous crimes against humanity. She could well be one of the spouses of the Nazis on trial at Nuremburg, who carried out the evil dictates of a psychopathic paranoid leader. She feels *for* him, "Poor Harry," when he feels nothing for his victims.

The atmosphere in destroyed Vienna, the plot of the dead man who goes on living in the sewers and amid the rubble, produced one of international cinema's great works of art that described the effect of war on the population, what Jean Renoir referred to as the inevitable corruption of war on all participants. Making the film in the winter rubble of Vienna portrayed the destruction as a background set. The people who profit from war and suffering don't care what suffering is created by their actions. Harry Lime, looking down from the Great Wheel at the tiny people below echoes the bomber crews when he challenges Holly Martins to care if one of those dots disappeared.

What Harry Lime does to evade capture is to descend into the sewer system of underground Vienna. He runs through the putrid slime, scurrying like a rat. His shadow always seems larger than his true form. What we can derive from *The Third Man* is the statement that combat, warfare, generates a destruction that does not stop when the war officially ends and the guns go quiet. The destruction continues among the victims, the citizens of the rubble and their offspring, their emotions numbed, bonded by shadows. Graham Greene, when asked to write the story, took a line from his notebook about a man who attends his friend's burial and then sees him again in the street. The metaphor of the man thought dead and buried but who continues to live in the shadows applies to the specter of war which rises again and again.

Thieves' Highway, 1949

There are some films that don't exploit the war veteran as protagonist, but instead subtly imply his veteran status. Such is the case with *Thieves' Highway*. The screenplay, by A. I. Bezzerides, was adapted from his novel, *Thieves' Market*.

Jules Dassin directed this complex action-drama. Dassin also directed the successful urban noir crime dramas *Night and the City*, set in London, and *Rififi*, set in Paris. Dassin left the United States as anti-communist paranoia began to heat up. He never returned. *Thieves' Highway* has terrific action sequences involving the produce truck, one a 1930s vintage open cab that seems to be falling apart and eventually crashes, and another, a surplus World War II six-by that collapses on top of Nick when he tries to repair a tire. The highway scenes seem quaint, set in post–World War II California, and featuring some harrowing races with trucking competitors to market with the load of golden delicious. The pre-freeway scenes of the San Francisco Ferry Terminal and the Embarcadero at the foot of Market Street are visions of yesteryear.

The basic plot of *Thieves' Highway* has an Odyssean ring to it. Nick (Richard Coute) has been away since the war, and when he returns, he finds his father (Morris Carnovsky) is crippled and dying, and Nick must restore his father's business by taking a shipment directly to the source of the corruption that injured his father. There, dog tired from driving many hours. (Fresno to San Francisco, in the days before the Interstate highway system, was a long drive.) He is taken in by Rica (Valentina Cortesa), who is an agent of the corrupt produce dealer, where he collapses in sleep. Tough guy Nick has a significant rapport with Rica, and she awakens him when she realizes that Mike Figlia (Lee J. Cobb) is selling his produce off his sabotaged truck. Nick wins the love of Rica and defeats the evil produce baron with his tough, steadfast, dogged perseverance. The character of Rica embodies the brutalized citizenry of war-torn Europe, when otherwise decent people found their morality compromised by necessity.

In a Lonely Place, 1950

World War II had a significant impact on the making of motion pictures in Hollywood. Not only were artists and craftsmen in short supply, set and costume materials were rationed, censorship was loosened, and lighting was restricted. A wave of pictures made during that time became known as film *noir,* so labeled later by French critics, because of the use of darkness, cynicism, violence, and confined spaces (Doherty, 1993). After the war, when the artists and craftsmen returned and materials became available, the movies literally lightened up, but the influence of *noir* prevailed into the 1950s — and has continued in a vein of American cinema (Martin Scorsese's Scorsisi's *Taxi Driver,* Roman Polanski's *Chinatown,* and John Dahl's *Red Rock West* are recent examples). *In a Lonely Place* was released in 1950 and, although its spaces are well lit, the mood remains dark and the influence of the war is the undeclared subject of the film, which is about a combat veteran whose anger alienates those who love him. This realistic look at Hollywood was adapted from a story by Dorothy B. Hughes, with screenplay by Andrew Solt. It was directed by Nicholas Ray.

Humphrey Bogart plays Dixon Steele, a talented and wealthy film writer who hasn't had a successful film since before the war. We first see him driving a convertible on a city street, stopping at a stoplight, when a woman passenger in another car recognizes him and greets him. Her husband in the driver's seat doesn't like the greeting and says so. Dixon and the driver exchange angry words from their car seats and Dixon opens his door to fight in the street when the other guy drives off. Then we see Dixon entering a posh bar in a restaurant where other movie people gather. He is sitting at the bar with his agent and a friend, a drunken actor. An obnoxious young director appears, bragging about his latest success and insults the actor, apparently a has-been. Dix, as he is known, shoves the boor into a table and is going to punch him when others pull him off. An actress sitting at a nearby table remarks offhandedly that Dix has a pattern of going off in such a fashion.

The plot develops as Dix takes a hatcheck girl (Martha Stewart) home with him, not for amorous reasons, but because she happens to have read the book he was supposed to read, with the idea of adapting it to the screen. She tells him about the story in the manner of an undereducated enthusiast, misusing words with delightful naiveté. After she leaves his apartment, she is murdered, and we next see Dix being awakened by a cop, who happens to be a veteran of the infantry unit Dix commanded. The detective, Sergeant Nicolai (Frank Lovejoy) declares to his police supervisor, "We spent three years together overseas." Dixon Steele, we learn from his police record, has a history of violent behavior, bar fighting, domestic disturbances, dating back to just after the war.

Fortunately for Dix, a neighbor in the same elegant, mission-style apartment complex, provides him with an alibi. The neighbor, Laurel Gray (Gloria Grahame) claims to have seen Nick saying goodnight to the hatcheck girl, who was later strangled, her body dumped on the side of the road. Laurel and Dix have a great rapport and provide sharp, witty dialogue in their repartee as they become lovers.

As the murder investigation proceeds, Dixon is the logical suspect. He is clearly capable of murder and has a pattern of behavior that is consistent with such an act. His temper is short and his actions are violent. Laurel begins to be afraid of him after another road rage incident, when he beats a young man unconscious. Dix is about to bash the man in the head with a rock, when Laurel diverts his attention and breaks him out of his altered state of consciousness. It doesn't seem to help Laurel when Dix tells her that he's "been in a hundred fights like that," as if to minimize the importance of this particular altercation. And when finally he terrifies her in a fit of paranoid accusations, they both realize that their relationship is at an end. The moment of that realization happens to occur at the dramatic moment when Sergeant Nicolai calls to inform him that the real murderer has confessed and Dix is in the clear.

In a Lonely Place has a tight plot with characters who are interesting and complex. Nicholas Ray directs women well and gives his female characters a chance to show their charm and depth. We don't know for sure if the war was a source of trauma for Dixon Steele, but his habits are revealing. For one thing, he usually doesn't answer his telephone. His vet friend, the cop, remarks, after Dix doesn't blink when told the hatcheck girl was murdered after leaving his apartment, that it's "hard to tell how Dix feels about anything." The detective gives a clue when he refers to their wartime experience as "the worst years of our lives," perhaps taking off on the ironic title of *The Best Years of Our Lives*. We are left with the feeling that Dixon Steele, however talented and successful, would today be ordered by the court into anger management or dragged into a therapist's office by a long-suffering friend or relative on the recommendation of a defense attorney.

Everyone around Dixon knows that he has a problem with anger, but no one can convince him to change. If he were referred to a counselor, as his faithful agent says he tried to do, Dixon Steele would present as a war veteran who does not trust anyone and manages to respond to every mindless jerk and hint of friction in his environment as though it were a bugle call to action. He might claim that he never starts fights, that it's always the other guy who gets what he deserved. He never backs down from a fight, perhaps because he is so out of touch with his feelings that he doesn't recognize fear or experience empathy, and doesn't pay attention to the signals that an explosion is imminent. We feel sad when the movie ends with the veteran walking away alone, realizing that he has just blown another good relationship.

Nicholas Ray was a student of Frank Lloyd Wright before he got into directing films and the gorgeous apartment building with its garden court was Ray's own home. *In a Lonely Place* was restored to excellent condition on DVD from many cans of film dug out of the Hollywood archives. It is an important war veteran film because it doesn't blame the war or the military and yet gives us a very real picture of a veteran who can't seem to cope in society.

Kansas City Confidential, 1952

World War II Marine veteran of Iwo Jima is out on parole after spending time in prison for a gambling beef. He is driving a florist's delivery truck. Every working day at the same time he parks in front of a flower shop, which happens to be next to a bank. We know all this quickly because his movements and that of the armored car removing money from the bank about the same time are being observed. The veteran is Joe Rolfe (John Payne). The guy who is timing everything is Tim Foster (Preston Foster), an ex-cop planning a bank heist. Foster hires three hoods, coercing each with knowledge of their criminal involvements. The hoods are a tarnished bunch of character actors: Kane (Neville Brand), Romano (Lee Van Cleef), and Pete (Jack Elam).

Joe is blamed for the robbery they pull off because the robbers use a mock delivery truck painted to look like Joe's, and pull up to do the robbery just as Joe drives off. So Joe is arrested and questioned, but released after the fake truck is found abandoned.

Interesting from the war veteran angle, Joe visits the proprietor of a diner, Winky's, to get information about the bank robbers. We learn from the proprietor's shady-looking brother, who delivers the lead to Joe, that he was helping because Joe had saved his brother's life on Iwo Jima. The proprietor has a significant limp as he hustles about behind the counter. Joe is identified as having received a Bronze Star and Purple Heart. No more is said about Joe's experience in the Marine Corps, but we see plenty of his fighting ability as he traces one hood, Pete, to a crap game in Tijuana. Pete dies in a struggle over a pistol, but gives Joe enough information to identify the rendezvous for the robbers in a Mexican coastal town called Borados.

This 1952 noir drama was directed by Phil Karlson, from a screenplay by George Bruce and Harry Essex. The drama has a clever way of twisting our moral support of justice being served. The leader of the robbers, Foster, is a former police captain who "got his walking papers" due to some infraction. He has set up the heist, getting the robbers to wear identical masks so they never see each other's faces, but he knows them all. What Foster wants is to set up the hoods for a betrayal, so that he can collect the reward money.

But Foster's scheme comes unraveled when his daughter, who is a lawyer studying for the bar, comes to Borados to visit her widowed father. Helen Foster (Coleen Gray) meets Joe while sharing a taxi from the airport to the hotel where the hoods are gathered. Joe poses as Pete, hoping that no one will recognize him.

If this plot seems familiar, it is perhaps because it has been repeated so often in films about war veterans. The veteran is a straight guy who does not brag about his war record and who runs into criminals and corrupt politicians. To name a few films with a similar theme from the same postwar era: *The Blue Dahlia, Bad Day at Black Rock, Thieves' Highway, Key Largo, Ride the Pink Horse*. The plots capitalize on the sacrifice and modest nature of the war veterans, which is played in contrast to the low nature of the non-veteran hoods. The theme of each of these movies centers on the solitary nature of the veteran's struggle to correct the wrongs being done. In each of these movies the veteran must rely on his wits and his crafty fighting ability. Also, the veteran is aided in his fight with some kind of material assistance from a woman. In *Kansas City Confidential*, the ex-policeman's daughter falls for Joe, in spite of all the appearances of being a hood himself, and in spite of his trying to drive her away with rough words. Usually the women involved has some kind of association to the criminals and, in that role, they are able to provide the information the veteran uses to win the day.

Films about war veterans of this postwar era, which spans the veterans' recovery from the Second World War that was hampered by the onset of the Korean War, have a tradition that tends to dramatize the veteran's alienation in his society and culture as a concrete assault upon his person. The veteran tries to do the right thing but is thwarted by dark forces that compel him to fight for justice, pretty much all by himself. He is either wrongfully accused, as in *Kansas City Confidential*, or prevented from doing a duty to the relatives of those who died in combat. The 2012 novel by Mark Halprin, *In Sunlight and in Shadow*, dramatized this conflict for the straight veteran trying to do business in a corrupt society, perhaps corrupted by the conditions of the war.

There were very few films of this era that portrayed the war veteran as having an easy time with adjustment. Apparently there's no story in that variation. Most veterans were given a challenge that they had nothing to do with creating. The alienation of the combat veteran of this era was, we gather from the contemporary scientific literature, poorly understood. Mood disorders, particularly involving alcoholism, were attributed to flaws of character. Families were reluctant to discuss the veteran's sleep disturbance and nightmares as if it were an unseemly disorder that warranted embarrassment and even shame. Veterans seldom took their troubles to the VA hospital, and even the VA hospitals of the era failed to link many disorders to traumatic causes, for such was the science of the time. DSM-II, the prevailing authority for psychiatric nomenclature, had, with almost hysterical denial, successfully muddled the issue of stress caused by trauma.

Films portraying war veterans made solid drama for the time and the veteran was easy for audiences to identify with as someone who had done his duty and was being misunderstood. In each of the dramas it took a pretty unusual woman to like the guy with the disturbance in his past. She knew a bit about the dark world that was imposed upon him, and by believing in him she played a significant role in aiding him in his fight.

Kansas City Confidential gives us a Marine veteran who knows how to fight and stand up for himself. The darkness that pulls at him is not of his doing, but is *out there*, a product of his society. Movies that have been produced about veterans of the current Wars on Terror in Iraq and Afghanistan do not resort to the Hollywood projection of the darkness. They have utilized insight into PTSD in the veterans and make drama from the personal struggles of the veterans to adjust. However, none of them, with the exception of *The Hurt Locker*, which dealt very little with the veteran at home and was all about action, have made money at the box office. *Kansas City Confidential* still gets seen as a fine example of Hollywood film noir.

Human Desire, 1954

Human Desire is a remake, directed by Fritz Lang, of Jean Renoir's 1938 classic *La Bête Humaine*, which starred Jean Gabin. Lang's version was written by Alfred Hayes. Both versions are adaptations of Emile Zola's novel. The title, *Human Desire*, is an interesting translation of what would literally be

The Human Beast. In this 1954 version the beast is Broderick Crawford, who plays an oafish railroad assistant yard master, Carl Buckley, who gets fired for carelessness. His wife is Vickie, played by Gloria Grahame, with her usual passion. She is a noir heroine who manipulates a train engineer, Jeff Warren (Glenn Ford), who has just returned to his old job after three years in the army fighting in Korea. The difference between the two versions, *La Bête Humaine* and *Human Desire*, is in the romance of the steam locomotive and the craggy features of the engineer Jean Gabin, versus the clean lines of the diesel and the placid features of Glenn Ford. When Carl is fired from his job he begs and coerces his wife to visit an influential man she knows to convince the yard master to rehire him. She does so reluctantly because of her sexual past with the man. In fact, she reveals that he seduced her when she was a girl of 16. Carl is wildly jealous of what happened and forces his wife to meet the man on a train, where Carl kills him with a knife. Jeff is also on the train as a passenger returning to the rail yard (dead-heading, as they say) and meets Vickie after she has witnessed the murder. At the inquest, Jeff lies to protect Vickie, and they begin an affair. Carl decompensates with alcohol abuse and gambling, and blackmails Vickie to keep her from leaving. He had his wife arrange the assignation on the train with a compromising note to her lover.

What is interesting, from the war veteran standpoint, is that Vickie tries to get Jeff to kill Carl, but Jeff finally refuses. She says, "You killed before," referring to Korea. Jeff replies, "The war — you thought I could do it because of *that*? It takes a different kind of killing and a different kind of man."

Director Lang creates some tense and passionate moments, but *Human Desire* is muddled, and the ending, with Carl strangling Vickie, is left unfinished. Glenn Ford's Jeff is no beast, in spite of what is implied by his exposure to combat. He seems placid and pleased to be driving his diesel locomotive.

Renoir's 1938 version is richer in characterization than *Human Desire*. The disorder that affects *La Bête* railroad engineer Jacques Lantier (Jean Gabin) is described by him as an inheritance from generations of alcohol-abusing men. Simone Simon plays Severine, the wife of the assistant yard manager. Severine, like Gloria Grahame's character, was sexually abused as a teenager by the man she is asked to plead for help to reinstate her husband's job. Renoir said that he wanted a beautiful but innocent looking woman to play the role of the female bound for revenge against her husband, so much so that she is willing to induce another man to commit murder. The richness of *La Bête* is that it dotes on the rail yards and steam locomotives as background throughout the film, which makes it a treasure for railroad enthusiasts. In preparation for the film, Gabin actually worked in the cabs of locomotives and drove the beasts, unbeknownst to passengers. *La Bête* savors the scenes of workers in their hostels as they prepare their meals and wash away the grease and grime of their work. The war veteran angle is not in the character of *La Bête*, but looms in the background; the movie, after all, was being filmed in 1938 as Hitler's armies were occupying Czechoslovakia, and Neville Chamberlain was negotiating appeasement.

Suddenly, 1954

Frank Sinatra plays the sadistic killer Johnny Baron, a man planning to assassinate the president of the United States, who is scheduled to make a train stop in the small town of Suddenly. Baron is an army infantry veteran who brags about winning the Silver Star and killing 27 men: "When I was in the army I did a lot of choppin'." He and two fellow gangsters take over a house near the railway station, holding its inhabitants hostage. They include the sheriff of the town, Todd (Sterling Hayden), who is also an army veteran (Johnny sarcastically calls him "a good soldier." Todd speculates that Johnny was discharged on a Section 8 because he was sent home before the war ended, unlike most in the infantry who had to stay in until the war was over.) Ellen (Nancy Gates), a war widow; her eight-year-old son, Pidge (Kim Charney); and Ellen's father, Pop Benson (James Gleason). Pop is a World War I navy veteran who happens to be a retired Secret Service agent.

As things turn out, the assassination is foiled by some rather dumb planning on the part of the gangsters. Pidge gets Pop's pistol and manages to shoot at Johnny, but misses. Ellen grabs the pistol and shoots Johnny and wounds him. Then the sheriff, the "good soldier," kills the would-be assassin. *Suddenly* was taken off the market along with *The Manchurian Candidate* after JFK was assassinated. The audience is left with a modern American theme that bad people, not guns, are dangerous.

The theme of the good veteran versus the bad veteran struggling over control of a gun had been articulated in Kurosawa's 1947 *Stray Dog*. One veteran becomes a gangster, the other becomes a cop, but in *Suddenly* we have the message that a person with a disturbed childhood, whose father was a "dipso" (alcoholic), and who was abandoned by his mother to an orphanage, can become unraveled by army training and combat. Johnny says, "Before the war I drifted and drifted. The war changed everything." Later he states, "When you got a gun in your hand you're a god." It was an important postwar message to convey that it wasn't that combat unnerved a soldier, it was a troubled childhood. When film director John Huston tried to make a case in his 1945 army documentary, *Let There Be Light*, that conditions in combat could cause mental illness, the army shelved his film and remade the documentary with a new director, calling it *Shades of Gray*, which conveyed the alternative message that poor parenting was the cause of combat fatigue (Early, 2003, pp. 70–71). Tragically, it seems many veterans believed that their problems adjusting to civilian life after World War II and the Korean War were not the responsibility of the federal government, but their own to deal with in private.

Nightfall, 1956

Nightfall is one of the many low-budget noir films of the postwar era that places the innocent war veteran in peril due to circumstances beyond his control. Aldo Ray plays James Vanning, a navy veteran of the Battle for Okinawa. "I'm back from the wars," he says. "I'm a vet." He had the misfortune to be camping in Wyoming with his friend, a medical doctor. They are about to break camp ahead of a forecasted snow storm when they go to the aid of two bank robbers who crash their car. The ungrateful robbers, John (Brian Keith) and Red (Rudy Bond) kill Doc and try to get Jim (a man of many aliases), to shoot himself to appear as if he's committed suicide. Jim refuses and is stunned by a ricochet shot from Red's pistol. The robbers drive off with a bag they think contains their robbery booty, but happens to be the doctor's bag. When they return, Jim has run off with the bag of money. This is all told in flashback as Jim is pursued by the robbers.

The theme is familiar as the veteran is driven underground by events outside his control. In *Nightfall* the veteran must assume aliases and keep moving to avoid harm while he waits for an opportunity to clear his name.

Nightfall was directed by Jacques Tourneur from a screenplay by Sterling Silliphant, adapted from a novel by David Goodis. The dialogue is snappy and the acting is good, but the plot has a sense of being conveniently contrived to fit a 78-minute film. Jim is also followed by an insurance investigator, played by James Gregory. The robbers, pretending to be policemen, dupe a lovely woman into luring Jim into a trap. The woman, Marie (Anne Bancroft), is a fashion model and Jim works as a freelance commercial artist. The robbers accost Jim and beat him, trying to get him to tell them where the money is hidden, but, as Jim explains to Marie later, he doesn't remember. He was stunned by the ricochet bullet and apparently suffered a concussion, so that when he ran off into the snow he could not recall where he left the bag of money. Jim finally fights off the robbers and flees again, seeking refuge in Marie's apartment. She is enticed to run off with him back via Greyhound bus to Moose, Wyoming, so that he can find the money and prove his innocence. The insurance man follows them, becoming convinced of Jim's innocence, and there is a final confrontation, in which the robbers turn on each other; Red kills John in a shootout, and Jim fights Red in and out of a snow-plow that is dramatically closing in on the shack where the insurance man and Marie are tied up. The film ends abruptly as Red is caught screaming in the snowplow's savage maw.

The veteran's changing identity, being mistakenly thought guilty, fits the Odyssean theme of the veteran's readjustment from combat to civilian life.

Elevator to the Gallows, 1958

When a nation engages in war, even wars on foreign soils, the impact is soon felt throughout the culture. Louis Malle made *Elevator to the Gallows* (*L'Ascenseur pour l'Echafaud*, as it was released in France; *Lift to the Scaffold*, in Great Britain) in 1957 about a "parachutist" veteran of the French–Indo China War and the war in Algeria. He is an employee of a war profiteer and conspires to murder his boss. His co-conspirator and lover is the boss's wife, Florence Carala (Jeanne Moreau in her breakthrough screen role). The war veteran is Julian Travenier (Maurice Ronet). He is the epitome of cool, as if he were disciplined to the point of emotional numbness. Julian carries out the murder by repelling off the side of the office building so that it appears the boss has locked himself in his office and committed suicide.

When Julian first puts the pistol in the boss's face, the old man says that he doesn't believe Julian has the courage: "In war, yes. But not in more impor-tant things." The arrogant war profiteer soon learns that is not the case. Before he shoots him, Julian says, "How many millions did you make in Indo-China? And now in Algeria? Respect war, Mr. Carala, they are your family heirlooms."

Louis Malle fashioned a terrific montage, cutting among the assassin who is trapped in the office elevator, two young thieves who have stolen his car, and Florence wandering through the wet streets of Paris in search of her lover.

The young car thief, posing as the war hero, meets and eventually mur-ders a German tourist and his girl friend using Julian's pistol. The police think Travenier killed them. The girl who accompanies the thief is an admirer of Julian, who, she says, has many war medals and "fabulous wounds."

Elevator to the Gallows was Malle's second film (his first was a documen-tary made with Jacques Cousteau), and it established him as an important director in the French New Wave. Louis Malle's career lasted until 1994, when he made *Vanya on 42nd Street*, and is marked by an impressive range and variety of important films. His second film about a war veteran who is mis-directed by his emotions was *Alamo Bay*, which he made in 1984, about a Vietnam War veteran fighting to save his fishing boat on the Texas Gulf.

A very great attraction of this film is the unique original score on the soundtrack by Miles Davis, said to be an improvisation played as the trumpeter watched the film. He plays throughout the film with a quintet, featuring Barney Wilen, René Urtreger, Pierre Michelot, and Kenny Clark on drums. The character of Jeanne Moreau duplicates that cool in her role as the classy woman picked up in a police sweep while wandering the streets not knowing her lover's fate. It is the kind of cool that captured many young viewers (this critic included) in the late 1950s. (Oddly, the film carried the ironic title *Frantic* in the 1958 U.S. release.)

A remarkable situation occurs in *Elevator to the Gallows*: the two lovers who occupy the film never meet. They briefly talk on the telephone in the beginning, but then they exist separately and are kept from further contact. Not only is the war veteran separated permanently from his lover by his deed of revenge, he is trapped like an insect in amber.

Elevator to the Gallows gives us the impression that the veteran is committing the murder out of love for Florence, but when Julian is about to kill her husband, he speaks of his contempt for the war profiteering, and it is his cool control of his emotions that allows him to return to the scene of the crime to retrieve his repelling rope, only to be trapped in the process.

Ed Harris, as Shang, the Vietnam War veteran in *Alamo Bay*, is also trapped in the emotions of war. His hatred for the Vietnamese émigrés drives him to attempt murder. His hatred is fueled by the racial bigotry of the KKK and their allies. The seething passion of Shang is a remarkable contrast to the controlled emotional vengeance of Julian in *Elevator to the Gallows*, yet both characters are drawn to their demise by dwelling on their war experiences. In Homer's *Odyssey*, the fearsome nature of the Sirens functions to draw war veterans to their deaths by the attraction of wartime memories. The blanched bones of warriors pile up at the feet of the Sirens who sing of the heroic exploits of the Trojan War. If warriors pause to listen to their songs, they will be trapped there and die.

The Vietnam War was particularly rich in ethnic and cultural differences between the Vietnamese and the U.S. troops. There was the unfinished business created by the U.S. pullout, which gave the veterans of that war a sense of loss that they felt they did not deserve. The Vietnamese people came to symbolize and to be blamed because of the failure of U.S. strategy. The Theory of Cognitive Dissonance (Festinger, 1957) suggests that the more effort and energy and money one puts into a task, the more one has to justify its value. The deaths, the wounded, the suffering, and the financial costs of conducting war generate such dissonance. The more the ambiguity regarding the justification for the war, the more dissonance is created by the efforts expended. And after the war, the war veteran must then deal with the relationship of the memories to the reality of the facts as they come to light. Anger, grief, hatred, revenge, all the emotions generated by combat, the symptoms of PTSD and depression, have to be related to as the product bought by the conduct of the war.

Lonely Are the Brave, 1962

Lonely Are the Brave is a fairly unique movie. Directed by David Miller, it is a story of a Korean War veteran, a cowboy, John W. "Jack" Burns (Kirk Douglas), who discovers that his friend has been incarcerated and is on his way to a two-year prison term. Jack starts a fight in a tavern to get himself arrested so that he can help his friend escape. As they are booking him, the police decide instead to let him go, but Jack, determined to help his friend, assaults the cops to ensure that he is locked up. But his friend, Paul Bondi (Michael Kane) decides to do his time (he was arrested for helping immigrants), and Jack, who can't tolerate being confined, escapes. There then begins an epic ride of a cowboy on a beautiful horse (Whiskey, who almost steals the show), pursued by a team of sheriff's deputies.

Sheriff Morey Johnson (Walter Matthau) is a deadpan character who rather admires the cowboy he is pursuing. In a classic scene found in many war veteran films, the sheriff's deputy reads the report on the history of the fugitive. He reports that Jack served in Korea, did seven months in a disciplinary company for striking an officer, was wounded in combat, and received a Distinguish Service Cross ("with oak leaf clusters"). What part the war experiences play is uncertain, but the cowboy is clearly at odds with modern society. He is at home on the vast plains with the cougars and squirrels, but he is out of place where the rubber meets the road. Traffic on highways puts him at peril and ultimately brings about his end.

The first scene in *Lonely Are the Brave* shows the cowboy asleep next to his saddle and horse. The scene could take place in 1875, but an increasingly loud roar is heard and the camera pans up to show the contrails of jet planes flying above. The picture on the wall of the sheriff's office is of President Harry Truman, which means the era depicted must have been 1952, although it is consistent with the personality of the sheriff, rather like Will Rogers, that he might be the sort who would keep a picture of Truman up for sentimental reasons. If the drama took place in 1952, it must mean that Jack was only recently discharged.

I don't know how much thought was given to Jack's war record. The Distinguished Service Cross decorations were unusual. The Cross is a very high award, second only to the Medal of Honor, and for any soldier to receive two, which is implied by "with oak leaf cluster," is rare. Is Jack's self sacrifice — sacrificing himself for his friend — a product of the war? We know alienation is normal and to be expected in veterans of foreign combat, and Jack's antipathy for authority was evidenced in the army. So what we see in this cowboy is alienation dramatized, the war veteran at odds with civilization.

Lonely Are the Brave was written for the screen by Dalton Trumbo, from a novel, *Brave Cowboy*, by Edward Abbey. Trumbo was one of those Hollywood figures who was condemned by the House UnAmerican Activities Committee, and blacklisted. He continued to work as a screenwriter, but underground, using aliases. Kirk Douglas was credited for breaking the blacklist hold on the film industry by having Trumbo write the screenplay for Douglas's previous film (as an actor), *Spartacus*, and insisting on Trumbo getting screen credit in his own name.

Gena Rowlands plays Paul's wife, Jerry, whom Jack visits before getting himself arrested. There is a definite sexual tension between the two. Their kisses are passionate, more than ordinary friendship would dictate. Jack's sacrifice for his friend is an act of self-abnegation that seems to state that he will give himself up for the sake of his loved ones.

The other war veteran in the film is a one-armed man who is sitting in the tavern where Jack goes to pick his fight. The one-armed man is a tough character who immediately takes the challenge and actually provokes the fight. Jack is reluctant to fight a one-armed man (Bill Raisch, who is described later as a "tough hombre") and so declares that he will only use one arm himself. His antagonist announces that he lost his arm on Okinawa. So the metaphor is established of two war veterans in a fight for no good reason, each fighting with only one arm. In fact, political wars since World War II, Korea, Vietnam, the Wars on Terror, have all been described derisively by some as fighting with one arm tied behind our backs.

Black and white photography by Philip Lathrup, in this film, is terrific. The scenes of the plains and mountains of New Mexico fit well the theme of the cowboy's last ride. It is also a repeating theme to show the war veteran at odds with society. It is done more subtly and with better quality than the later *First Blood*. It has some of the heartfelt loneliness of John Ford's great epic *The Searchers*, in which John Wayne plays a U.S. Civil War veteran, who shows that he is in love with his brother's wife, and is burdened with the task of retrieving his young niece who was kidnapped by Native raiders.

These movies repeat a theme that flows through the history of film depicting the war veteran who returns from combat and finds that he does not fit in well with the society of his homeland. *Lonely Are the Brave* is exceptional in depicting the veteran who reveals his yearning love of a woman that he cannot acknowledge. In Clint Eastwood's *Absolute Power* we see a war veteran whose war record is also revealed in a police report, still mourning the loss of his wife and alienated both from his society and from his daughter, who he struggles to reach. These themes of the alienated war veteran are touching reminders of the common experience of returning to the homeland from war.

The Long Goodbye, 1973

The Long Goodbye was Raymond Chandler's last major work of his series of successes in writing detective novels. It was published in 1953 in Great Britain and 1954 in the United States, just five years before his death. His last novel to be published, and his poorest, *Playback*, written over several years, was adapted to a novel from his screenplay, and finally published in 1958.

The title, *The Long Goodbye*, is meaningful as a war veteran's long farewell to war. The novel was adapted to film by Robert Altman and released in 1973, starring Elliot Gould as a rather unpleasant, shabby, chain-smoking private detective Phillip Marlowe. The plot of Chandler's book concerns a war veteran, Terry Lennox, who is a shambling drunk when he meets Marlowe by chance outside a nightclub. Terry has been abandoned by his wife and Marlowe takes him home and helps him sober up. They become friends.

Terry is a veteran of World War II and was part of a British Commando unit that met a bad end in a campaign in Norway early in the war. He was wounded there and had a severely scarred face as the result of an explosion. He saved the lives of two members of his unit, who figure in the novel's very complicated plot. (Altman's adaptation deleted all reference to the veteran status of Lennox and, with it, lost the core of the meaning from the plot.)

There are a couple of parallels in this work of fiction with author Raymond Chandler's personal biography. Chandler received a concussion and was taken out of action in World War I as a U.S. citizen fighting with Canadian forces in France, similar to his fictional American, Terry Lennox, who volunteered to fight with the English. (Chandler had been educated in English prep schools and they left their mark on him.) Also similar to his character, Lennox, author Chandler was subject to long, debilitating drinking binges.

Phillip Marlowe becomes involved when his friend asks his help fleeing to Mexico. Marlowe finds out that Terry's estranged wife has been murdered and, later in Mexico, Terry confesses to the murder and appears to commit suicide. Everyone, including the police and Terry's war buddies, want Marlowe to quit the investigation, but he persists.

As it turns out, Terry's suicide was staged by his two war buddies whom he had called upon for help. And how could they refuse the man who saved their lives? The suicide was staged with a note left so that he would be blamed and the investigation stopped before it led to implicating his lover's husband, another drunken novelist.

Terry appears, finally, in disguise to Marlowe, which the detective readily sees through. We get a sense of the war veteran as a kind of cipher, a character in disguise who is not as he seems. To a certain extent perhaps every veteran who has spent any time in combat is a master of disguise in the sense that he or she must contain memories that are destabilizing in their juxtaposition with the contemporary reality. The presence of death and the potential for guilt are factors that can dog a veteran of combat and create self sacrifice as a meaningful option.

Chandler never acknowledged any negative influence on his postwar adjustment that was caused by his participation in combat. He called such posttraumatic symptoms "old soldier nonsense." We do know that his Canadian Expeditionary unit participated in combat so heavy in losses that it had to be disbanded due to depletion before the end of the war. He had a certain "old soldier" cynicism. He wrote in a letter to a friend (Chandler, 1981): "I read these profound discussions.... Who cares? Too many good men have been dead too long for it to matter what any of these people do or don't do." Chandler only began to drink heavily after the war when he was working as an executive for a California oil company. He married an older woman in fragile health and was loyal to her until her death, although he may have had a few drunken flirtations along the way (Hinley, 1997).

To wear a mask, to adopt a disguise, is not necessarily to be duplicitous if the goal is to survive in a peaceful environment. Some veterans in treatment refer to a kind of shadow character who is mostly submerged, suppressed, corralled. It is not sufficient to describe this shadow character as memory, because it is more than that: it is a complex of memories, such as Carl Jung described, that is strong enough to have a personality. It may merely sit back and hector, like Hyde to Jekyll, but sometimes it may manifest in behavior. If consciousness is lowered, or if circumstances become perilous, the mask of civility may dissolve. (See Jung, 1969, p. 92, for a review of his theory of the Complex.)

In the case of Terry Lennox in *The Long Goodbye*, the mask of civility required him to drink heavily, but when the mask dissolved he didn't turn to violence; he responded by protecting his loved one by sacrificing himself, taking on the blame for murder and staging a suicide, which was an act that required him to don a disguise.

People who are intellectually agile, who have what we used to call "good ego strength" (an ineffable quality made visible by measurement) and who encounter traumatic circumstances in war, have the capacity to wear a mask of civility that disguises their wartime values. Underneath that mask is the one who could fight beside you and then, with flat affect, watch you die, then go on fighting.

The ability to adjust well, to wear the mask of civility and escape diagnosis, does not mean that symptoms will not become paramount when stress levels are raised. One of the effects of good adjustment is that symptoms go undetected and untreated. Symptoms in hiding are then unmitigated by the benefit of experience and remain raw and as uncivilized as a masked Dionysian reveler.

Blessed by Fire, 2005

If there is a Universal Soldier, then there must be a Universal War Veteran. The Argentine film *Blessed by Fire* presents another story of the aftermath of war, which is played out in the lives of the war veterans. During the opening credits we see a political demonstration and a reporter, Esteban Leguizamón (Gastón Pauls) at work in the streets, documenting the event. The scene cuts to an ambulance, siren blaring, as it navigates the city streets.

Later, Esteban receives a phone call in his office and is stunned by the message. Esteban is a veteran of the 1982 war in the Malvinas Islands that the British claimed and called the Falklands. He experiences a series of flashback memories as he rushes to the hospital ICU where Alberto Vargas (Pablo Riva) has been taken. Vargas is a fellow veteran who has attempted suicide. Esteban had struggled mightily to save Vargas during the war, when Vargas was severely brutalized by abusive officers and wounded in the final days of the battle.

Esteban is confronted by his memories as he assists Marta (Virginia Innocenti), who found Vargas and called Esteban. Vargas had overdosed on alcohol and drugs. In his voice-over narration, Esteban states that more than 290 veterans had committed suicide, more than were killed on the island during the war. As memories occupy his consciousness, we learn why there were so many suicides. As Esteban explains, "The Malvinas came back again — and covered everything."

Esteban is unable to sleep. His memories describe the suffering of the men who were drafted and sent off to the islands to await the British landing. Argentina had seized the Malvinas from Great Britain, just as the British had seized the island 150 years previously, and called it Falkland. The Malvinas Islands are close to Antarctica. The soldiers dig bunkers, three-man fighting holes that guard the shoreline. They live in the mud and cold without adequate food or protection from the elements. Three soldiers, suffering together, capture and kill a sheep. They cook and eat the meat, and when one soldier, Vargas, tries to bury the sheepskin, he is discovered by the sergeant. As part of Vargas's punishment, he is beaten and staked out in the rain and mud until he becomes ill.

Esteban talks to Vargas, who is unconscious and sustained on life supports in the hospital ICU: "Since I've seen you, I keep going back to the islands." In the battle that finally comes, the Argentineans are routed in a brutal slaughter. In announcing the surrender to the assembled mud-spattered, weary survivors, the colonel, after praising them for their deeds, foretells their fate: "What you have experienced here will be with you forever."

Blessed by Fire (*Luminados por el Fuego*) was directed by Tristán Bauer. The reporter's flashback memories are about three hapless grunts, Esteban himself, Vargas, and Juan (César Albarracín). Juan, the youngest and a recent father, is killed in the battle. Vargas, who suffers from the torture and abuse of the officers, is severely wounded. All three suffer the deprivation of the long period of desolate watch on the coastline, living in a muddy hole without adequate clothing. Every once in a while a British Harrier jet rushes by and drops a bomb, an ominous omen of the overwhelming superiority of their opponent. The officers commanding them are presented as brutal cheerleaders, taunting and goading the soldiers with demeaning epithets.

After Vargas dies, Esteban takes his identity tag back to the Malvinas. He visits the twisted wreckage of the battle and finds the bunker above the beach where he lived and suffered with his friends. He discovers the artifacts that remained: a stashed photograph, Juan's treasured watch. The movie ends with Esteban sobbing, crouched in the abandoned fighting hole.

The role of Marta is one of a war veteran's mate, another universal character. She is Penelope, waiting for Odysseus. Her face shows an impressive range of expression. Although she is overshadowed in the drama by Esteban's nightmarish flashbacks, she relates her long, patient struggle to cope with her lover's self-destructive postwar habits.

The suffering, begun in war, continues in the war veterans, and the meaning that they give to their suffering is irrevocably tied to the meaning of the war. The fight for the Malvinas was lost by Argentina. It was a one-sided fight and an ignominious defeat that was the doomed product of their president's ambition. The chaos of the brief battles, which were depicted as nightmare scenes reminiscent of Goya, are bracketed by the ordeal of anticipation and the panic and fatigue of the final rout and defeat. What positive meaning can be given to such an experience? Esteban, who has struggled so mightily to save his friend, sees him let go of his own life, as if his near-death struggle years before had locked him into a life fated to finish this way. Marta, Vargas's mate, is drawn into his suffering. Esteban can only grieve for his friends who never left the island, and for the memory he bears that is tied to their fates.

Harry Brown, 2010

Michael Caine, an actor who is also a 77-year-old Korean War veteran, plays an aging Korean War veteran who happens to live in the very neighborhood of housing projects where Caine grew up. Caine's character is Harry Brown, a man whose wife is dying of dementia. He portrays the weary bearer of sad duty as he visits his wife and tries to make conversation. He plays chess with an elderly friend at a pub. The feeling is that they have been playing together for many years. His friend, Leonard Attwell (David Bradley), confesses that he is afraid of the young thugs who hang out in the project, called The Estate. Each scene of plot development is alternated with scenes of thug violence and intimidation. (Caine even confessed he'd also been in a youth gang when he lived there.) What develops is a vigilante plot when Harry's wife dies and his friend is murdered in gang violence. The double blow is too much for Harry and he reverts to his warrior identity. Earlier he had said to his friend, "The Marines were a lifetime ago. I was a different man then." And then he adds, "Once I met my Kath, I knew that all that stuff had to be locked away." But as he seeks to buy a gun in a scene reminiscent of *Taxi Driver*, Harry gets in a shootout with the traffickers, and as he is killing one man, he tells him the story of how he watched his friend die that way in Korea. He then adds piquantly that he's never told anyone that story.

Harry takes away a bag of pistols from the traffickers and sets fire to their dwelling. But age and infirmity in the form of emphysema take their toll on Harry and one of the investigating police officers develops a hunch that Harry is behind the sudden increase in dead thugs. Harry's actions put him in the hospital after he passes out while chasing a thug, but he doesn't stay long and leaves AMA to complete his vendetta.

Harry Brown was directed Daniel Barber from a story by Gary Young. The thugs are made unredeemably ugly, but carefully portrayed as Caucasians of indeterminate European ethnicity. They infest the housing project like vermin, and the residents have to go around them to avoid being abused. The director took scenes also from *A Clockwork Orange* (1971), although most of the gang brutality is implied rather than shown, much of it shown at great distance.

There are also echoes of past Clint Eastwood movies, particularly his recent *Gran Torino*, about an aging Korean War veteran who decides to take on gang violence after his wife has died. The problem with *Harry Brown* is that, except for Caine's Harry, the movie is otherwise bleak and ugly. One of the police inspectors, Alice Frampton (Emily Mortimer), seems courageous but out of place amidst the brutality. The police are seen as ineffectual and unable to protect the residents of the housing project, while the police spokesman insists that all is under control.

There isn't much discussion in *Harry Brown* about alternative measures that might be taken to clean up The Estate. Harry appears to be isolated from other residents and has only one friend. One of the consequences of "locking away" memories of combat is that the veteran narrows his consciousness, limiting the expression of his personality. The combat memories do not become integrated to fit the context of the whole of the veteran's life. The movie gives us very little of what Harry's life was like, except that he is living on a fairly meager pension that restricts his choices for housing. He seems to have no other friends or family.

In the United States, the status of the war veteran has increased considerably since 9/11. It was repeatedly noted by politicians and news reporters that the street vendor who recently alerted the police to the Times Square car bomb was a Vietnam War veteran. There was something remarkable about the veteran of one war being on the lookout for terrorists. The low-budget film *Land of Plenty* is all about a Vietnam War veteran patrolling the streets of L.A. looking for terrorists. All war veterans are now called heroes and thanked for their service. It was not long ago when status as a war veteran was distrusted and military service was not regarded as so noble, but rather a lower status blue-collar job (for instance, in *From Here to Eternity*). With wars in progress over a period of years, a nation becomes populated with warriors turned civilians. Some might say it keeps us safe to have old warriors in our midst.

Harry Brown ends with Harry walking toward an underpass which, all through the film, had been populated by thugs, such that a traveler risked life and treasure to pass through. The underpass now is deserted, we assume, but for how long? Harry, for all we know, is still armed. If it is true that revenge is not quelled, but rather strengthened by acting it out, then it is only a matter of time before more thugs meet Harry Brown.

Movies and stories about war veterans reverting to vigilantism are as old as the medieval ballads about Robin Hood and as recent as the popular novel *In Sunlight and in Shadow*, by Mark Halprin. They hint at hidden nobility, once manifest. In Robin's day, however, it was all about resistance to taxation that was imposed to keep a professional army in the field. When the war veteran becomes a warrior again, when the standing authority is weak and distrusted, it then becomes a question of how good the veteran's judgment is. We can see that Harry has been worn down by his wife's dementia, which implies a long draining away of their relationship. When Harry's chess partner is killed, he has no one else with whom to associate except the pub bartender. Opting to return to violence is a raw, uncivilized form of the warrior status that was kept primitive by repression. The viewer of *Harry Brown* has no choice but to root for Harry, who is volunteering for active duty once more.

Robin Hood, 2010

There is an archetypal theme that appears in various forms in films and stories about war veterans returning to their homeland. The veterans who have changed so much, or been away so long, that they are no longer recognized, not even by their spouses. The veteran returns disguised as someone else. The plaintive note of the spouse that plays to this archetype is, "You are not the person I married." And even the warrior-turned-veteran, as the opening quotes by E.B. Sledge and Salinger's Sergeant X attest, has been changed so much by the war that he or she no longer even thinks as the same person.

This motif is found in Sir Walter Scott's *Ivanhoe*, when the veteran returns from the Crusades disguised as a pilgrim. The French film, *The Return of Martin Guerre* and its U.S. Civil War version, *Sommersby*, exploited the idea that, in earlier times, there was no likeness of the veteran aside from the memories of those who knew him many years ago. This doubt about the veteran's identity is first found in Homer's *Odyssey*, when Athena disguises Odysseus as an old beggar, fooling even his wife (Murnaghan, 1987). Odysseus arrives home to spy anonymously on his household. The 1946 noir film *Somewhere in the Night*, directed by Joseph L. Mankiewicz, takes the theme a step further by having the veteran enlisting in the army under a false name, being involved in a combat explosion that wounds him, causing amnesia and requiring plastic surgery on his face. He then returns to a mystery of discovering his own identity. The 2001 film, *The Majestic*, makes an interesting wrinkle in the theme by having Jim Carrey play a man who crashes his car in a storm and develops amnesia when he is rescued and taken into a town. There he is mistaken for a local hero of World War II who never returned from the Normandy Invasion. Jim Carrey's veteran doesn't know who he is and goes along with the townspeople's adulation. (Written by Michael Sloane, *The Majestic's* main character, Peter Appleton, is a Hollywood writer in 1951 who is under investigation by the House Un-American Activities Committee, which, in fact, did drive some well known movie writers into hiding where they had to work under a pseudonym.)

In Richard Rush's 1980 *The Stunt Man*, a Vietnam War veteran (Steve Railsback), running from police, happens upon the set of a war movie after he has accidentally caused the death of the movie stunt man. The film's director, played by Peter O'Toole, hires the veteran, who has eluded his searchers, and has his make-up crew transform the scruffy veteran into a stylish Hollywood stunt man and places him in perilous predicaments involving a World War I pilot who is escaping from Germans.

Ridley Scott's richly produced 2010 version of *Robin Hood* exploits the theme of the war veteran returning in disguise. Robin Longstride (Russell Crowe) is an archer in King Richard's Crusade. The plot, written by Brian Helgeland, has King Richard's army on its marauding way home from the Holy Land, assaulting a castle in France, where the king is killed by a crossbow dart shot from the castle wall. Historically, according to historian John Gillingham, Richard the Lionhearted did, in fact, die while reconnoitering a castle for assault in France, but only after he had returned to England and reclaimed his throne. He was actually taken prisoner returning from his Crusade by a German nobleman and held for ransom (Gillingham, 1999, p. 222).

In *Robin Hood*, the 2010 movie, Robin was not in on the final assault on the castle. He had been put in stocks as punishment by King Richard for impudence, criticizing (when asked by the king) the Crusaders for wonton killing of Moslem civilians (thus giving the old theme a current feel, harkening to the ongoing wars in the Middle East, and giving Robin a rather insufferable righteousness). In the distraction of the king's death, Robin and his warrior comrades, Little John, Alan, and Will Scarlet, escape from the stocks and ride to the coast. On their way they happen upon the aftermath of an ambush of a knight who was transporting the king's crown back to England. The ambush was carried out by a traitor named Godfrey (Mark Strong) and is interrupted by Robin's rogue group, who drive off the ambushers. A knight, Sir Robert Loxley, is mortally wounded, but dies only after making Robin promise to return his sword to his father. Robin then poses as Sir Robert and they proceed back to England with the king's crown and the dead knight's sword.

Robin is partly honest when he delivers the crown to the new king, John, and the sword to the knight's father, Sir Walter Loxley (played with nostalgic charm by Max von Sydow). But Sir Walter asks Robin to continue to pose as Sir Robert, and enlists Marian, the late knight's wife, in the deception so that she will not lose her husband's land upon Sir Walter's death, all of which makes for quite a complicated and ultimately confusing plot.

In an odd and seemingly anomalous twist, a band of boys is roaming the woods, and their meaning and purpose is unexplained, except to suggest that they were war-neglected children driven to the wild by poverty. This version of *Robin Hood* purports to tell how the legend started when King John pronounced Robin and his friends as outlaws. The advantage that Ridley Scott and his writer have is that there are no biographical facts beyond a few medieval ballads that give very little detail about the character and activities of Robin Hood, and these ballads do not say anything about Robin being a veteran of the Crusades. The ambiguity has led to many versions of the mythical outlaw (Holt, 1982; Knight, 1994), and each version seems to play to its own era through the lens of the 12th century. The 1938 version of Robin

Hood, *The Adventures of Robin Hood*, starring Errol Flynn and directed by Michael Curtiz, played to the Depression audience with scenes of banquets and abundance provided by Sir Robin of Loxley rebelling against the evil taxations of Prince John. In that version, a benign King Richard returns and justice is restored to the land. In the current version, Scott and his writer, Helgeland, have created a confusing plot that triggers the theme of the war veteran returning in disguise to take up the cause of the oppressed who are burdened by the taxes that pay for foreign wars.

Scott's version of Robin Hood seems determined to please the moviegoing public, giving Marion (played by lovely Cate Blanchett) a sword to fight with, and having her entering the final battle of the English fighting French invaders on the seashore, still slim even in her battle armor. In the finale, Robin fires the arrow that improbably nails the traitor fleeing from the fray on his horse. The traitor is poetically shot in the neck, as was the king. (King Richard was shot in the shoulder, and the wound became infected.) The producer's gift for authenticity also fails when Robin states to his comrades that there is no difference between a knight and a common man. This was a remarkably uncharacteristic thought in the Middle Ages, but a definite crowd pleaser in today's egalitarian society. Scott's *Robin Hood* has the treacherous King John prevailing and declaring Robin an outlaw.

There being several ways a person is changed by combat (e.g., being away a long time, witnessing and participating in events that are traumatic or at least out of the norm and not shared by homebodies, aging through momentous and extremely stressful war experiences, becoming familiar with death), returning in disguise is the poetic symbol that describes the change when the warrior becomes a veteran. The disguise is to pose as a normal citizen that the veteran once was. A movie, like the aforementioned *Harry Brown*, warns what could happen when the mask comes off.

In this version of *Robin Hood*, Marian is something of a begrudging Penelope, when she agrees to the deception of Robin Longstride pretending to be her husband. Of course they fall in love after some initial resistance, with a weak erotic undertone, in which he sleeps on the floor of her chamber in his pose as her husband. It brings up the other side of the war veteran's return, that is, the willingness of the family and friends of the veteran to absorb change brought by the war. In *The Dry Land*, the veteran's spouse and his friend watch in helpless anguish as the veteran descends into a spiral of alienation. In *The Majestic*, the townspeople, the veteran's father, and even the veteran's girlfriend, are willing to accept change, overlooking the fact that this veteran who was washed ashore like Odysseus at the mouth of a river is not their hero. In *The Stunt Man*, the veteran on the run is exploited for the purpose of making an anti-war film.

Occasionally there is a news item about some celebrity or politician who claims to be a war veteran who really isn't, or was a veteran, like Jim Carrey's character in *The Majestic*, but just not in combat. Apropos of *The Majestic*, it was the infamous Senator Joe McCarthy who initiated national sensation by claiming to know of Communists in government, who claimed also to have been a B-29 tail gunner, but in fact never was in combat, although he implied that he was. Politicians point modestly or boastfully to their war record, if they have one, though some, like the senior President George Bush and Senator George McGovern, avoid or minimize mention of their war record. Some, like Senators John McCain, Daniel Inouye, and Robert Dole, can't minimize their battle scars. It is a common folk wisdom that the guy at the bar that boasts about combat was not there.

The disguise that the veteran wears is the mask of civility that allows him or her to get along as well as can be, to keep in check the memories of wartime and the accompanying emotions, hopefully not in a secret room and not inaccessible.

Shutter Island, 2010

Shutter Island is a very dark suspense film by Martin Scorsese that uses surrealism to convey psychiatric medical abuse in the wake of the experience of wartime atrocity. Set in a mental institution on a remote island in the ocean off Massachusetts in 1954, the story concerns Teddy Daniels (Leonardo Dicaprio), a U.S. federal marshal who has been assigned to investigate the disappearance of a female patient. Flashbacks indicate that Ted was a soldier in a World War II army unit that liberated Dachau. According to his memory, he and other soldiers in vengeful fury lined the Nazi guards up and shot them. Ted is first presented as a victim of seasickness on the boat that takes him to Shutter Island. Once there, the mystery of the disappearing patient is explained to him by the chief of staff, Dr. Cawley (Ben Kingsley).

Shutter Island was written as a screenplay by Laeta Kalogridis, from a novel by Dennis Lahane. The plot is structured to be a mystery that gradually evolves into surrealistic dream sequences couched in a reality so spooky that the viewer becomes unsure when the dream ends. What Scorsese presents, however, is a story of a war veteran who has been influenced by the terrible traumas of war, including the climax of the death camp. In one memory sequence, he witnesses the botched suicide of the camp commandant who has attempted to shoot himself in the head, but only succeeds in defacing himself. Ted sees the man trying to reach his pistol and nudges it away with his boot, to watch him slowly die.

Dr. Cawley makes an interesting statement that having trauma in one's life allows psychiatrists to attribute psychosis to a cause. The plot of *Shutter Island* is constructed so that the puzzle of Ted's memory and reality remains confused. The era in which the film takes place is one of witch hunts for communists in high places and there is even suspicion about the island hospital being funded by a grant from the House UnAmerican Activities Committee. The postwar atmosphere of hallucinations blending with reality is similar to the 1990 *Jacob's Ladder* by Adrian Lyne, which depicts the Vietnam War veteran decompensating into psychosis because of wartime traumas. In that film the soldiers go berserk in combat because of government experimentation with a hallucinogen that makes them more aggressive. In *Shutter Island* the soldiers may have retaliated for the horrible atrocities committed by the Nazi guards, committing an atrocity of their own by murdering them.

There is a bit of truth in the sensational plot that horrible trauma can be encapsulated if it is not integrated, causing suppression of the memory and leaving the veteran with fragmented memory and dissociation (Lanius et al., 2010). The veteran, not having integrated the memory, may function well until stress again becomes unbearable. In this case Ted commits another atrocity — or does he? Scorsese never gives us a definitive statement.

Surrealism, the blending of dream symbolism and the irrational with logical reality, was a significant movement that influenced cinema after the First World War. Spanish filmmaker Luis Buñuel carried on the tradition throughout his long career. There is an affinity in surrealism for traumatic memory and nightmare to reside alongside everyday life. Many films that depict war veterans adopt surrealistic flashback and dream segments to refer to the traumas of combat, taking the viewer into the memory: *Gods and Monsters*, *The Man in the Gray Flannel Suit*, *Missing in America*, and *The Tunnel*, a short film in *Akira Kurosawa's Dreams*. Movies, as Buñuel demonstrated early on, lend themselves to visual confusion of the past, the unconscious memory, with the conscious present. Veterans like Tom Rath in *The Man in the Gray Flannel Suit*, who strive for conformity and material success and nonconformist recluses like Jake Neeley in *Missing in America* are both prone to suppression of traumatic memory and both men are disrupted by the powerful attraction of symbolic events, as is Ted in *Shutter Island*.

Mesrine: Killer Instinct, 2010

There has been discussion in the past about the psychic consequences of participating in excessive violence, killing, and torture (Grossman, (1995,

2009). The story of Jacques Mesrine, based on his memoir *L'Instinct de mort*, opens with his participation as an army-enlisted man in the interrogation-torture of Algerian prisoners. They bring in one prisoner's sister, after beating him severely, and threaten to shoot her if the prisoner doesn't give the desired information. Mesrine is ordered to pull the trigger.

Mesrine: Killer Instinct is the first of a two-part, four-hour film, with the second part, *Mesrine: Public Enemy*, completing the story. Directed by Jean-François Richet, Jacques Mesrine is played with gripping determination by Vincent Cassel. From that traumatic encounter with wartime torture, Mesrine as an army veteran is unable to return to living with his parents and working with his father at a lace factory. He partners with another robber and begins a life of crime. He is introduced to a criminal gang leader, played by Gerard Depardieu. Mesrine's violence continues, although he marries a sensitive Spanish woman (Elena Anaya) and starts a family. Mesrine cycles though naïve sentimentality and periods of violent brutality. He eventually brutalizes his wife in a repetition of torture. He partners with another woman, Jeanne (Cécile de France), and boldly and brutally robs a casino with her. They are both caught, convicted, and sent to prison. He flees to Québec and is caught there on a violent kidnapping charge and is sent to prison, where he is brutally tortured by his Canadian guards. He stages a bold breakout from the prison and even more boldly returns in an attempt to liberate his comrades in the prison yard, ultimately causing many of the prisoners to be shot down in the gun battle with the guards.

Recent news stories of WOT veterans using a form of water-boarding torture to discipline their children give us a chilling reality of the traumatic psychological damage done by the practice of excessive violence, not in direct combat, but employed in the interrogation of prisoners. Neither of the news stories stated, though both implied, that the veterans had been exposed at least to training in "enhanced" interrogation techniques. It is also possible that when a nation resorts to torture as a matter of policy, it reflects a source within the society that is disordered.

Jacques Mesine's parents are judgmental when he returns to them from the army. They want him to work at a job, raise a family, and be honorable. His father is portrayed as a weak and passive man who is scorned by his son, so it is unlikely that abusive discipline was employed in Mesrine's childhood. He leaves home in anger, but later asks his parents to take care of his children when he has to flee the country as a fugitive.

The great French gangster movies of Jean-Pierre Melville and Claude Sautet have the moody toughness, but not the graphic brutal violence employed by Richet. What is most chilling, of course, is that this is based on a real French criminal who began his violent career in overseas military combat.

Fairy Tale: A True Story, 1997

There are several relatively recent movies that illustrate the encounter between the war veteran/Creature and the Child, who, as we see, varies in gender and age. A wonderful illustration is in a scene in the beginning of Charles Sturridge's 1997 movie, *Fairy Tale: A True Story*, that takes place on a train in England immediately after World War I. Young Frances (Elizabeth Earl) is on the last part of her journey from South Africa. Her mother is dead and her father is missing in action. She is traveling to live with her cousin, Alphy, in England. She walks through a car full of wounded war veterans looking for someone to play Cat's Cradle with her. She sits in front of a corporal who has part of his face shot away. The scene is designed to be shocking, but Frances is unfazed and invites the wounded war veteran to play, a virtual imitation of the scene at the lake between Frankenstein's Creature and Little Maria.

Fairy Tale: A True Story is about a popular contagion in England following the collective trauma endured in the war. Alphy's father is a photographer and the girls borrow his camera to photograph their playmates, the fairies. The pictures they take create a national sensation, and the girls, because they are symbols of innocence, are taken as psychopomps, guides to the spirit world. They are sought after by newspaper reporters chasing the story. At one point the disfigured veteran from the train appears in the woods in time to drive a persistent, intrusive reporter away from the girls. The film lets us play with the idea that fairies are real. Fairies were thought, then, by the British folk wisdom as being Hermes-like envoys to the afterlife. With the emphasis on the wounded war veterans, the nation seems to be in a wounded state of grief, wishing for a way to connect with the lost boys.

Young Frances in this story seems totally naïve and unfazed by the smoky car full of strange, wounded men. She connects with the disfigured man just as she connected to the lost boy, her cousin's late brother. She is willing to play with anybody who will hold his fingers out for Cat's Cradle.

Sundays and Cybele, 1962

The story of the Creature and the Child can be seen in several variations. One of the richest is the 1962 French film *Sundays and Cybele*, directed by Serge Bourguignon, with Hardy Kruger as war veteran, Pierre, with Nicole Courcel, as the girlfriend, and Patricia Gozzi as Cybele. Here the war veteran was a pilot in the French-Indochina War who crashed into a village and thereafter relives the crash and the visual memory of a girl in his path.

Cybele's mother has abandoned her daughter to join a circus. Her father doesn't want her, nor does her grandmother. Her father is leaving her at a Catholic boarding school. He promises to return every Sunday, but leaves her a note in her satchel admitting that he will not be back.

Pierre is living with his girlfriend, but seems uninvolved and numb. Seeing his girlfriend off to her job as a nurse (she was his nurse when he was hospitalized after the war) at the train station, the veteran meets Cybele being taken to the boarding school. He follows them after the father asks directions. He picks up the satchel left by the girl's father at the gate and learns that the father will not be back, that Cybele is abandoned. Pierre returns on Sunday and is mistaken for the father. Cybele goes along with the ruse, as she has been waiting a long time.

It is winter, nearing Christmas in the suburb of Paris, and director Serge Bourguignon makes the veteran's visits to the girl a lyrical piece of visual art. He perfectly captures Cybele's willing enchantment and Pierre's childlike responses as he carries her limply in his arms along a path in the park (evocative of Little Maria's father carrying the girl's body through the village in *Frankenstein*, and of Beast carrying Beauty after she has swooned at first sight of him).

They meet every Sunday. Snow and frozen ponds in the park become the scenes for their enchantment, until their relationship is misunderstood by others as perverse. Pierre seems to be brain injured he is so numbly innocent. Cybele is fully invested in the romance and, when Pierre is shot dead by the police, Cybele has lost her connection to the world. Pierre seems impotent, but the fact that he has an adult girlfriend suggests otherwise, although she was his nurse. Perhaps the best expression of his involvement with others is disinterest.

Cybele's motivation is clear. She is in love. She is enchanted by her own play. Pierre is paying attention to her. Pierre cares for her and they are on the same wavelength. The plot gives us an excuse to understand the veteran's fascination with Cybele as posttraumatic association to the Vietnamese girl about Cybele's age in the path of his crashing aircraft. But what is important to the theme is that Pierre can connect with someone with feeling that makes him seem happy. His contact with the abandoned child connects him again with his feelings that constitute the joy of living in the world.

Desert Bloom, 1986

A realistic family variation of this theme of the Creature and the Child takes a representative twist in *Desert Bloom*, in which Jack, the World War II veteran, played by Jon Voight, is struggling to relate to his family while in the throes of alcoholism and PTSD activated by a hot war in progress in Korea. Jack runs a gas station on the outskirts of Las Vegas, Nevada. His 13-year-old stepdaughter, Rose, one of the desert blooms, is played by Annabeth Gish. The film is largely from her point of view and her voice-over narrative tells of her struggle to relate to the suffering of her remote and frequently overbearing war veteran stepfather. The "beast" in Jack comes out in his wrong-headed, violent application of discipline, fueled by alcohol addiction and posttraumatic flashbacks to the Battle of the Bulge.

A MacGuffin for this 1986 film, directed by Eugene Corr, is the detonation of an atomic bomb (another desert bloom) at the test range near Las Vegas. Corr gives us a feel for the naïveté at the time regarding nuclear energy. Rose tries to relate to Jack, and stumbles. When Jack finally goes to rescue Rose, who has run away on the eve of the bomb test, they succeed in establishing a bond of sorts. An awkward, wary relationship of understanding and appreciation seems to have developed.

Throughout *Desert Bloom*, alcohol addiction complicates the PTSD symptom picture. The complication is seen often enough that addictions, along with mood disorders, are associated with PTSD. Jack is not very intelligent, but aspires to be, and he thinks he's getting there. When he is sober he is socially reserved, pedantic, and awkward with expressions of feeling. When he is drunk, he is crude and violent. The new war has apparently impaired his ability to cope and he experiences a flashback of a traumatic reenactment of being caught in an artillery barrage.

The validity of *Desert Bloom* is that the war veteran and the child, bonded together in family ties, keep trying to connect in a feeling way. Finally, Jack has the opportunity to rescue his stepdaughter and it is almost as if the peril gives them a new way to connect, whereas before, his attempts to show he cared were misdirected into anger, and her attempts to show she cared were deflected by his defensiveness. The film leaves the viewer with the sense of hope that the delicate relationship between Creature and Child will, if nurtured, grow and eventually bloom.

Little Lips, 1978

Little Lips describes the sexual attraction in the relationship between the veteran and the child. *Sundays and Cybele* and *Lawn Dogs* skirt the issue by showing that the sexual interpretation of the relationship was a mistaken collective perception. *Little Lips* is a step closer to perversity, saving itself by the traditional dodge of the veteran's impotence. He cannot perform as other men, the doctor pronounces sadly, yet he is brought out of his post-combat numbness by a 12-year-old war orphan, Eva (Katya Berger), who is living with his domestic help. The moody veteran, Paul (Pierre Clémenti), has survived World War I on the German side. Wounded in combat, he returns to his rural estate kept by caretakers who continue to care for him. Paul lives in isolation and seems troubled by dream scenarios of gross, lustful desires (not of combat, as one might expect). The pistol that he unpacks gives him pause that implies both wartime memory and threat of self harm.

The brooding veteran becomes enchanted by the girl in a series of sexually provocative scenes, edited for censorship, but intended to appear salacious. The veteran is literally pulled back from gothic suicide by Eva. As he stands on the edge of a precipice, she approaches him like a messenger from Athena, and takes him by the hand. Paul finally does kill himself when he discovers Eva in the arms of a local gypsy boy, who is closer to her own age.

The theme of the Creature/veteran and the girl is one of the mutual attractions of the traumatized veteran becoming inspired, his spirit awakened by a traumatized child, and the child's need for connection with her lost security. He is evidently inspired by the child's innocence, and sees in the child his own innocence that was broken off by his experiences in combat. After Paul develops a relationship with Eva, he is transformed, in a series of scenes, from his depressed moodiness to become a man capable of feeling happy. He begins to write. In a very sappy scene, after Eva leads him to her hideaway, an abandoned cottage, Paul tells her about the story he is writing and describes it as *their* story.

That Paul is sexually impotent from a war wound is a familiar symbol in war veteran stories that suggests the wounded veteran's loss of feeling (e.g., *The Sun Also Rises* and *The Lucky Ones* and, strongly implied in *Cutter's Way* and *The Big Chill*). Shephard (2001, p. 148), a journalist not a clinician, asserts that impotence was one of the "principal side-effects" of shell shock, although it could also be interpreted as a symptom of depression in all the cinematic cases cited above. Paul also exemplifies the vulnerability that is created by caring for another, when caring is interpreted as sexual attraction. Paul's suicide seems to be a brittle failure to adapt, and the film, unfortunately, gives us no understanding of the war traumas that lead to his death.

Gran Torino, 2008

When I was stationed at Thule Air Base in the winter of 1961, we had a base-run television station that played reruns of 1950s TV series. *Rawhide* was my personal favorite, although there wasn't a lot of competition. I watched a character named Rowdy Yates who had a rough kind of rawhide charm.

Rowdy was played by Clint Eastwood, who then went on to stardom via westerns made by an Italian director, Sergio Leone, in Spain, the so-called Spaghetti Westerns, in which the emotionally numb heroes spoke sparse dialogue, and in which brief violence was interspersed with long periods of menace.

Since then, Clint Eastwood has enjoyed steady employment as a movie actor, capitalizing on roles that tended to appeal to the stereotype of the tightlipped man of few words, vicious and dominant — a strong man who cares not what you think of him. He began directing films with the 1971 California thriller *Play Misty for Me*, in which he portrayed a victim of a mad woman. *Gran Torino* is his 29th film as a director. Here he plays Walt, a retired auto worker, just widowed, who has difficulty adapting to change. Walt is a Korean War veteran, who served with the First Cavalry in Korea, the first Army division sent to Korea and the hardest hit by the Chinese entry into the war. Walt lives in a Detroit suburb that has transformed from ethnic European, predominately Polish, to Southeast Asian, predominantly Hmong.

Eastwood has a tradition of politically incorrect humor, particularly when using satire. At age 78, he expanded that character. Walt sits on his front porch smoking cigarettes, drinking Pabst Blue Ribbon beer from crushable cans, and spits out insults at his Hmong neighbors. His prized possession is a pristine 1972 Ford Gran Torino, which is parked in his garage, frozen in time like an insect in amber.

Gran Torino begins at a Catholic funeral mass that is conducted by a 26-year-old red-haired, baby-faced priest (Christopher Carley). The contrast is immediately captured in cuts at the funeral between the grizzled Walt and the boyish priest. In a surprising way, the priest becomes a strong character who confronts Walt repeatedly with his late wife's wish that he return to the Catholic sacrament of confession.

Walt's war record is revealed in two stock ways: when he confronts the Hmong gangsters with his rifle, he shouts that he shot (insert ethnic slur) "like you and used the bodies for sandbags!" He later admits that he killed 13 enemy soldiers. Kids going through his trunk in the basement after the funeral discover his medals. He later pins his Silver Star on a Hmong neighbor, Thao (Bee Vang) whom he befriends. Walt tells him about the horror he felt while killing enemy soldiers who were trying to surrender. The film is driven to its conclusion when he acts out his guilt in a final gesture of self-sacrifice.

Critics have suggested that Eastwood is using his old Dirty Harry stereotype and has taken it to its conclusion in Walt. African American movie director Spike Lee, in a recent *New Yorker* interview, criticized Eastwood as a racist for not casting any African American actors in his 2006 Iwo Jima films (*Flags of our Fathers* and *Letters from Iwo Jima*). It is an undeniable oversight in a film like *Flags of Our Fathers*, which gave a great deal of care to achieve period authenticity, to have neglected the racial makeup in casting, and it was Eastwood who had the final say. *Gran Torino* is an Eastwood critique of racial and ethnic prejudice. Walt, in one long scene, stops his truck to confront four African American toughs who are molesting his Hmong neighbor, Sue (Ahney Her), and humiliating her Caucasian friend. Walt rescues her and dominates the toughs with the aid of his semi-automatic pistol, an undeniable reference to his famous *Dirty Harry*'s "Make my day" scene, which also involved Eastwood's character menacing an African American criminal into submission. So, while *Gran Torino* is a satiric critique of ethnic prejudice, the only African Americans of any prominence are portrayed as gang-bangers who are chased off by Walt in a furious exchange of racial slurs.

Eastwood makes a joke out of exchanging ethnic barbs with his Italian barber under the pretense of teaching Thao to act like a man. The joke runs thin, however, and ends up being unconvincing. It is extended later when Walt takes Thao to a construction site to get him hired by a foreman friend. Thao wins the job by mimicking stereotypical man-talk.

Gran Torino was shot in 32 days. (Remember Eastwood was 78!) Director of photography was Tom Stern; the story was by Nick Schenk. Eastwood only bought the script in February of 2008. It did not have the polish of his more carefully done work, such as *Mystic River* and the more recent *J. Edgar*, and scenes like the barbershop banter would have benefited from some additional takes. The final denouement, in which Walt acts out his war-time guilt, could definitely have been improved in order to be convincing. For all his skill and craftsmanship, Eastwood is a Hollywood product who has a penchant for blazing finishes.

One poignant aspect of *Gran Torino* is the alienation and antipathy that Walt shows toward his sons and their families. Eastwood gives the characters no sympathetic depth. Family therapists would wonder if PTSD wasn't a factor in Walt failing to provide a more accessible father. Survivor's guilt, which Walt definitely carried, has as one of its syndromes the tendency to drive away love and avoid affection. His two sons turn out to have values that are a statement about alienation. One son, Mitch (Brian Haley), in an apparent ploy to get possession of his father's house, tries to convince Walt to consider entering a retirement community. Walt and his son have no emotional rapport. But Walt does allow himself to feel again through the Hmong family whom he comes to protect. They are grateful. Neighbors feed him and bring him gifts that open his closed heart with their abundance. The emotion we see in Walt is a wake of years of emotional withdrawal, with perhaps the exception of his relationship with his wife. Walt apparently gave way to his passions in Korean combat. We would all forgive him that, but our judgments are not relevant. He judges himself. He believes he is the only one who knows what happened, although we know from many studies that witness testimony is highly biased and hardly a recreation, but rather a recollected version of what actually occurred.

All that finally matters is the wake of all the years since combat when veterans like Walt have piled proverbial sandbags around their existence, creating bunkers and perimeters around their conflicted emotions. What surprises viewers of *Gran Torino* is that when Walt finally does confess to the priest, he confesses the most mundane sins. The priest, anticipating more, asks "Is that *all*?" and then assigns ten *Our Fathers* and *Hail Marys* as penance. Walt doesn't mention his killing in combat. Perhaps he doesn't regard it as a sin against his Catholic faith, but it is certainly part of his soul wound. He believes that he killed men he didn't have to kill. No one else is judging him. He is judging himself and it drives him to sacrifice himself when all his cards are played.

Pardon the card game analogy, but *Gran Torino* presents a dilemma to health care professionals. When someone with survivor's guilt is in mourning for his late wife, when his culture and his neighborhood have changed to the extent that it is causing him an increasing sense of alienation, and then he is given a terminal diagnosis of lung cancer and he sees a way that he can achieve a final outcome that helps his neighbors survive, is it all right that he sacrifices himself, drawing fire, provoking a gang killing? The gang is put in jail and the pressure on the family relieved, but what we have seen on the screen is a violent version of assisted suicide.

There is a ring of a novice psychotherapist in the character of Father Janovich. When brutality strikes, when the gang beats and rapes the Hmong neighbor, the priest is drawn to the idea of revenge, even though it is alien to his beliefs. For Walt, the situation is that he is dying, and he carries with him a 55-year-old psychological trauma. He acts out his trauma guilt by becoming the victim of violence.

A killer of war veterans is the traumatic imagery of death. Hyperarousal and trauma memory combine to foster symptoms that lead to emotional isolation, which is experienced even in socially active veterans. Walt is an example of a war veteran who adjusted fairly well to a life of peace. He worked until retirement. He took obvious pride in his possessions, as the film's title suggests. But the nature of PTSD pathology takes its toll. He has grown alienated from his relatives. His wife, whom he evidently loved dearly, has died. He lives alone with his dog and is alienated from his neighbors. He finds himself surrounded by people who look to him like his old enemy at a time when he has aged to infirmity.

The scene of suicide by a hyperaroused enemy is suggestive of what Walt described to Thao as the scene of his trauma in Korea, killing enemy soldiers who are trying to surrender. The priest and the psychotherapist are confronted with the same problem of understanding the combatant's trauma imagery and translating that knowledge into customized guidance. We therapists are as lame and pedestrian as Father Janovich when we offer the few tools we have (insight, group therapy, substance abuse counseling, meditation). Father Janovich offered the Catholic sacrament of confession, but Walt didn't confess the traumas of Korea, although paradoxically, the act of confession, according to his faith, absolving him of sin, cleared the way to suicide.

All a therapist can do is take the time to see the situation through the veteran's eyes. Walt is not a very personable man. He doesn't disclose much. He has so closed himself off from his sons that they are not like him at all. Father Janovich finally sits down with Walt and drinks beer with him, but he can't fathom the nature of Walt's trauma, because Walt hasn't disclosed it.

Walt makes humor out of hostility. People around him regard him as a curmudgeon. Only his dog seems to warrant his endearment. Thao, who is an American-born Hmong, is raised in a family of recent immigrants. He must make a cultural leap if he is to adapt. A piece of irony, pointed out early in the film, noted that the Hmong immigrated in large numbers because they were Allies of the American forces in the war in Vietnam. Walt, in his closed mind, lumps all Asians into a stereotype, but the distinction was not lost on him. The Hmong gang members ridicule Thao for gardening, which, in their old-world culture, is considered women's work, and Walt is quick to point out with derision that Thao's mannerisms are effeminate.

In the final scenes, as a kind of postscript, Walt's will is read to those assembled. Thao and the priest are there and it is declared, in Walt's characteristically salty language, that his house is to go to the Church and his Gran Torino is to be given to Thao. It has been established early in the film that the car was a desired object in both cultures. Walt gives nothing to his family. He never forgave his auto-sales son for selling "rice-burners." That cultural divide cannot be bridged. The veteran cannot relate with intimacy to his family, and they move so far away they no longer share anything.

Absolute Power, 1997

Gran Torino is Eastwood's second film to deal with guilt in the aging war veteran. His 1997 *Absolute Power* portrays the Korean War veteran who is living quietly after a career as a burglar and an incarcerated felon. He appears to be creative but is socially isolated, even from his own daughter. David Baldacci published his novel about corruption in high places, *Absolute Power*, in

1996. Clint Eastwood's feature film interpretation by William Goldman was released the following year. The film adaptation greatly simplified the Baldacci plot, combining two key characters into one and focusing on the starring role of the highly principled thief. The core of the plot concerns a 66-year-old Korean War veteran, Luther Whitney (Eastwood), who is a compulsive burglar. He has been convicted and sent to prison on three different occasions. His wife has died and his daughter (Laura Linney) has shut him out of her life, although he secretly monitors her daily activities as a prosecuting attorney. Luther has been inactive in his chosen line of work for the past 20 years, but is drawn into one last burglary. Baldacci writes:

> He wondered again, for the hundredth time, why he had continued his criminal activities. It certainly wasn't the money. He had always lived simply; much of the proceeds of his burglaries had been simply given away. His choice in life had driven his wife mad with worry and forced his daughter from his life. And for the hundredth time he came away with no compelling answer to the question of why he continued to steal from the well-protected wealthy. Perhaps it was only to show that he could [p. 77].

Luther was an army ranger during the Korean War and the author gives a clue to understanding his motivation as a thief: "Not a violent person, his entire adult life had been spent right on the edge of danger" (p. 211). Eastwood's film fleshes out Luther with some of the qualities of Hermes by portraying him using many disguises and tricks to capture the crooked politician and his accomplices. Luther is accused of murdering the young wife of a fabulously wealthy man when he is trapped in the bedroom behind a one-way mirror where the loot is kept. He witnesses the man he recognizes as the president of the United States (Gene Hackman) having violent sex with a woman. The woman is about to stab the drunken president when his Secret Service agents intervene, killing her in the process.

Cynical as the plot sounds, there have been so many scandals in and connected to Washington D.C. involving sex and larceny that adding murder is not a fantastic exaggeration. The character that has evolved in Clint Eastwood's roles as an actor and director depict a man who is alone, sometimes an unnamed stranger who fights bullies and tyrants, a man who shows little emotion but much determination and grit, and then slips away into isolation again when the job is done. The character of the war veteran burglar who lives alone and is estranged from family is taken from the Baldacci novel and made the centerpiece of the film appealing to the archetype. What makes the theme archetypal is its application down through history as the lot of many veterans of foreign wars. Veterans returning from wars that were fought on foreign soil had the task of reintegrating into their homeland after experiencing the traumas of combat. There is an inevitable alienation, given that the veteran has experienced death and destruction no matter what the cause or justification of the war, while the civilian population to which he or she returns has not had those traumatic experiences.

Essential in this archetypal play down through the ages is the perception of the veteran as having special attributes that are not necessarily displayed or even called for in domestic life. These attributes have to do with the training and extreme experiences demanded by prolonged combat. Also essential in these stories, so well captured by Clint Eastwood and other popular filmmakers, is the perception that power and control are exercised by the unscrupulous and unprincipled. The romance of fiction embellishes the lone veteran to call upon the skills and discipline developed in combat to fight for justice.

Of course, the romance of fiction novels and film is depicted in large strokes. *Absolute Power* is about a felonious president of the United States brought down by an aging war veteran with extraordinary attributes of stealth and expertise. Everyday war veterans live more mundane lives in which they may not even be identified as alienated, although they usually harbor unshared memories of combat and hold civilians to a wartime standard seldom met.

Baldacci's book and Eastwood's film focus on the hypocrisy of politics which results in a moody cynicism. Baldacci puts the line in the mouth of the police detective (well played by Ed Harris): "Hell, I don't know why we should be surprised at what happened. You know what kind of person it takes to run for President? Not normal. They could start out okay, but by the time they reach that level they've sold their soul to the devil so many times and stomped the guts out of enough people that they are definitely not like you and me" (p. 466). Ruthlessness in the application of power is justified in warfare, but when it is applied in civilian life, it is seen as immoral. The veteran of combat holds back and keeps hidden what is seen as exploited by the less principled.

Eastwood ends his film version of *Absolute Power* with the war veteran, seemingly at peace, sitting and sketching his daughter as she lies injured in her hospital bed. The errant Secret Service agents-turned-assassins have attempted to murder her by pushing her car off a cliff. Although she has undergone great abuse because of her association with her father, their relationship seems to be healing.

True Grit, 2010

The movie myth-makers, the Brothers Coen, have produced another examination of the American way of death in their spirited adaptation of Charles Portis's novel *True Grit*. In doing so, the brothers revise the 1969

Henry Hathaway–John Wayne tradition that death looks good in the presence of a hero. The plot involves a 14-year-old girl whose father is killed and who subsequently has to hire a knight errant U.S. marshal — a man with true grit — to hunt down the killer. The movie shows that truly *she* is the one with the grit.

The Coen brothers continue to explore the American culture of grim death that they began in 1984 with their first noir drama of dark humor, *Blood Simple,* and reinforced with bloody mayhem in the more recent *No Country for Old Men.* Underlying the drama of *True Grit* is the archetypal theme of the Beauty and the Beast. The girl is Mattie Ross. In this version she is played by 14-year-old Hailee Steinfeld, who sets out to see justice (not revenge) done to her father's killer. She finally hires a drunken, brutish, foolish man who works as a lawman, one Rooster Cogburn. Jeff Bridges plays the nearly reprobate drunk with an air of the trickster that was lacking in John Wayne's characterization.

Death dominates the story. Mattie, when she comes to claim her father's body, finds that she has to spend the night sleeping in a coffin in the undertaker's parlor with corpses. She witnesses the deaths by hanging of three men convicted after their capture by the marshall. On her journey with the marshall and the erstwhile Texas Ranger, La Boeuf (Matt Damon), one man after another is killed by gunshot, their bodies left in grisly display. The context is emphasized when Cogburn and La Boeuf briefly discuss, while on horseback, their war veteran heritage. They were not on opposite sides in the U.S. Civil War, but the tension from the memory of animosities rises precipitously between them as they talk, when La Boeuf learns that Cogburn was with Quantrill's Raiders, who were accused of murdering civilians as irregular troops. They are on the same side now, also, with the same dangerous job to do, repeatedly killing men to do it. (It is worth noting that serving with Quantrill became a career booster for Rooster Cogburn later when he joined a Wild West show with other gunmen who got their start in the Civil War.)

A mark of the change that took place in Hollywood casting between the 1969 Hathaway version and the Coens' is the choice of the actor to play Mattie. Hathaway has 21-year-old Kim Darby cast as the young teenager. The Coens, in their wisdom, chose Miss Steinfeld, who was a girl of the appropriate age tasked to play opposite some rough characters on a perilous journey of her initiative. The two lawmen ride off without her, disdaining the prospect of bringing along a girl. Mattie shows her grit when she plunges into a river and fords it with her horse, defying the ferry boatman who refused to transport her — all in the view of Cogburn and La Boeuf, who are impressed.

The Coens are faithful to the Portis novel, lifting clear, grammatically correct dialogue without the evidence of regional accent or frontier slang.

The action takes place at the end of the 19th century, when the country west of Arkansas was Oklahoma Territory, considered a wild refuge for outlaws and Civil War veterans. The Coens call our attention to a cultural fact that Americans are prone to resorting to violence as a means to an end. French film critic Andrè Bazin (1967, p. 148) observed about American films that the Civil War is our Troy and the stories of the Wild West are our myths. The migration west is our *Odyssey*. When an apparently crazy man can gun down 20 people outside an Arizona market, one clue we have that this is not 1875 is the number of rounds he is able to fire before he is tackled.

When Rooster Cogburn and Ranger LaBoeuf discuss their respective roles in the war, the tension seems to come from Rooster's participation in an operation that was deemed murderous because it involved the killing of civilians. It seems that as our population increases, the firearms manufacturers adapt, as if from a genetic mutation of technology. Firearms seem to be the method of killing in America. In China a madman takes a knife, in other lands perhaps a machete or an IED. A madman wielding a blade can also be terrifyingly effective. In Japan, after the introduction of firearms, a hiatus of many years developed where guns were not used, because the sword was deemed not only more effective, but esthetically more pleasing.

Some say that killing with firearms is made easier if one practices regularly on video games. It is easier to pull the trigger if it is impersonal and from a greater distance. There is a spooky similarity between the alleged killer who shot up the gathering recently in Arizona, posing as he did the night before with his weapon in position suggestive of sexual prowess, and Travis Bickle, in the classic film *Taxi Driver*, posing in front of a mirror as if in a street confrontation. Both gunmen, one fictional, one real, seem to be captivated by an ancient archetype, the sort that seeds the delusions of psychotics. Now, in America, as well as around the world, the would-be killers can post their pictures on a web page prior to their carrying out their madness. Movie makers help promote the myth, and celebrities, real or would-be and delusional, pick up the symbolism because it is so alluring.

Waltz with Bashir, 2009

Waltz with Bashir begins with a pack of 26 dogs running through dark streets, eyes glowing brightly, knocking over café street furniture, frightening pedestrians. The dream is told by a veteran of Israel's 1982 war with Lebanon. The interviewer is the documentary's director (and writer and producer), Ari Folman, in animated form. He is attempting to glean from his subject memories of the war. Although the veteran recalls being in Lebanon, he has no specific memories of the massacres that took place in the Palestinian refugee camps in West Beirut. All he has are nightmares.

Ari Folman explains in an interview that he decided to make the film about himself. He advertised on the Internet to find veterans who participated in the war, and sought to interview other veterans whom he knew personally. He took along animators when he went to interview the veterans, and the animators drew not only the scenes of the conversations, but the scenes of the battles and occupation that the interviewees were describing. Folman stated that as he pursued his task, memories began returning and he experienced hallucinatory flashbacks. He states at one point in the film, "I'm starting to remember. I've met people. I've heard stories. Stories about myself. I don't want to believe them."

Many of the scenes are described in surreal depictions. Folman likened his combat experiences to being on a bad acid trip — "the most surreal thing on earth." The worst of the traumas, which seem to be at the basis of his dissociation, was the witnessing of the massacres of the Palestinian refugee camps of Sabra and Shatila, which were perpetrated by the Christian Phalangists who carved crosses into the chests of the corpses and prisoners. The Israeli soldiers, he said, formed circles of witnesses. "Where were you in that circle? At age 19, you took the role of the Nazi." The director's family members were killed at Auschwitz.

One veteran confesses that he'd been waiting for someone to ask about his experiences in combat. He told the story of having his tank attacked with an RPG, the crew evacuating and running for the ocean. He alone survived to swim. He said that he normally couldn't swim 100 yards, but he was so scared that he managed to swim back to his unit's base — six miles by his estimate. He said that he feels guilt whenever he meets the families of the dead. Folman's narrative touches on the terrible collateral damage when, for instance, a village is destroyed by aircraft attacking a car loaded with terrorists.

Folman, in his commentary that is featured on the DVD, described his bizarre homecoming when he was on leave. He said that it was a mere 20 minutes' distance from the combat zone to the town where he lived. In the film he is depicted as being isolated among his young age peers who didn't care about what was going on in the war.

The director changes his technique at the end of *Waltz with Bashir*, using straight documentary footage of the corpses and mourners in the refugee camps. He said that it was his intention all along to leave the viewers with those scenes. It is as if, in the end, he did not trust the skills of his animators. This is reminiscent of advocates and clinicians who feel that they have to hit their audiences over the head with graphic descriptions of the traumas that were perpetrated on their clients. It is a display of anger intended to wake everyone up and experience the reality. He wanted to create "a chronology of the massacre." He said the Israelis are to blame because they did not stop the massacre. He speculated that such things are beyond the system of the ordinary human brain: "What do you do after you realize there is a mass murder going on?"

Waltz with Bashir pays tribute to Francis Coppola's *Apocalypse Now*, Folman's favorite film. He captures the surreal and cinematic beauty of flares burning in the night sky and the bizarre destruction that a squad of infantrymen can inflict on a passenger car that happens into a free fire zone. The *Bashir* of the title refers to the candidate for president of Lebanon who was assassinated by a Palestinian terrorist, an action that was credited with touching off the war in Lebanon. Bashir's picture is everywhere in Beirut in the form of huge posters on the sides of buildings, pasted on trucks and even the butts of rifles.

Folman deserves credit for the boldness of his creative effort, that of integrating his wartime experiences into a collective effort that could be shared with the world. I don't have a personal affinity for film animation, but I feel that *Waltz With Bashir* is a riveting and powerful statement made arguably better because it is animated. Describing his condition as "post-traumatic sketch disorder," he compares himself to the veterans of Vietnam, the Soviet Union, Afghanistan, and Iraq, as well as U.S. and Soviet forces who fought in Afghanistan, and U.S. and British who ask "What am I doing here, and why?"

Made in Dagenham, 2010

This British film dramatizes a 1968 labor strike that actually occurred at a Ford manufacturing plant in which 187 women machinists sought to establish a pay scale equal to men. It is a well-made, emotionally moving film of a true event that changed the way women were regarded in the workforce throughout the industrialized world. Albert Passengram (Bob Hoskins), a factory union official supporting the women, identifies himself as a war veteran who fought Rommel, said that, in the context, he wasn't afraid of what was happening. His reasons for supporting the cause are personal — he was raised by his single mother, who supported him by performing hard work at unfairly low wages.

Made in Dagenham was directed by Nigel Cole from a screenplay by William Ivory. It features Rita O'Grady (Sally Hawkins) as one of the women operating sewing machines in a factory making seat covers for Fords. She and her husband, Eddie (Daniel Mays), who also works at the factory, live in a housing development known as The Estate. (A more peaceful Estate than we saw in *Harry Brown*.) Rita appears at first to be a timid, friendly woman, busily caring for her two children when she is not working at the factory. She is drawn into the role of leader in the labor dispute when the other shop steward, Connie (Geraldine James), refuses to do so. Connie's husband, George (Roger Lloyd Pack), a veteran of World War II, suffers from nightmares in which he lunges out of bed and grapples with his wife in a terrible agony. Connie is a principal in the strike, even as Rita takes over the role as spokesperson. Both women must juggle their family responsibilities with the increasingly demanding duties coordinating the strike. Eddie is for the most part supportive of his wife, who had supported him in previous labor disputes on the men's side. However, he is tasked by the increasing burden of house-husbandry and wage loss as the factory is closed. Connie is an older woman, and her husband is emotionally more dependent and needy, and, although he supports her, he clearly is not doing well. He was an RAF gunner on a flight crew and bailed out, wounded and close to death, during the war. As the strike draws Connie further from him, he commits suicide, hanging himself in their little apartment. It is another death that appears to be the result of the war, but not one for the record.

Rita's growth as strike leader is quite moving. We see her first trying to confront her son's school teacher who had beaten the boy. When the teacher is adamant and condescending, she backs down. Gradually, however, she finds her voice, and when she is brought along to a meeting between union officials and the Ford administrators, she balks at the union man who is a toady to the Ford representatives, and speaks out about the injustice of the inequality of pay between men and women at the plant.

Throughout the film the women must deal with sexist comments and the condescension of men. Even the British government's secretary of state (played by Miranda Richardson with the verve and force reminiscent of Margaret Thatcher) has her own experiences as a victim of sexism.

It is worth dwelling on the role of the war veteran's spouse, Connie, because she is put in terrible conflict by her husband's suffering. He needs her support and is dependent on her to keep her domestic routine. Rita points out that all the women workers have to deal with problems as they assert their rights, but Connie's conflict seems to be more profound. When her husband follows her out the door as she goes off to her strike gathering, she reminds him of his history, when he did his duty to serve in his country's defense. He responds that he's not sure if he would do it again if there was another war, and she retorts, "Oh, yes, you would. You would do your duty." But when he hangs himself, she feels an awful guilt in her grief. When Rita urges Connie to participate, she says, "You've got a life, too. You've got to live it. Can't have the war destroying *two* people."

When Rita speaks to the union members assembled at a national meeting, she alludes to George's military service and says, "It was a matter of principle. You have to stand up. You have to do what was right, because otherwise you wouldn't be able to look yourself in the mirror." She challenges the union members, half of whom are men: "When did that change? When did we decide to stop fighting? We're not separated by sex, but only by those who are prepared to go into battle."

Those of us in the field of psychotherapy often see that the more severe the veteran's posttraumatic symptoms, the more alienated and socially avoidant he becomes. The veteran's dependence on his domestic partner increases in correlation with his PTSD symptom severity. She becomes his social front. She deals with the trades people and relatives. She schleps the kids to-and-fro. She prepares the holiday activities. She accompanies him to his medical appointments and talks to the doctors when he shuts down. She watches and monitors his symptoms and keeps track his medicine. She intervenes with the children and explains to them and the neighbors that her husband is a war veteran who has problems. Because of all these duties, her life is limited and buffeted by his symptom fluctuation. The fear that she harbors is just what Connie experienced when she returned to her apartment and found her husband dead.

As previously mentioned, *Made in Dagenham* is based on a real event in history. The closing credits feature the now-elderly women describing their experience in the strike and shows newsreel footage of their accomplishments. As one of these women says proudly, "We really are ladies." Groups for spouses of veterans would have a proper place in that pantheon.

In 1970, the British Parliament passed the Equal Pay Act, which has influenced the status of women workers in the industrialized world. The allusion to the sacrifice of war veterans proved to be a rallying cry for the cause.

Coriolanus, 2011

Ralph Fiennes adapted William Shakespeare's play *Coriolanus* to film, released in 2012, with great success. This is the story of a Roman general, Caius Martius Coriolanus, played by Fiennes himself with fierce intensity. The film modernizes the story, which takes place in a city called Rome, that is located somewhere in the Baltics. (The movie was filmed in Serbia.) The scenes of combat show modern urban assault methods. The Romans are fighting a border dispute with the Volscians, who are led by an equally fierce opponent, Tullus Aufidius (Gerard Butler).

Shakespeare's play and Fiennes's adaptation make the story interesting from our perspective, because Caius Martius is considered to be a national hero who leads his troops with inspiring example. His leadership gains him the honorary sobriquet of Coriolanus, named after the city, Corioli, that he has conquered. However, when he returns to Rome and is praised by the Senate and invited to run for political office, he cannot condescend to ingratiate himself to the citizens. The populace has been hungry and demonstrating in the streets for bread, a condition that was historically true in Shakespeare's time. Caius Martius meets the demonstrators with contempt. He shouts at the crowd, "Get you home, you fragments." Although he is a great fighter and a national war hero (literally personally attacking a strong enemy position when the troops were hesitating), he cannot adapt his talents to a second career.

Coriolanus has two truly stellar co-stars: Brian Cox plays the slick politician Menenius with believable flair; and Vanessa Redgrave plays Caius's mother, Volumnia. Her son is literally the light in her eyes. "His wounds become him," she purrs. "He has large scars to show the people." When she sits beside his naked torso, wrapping his wounds with gauzy bandages, their intimacy seems erotic, such that when his wife, Virgilia (Jessica Chastain), opens the door and sees them together, she discretely closes it again.

When Coriolanus is rejected by the citizens, who are angry at his pride and contempt for them, they rebel and cry out for his banishment. Fiennes plays the scenes of Coriolanus vis-à-vis the crowds as if he were a highly talented introvert whose genius does not extend to social poise. He can be hard, he can turn his intensity to a high pitch, making him violent and fearless, but he cannot charm his constituency. He is awkward and his words stumble out. "I would be council!" he shouts, when he campaigns for their votes. The citizens respond from the crowd: "He fought our enemies, but he doesn't love us."

When the senate meets to publicly laud Coriolanus on his return to Rome from combat, he walks out of the hall rather than listen to the president recite his accomplishments. Here, Fiennes does a nice touch. As Coriolanus is waiting outside the council chamber, alone, hearing the echoes of the president's praise, a deep rumble drowns out the voice as a janitor pushes his supply cart noisily down the hard floor of the institution's hall, giving the warrior a wary look that presages his fate.

Fiennes's *Coriolanus* adaptation to modern Europe works and has some application to the United States of today, and could be seen as applying to many combat veterans who return from overseas conflict. They are lauded as heroes, often applied as an impersonal appellation, only to find themselves unable to do civilian work and adapt to the customs and expectations of everyday life. (No less a personage than General Douglas MacArthur encountered this kind of reception when he returned to the U.S. after being fired from his job commanding the Allied forces in Korea. MacArthur also had a mother who effectively managed his career, even renting an apartment near West Point when he was a cadet. MacArthur had the good fortune of not returning home at the end of World War II, but instead took command of the Occupation of Japan, where he could reign more suitably as an all-powerful figure who was above the people.)

The weakest aspect of Fiennes's otherwise-excellent film is his treatment of the Volscians. When Coriolanus is banished from Rome, he offers his services to the Volscians. He and the Volscian leader, Aufidius, have a competitive hatred of each other. They have fought to a draw previously, both being knocked unconscious by a mortar blast as they fought bloodily with knives, their seconds hauling them off. Fiennes doesn't seem to quite appreciate the Volscians any more than did Shakespeare. The warriors are depicted as rabble. (Their pre-battle ceremonies are like the bunker party of *Platoon*, with electric guitar blaring, a frenzy of Dionysian revelers. If you saw the 1981 German film *Das Boot*, you will appreciate the parallel, when troops party before going to battle.)

Fiennes retains Shakespeare's emphasis on the wounds that Caius Martius incurs to become Coriolanus. His mother and the councilmen laud them, but Coriolanus conceals his wounds, not from shame, but out of respect for the suffering they caused him. Each wound has its own history, some causing the blood that masks his face in battle, some hidden and, therefore, all the more intimate.

John Logan must be credited with a skillful adaptation and modernization of the play. But he couldn't improve on the Bard's lines:

VOLUMNIA: O, he is wounded, — I thank the gods for 't.
MENENIUS, THE POLITICIAN: So do I too, if it be not too much. — Brings a victory in 's pocket, the wounds become him.

And it is Menenius who recognizes the warrior who is attempting to tame his temper, when he says with a certain ominous warning: "He's a bear indeed that lives like a lamb."

Postscript

I wanted to give a perspective of history to this topic of alienation in war veterans, and so I have presented it here in a variety of ways, and have relied mostly on movies of the 20th century, partly because they reflect not only the various situations of the war veterans, but also of the culture surrounding them. Essentially, this alienation exists in the veteran in the form of a sense of being different from others in the culture and society in which he or she was once familiar. Alienation is enhanced by the veteran feeling isolated from others because of the experience of combat and it is helpful to see the broader context of the universality of this feeling among war veterans. Japanese film director Akira Kurosawa demonstrated the alienation in the form of historical settings, as the samurai warrior who is "discharged" from service and wanders, unconnected, in a society to which he does not belong and must sell his warrior services to survive. In *Stray Dog*, Kurosawa presented a more complex dual *après guerre* setting in modern Japan of the veteran who overcame his alienation to seek conventional employment in contrast to the veteran who strayed into further alienation and crime. This theme was repeated in a U.S. *noir* setting in *Suddenly*.

The veterans of the Wars on Terror (the 1991 Gulf War, and the wars in Iraq and Afghanistan) are shown largely as struggling with alienation caused by their combat in foreign lands that impedes their settling back into peaceful coexistence with family and friends, often despite a friendly homecoming. Electronic media, along with the ongoing nature of the wars, serve to keep them conscious of their combat experiences. The veterans express antipathy in reaction to the over-psychologizing, if you will, of the Vietnam War veteran. The veterans of Iraq and Afghanistan combat insist that their reactions are normal —(they would take the "D" out of PTSD)— and they are normal for combat veterans, but that is not to say that their reactions are not problematic, since the society to which they return does not share their norm. The innocence of American society is kept sheltered through a consensual censorship, a form of denial that keeps the ugliness of warfare away from everyday life and may be a factor behind the high rate of suicide among combat veterans.

Many films of postwar adjustment portray the war veteran as buffeted by events in culture. Films of the 1930s era of the Great Depression dramatize the veteran's difficulty finding his place again in society. Films of the *noir* era of the decades following World War II show the veteran battling criminal forces to reestablish his place. This era, I have contended, portrays the veteran as essentially whole, but prevented from settling down by elements in his environment. Films of the *noir* period used the war veteran as a plot device that pitted him against criminals, often presenting him as a falsely accused, righteous figure who had to prove his innocence. This *noir* era was culturally dark, while the veteran, who had, in a sense, fought the forces of darkness on foreign shores, had to establish his place to build a better society, a very Odyssean theme. Films of this era seemed largely to be siding with the veteran, dramatizing his alienation as the understandably right position to take for the times. Alienation was seldom seen as a psychological struggle with posttraumatic memories. More often, if the veteran was deviant, as in *Suddenly*, he was shown to be a product of poor parenting. *Lonely Are the Brave* shows a veteran literally at odds with his modern society, a cowboy just back from Korean combat, who fights authority and defies containment.

The era of the Vietnam War was foreshadowed by the Korean War veterans and a time in which war was an unwanted imposition on a tired society seeking peace yet harboring persistent perceptions of threat (Pash, 2012). The veteran of World War II was a more commonly encountered product of a war that had to be fought. He was one of a massive population upheaval, a national effort in which his settling down was part of a national settling. The Korean War and the Vietnam War were the products of political campaigns against Communism that did not have national consensus. The Vietnam War famously divided the nation (or perhaps it should be said that it exposed a division in the nation). The veteran was vilified, if not personally, at least collectively, as being responsible somehow for the war being fought. World War I veteran Ford Madox Ford had an insight into the Vietnam War generation when he wrote about the division that existed after his war between those who fought and those who stayed at home and afterwards wished they had fought. His war veteran character, Christopher Tietjens, in *Parade's End*, says,

> After the war was over the civilian population would contrive to attach [discredit] to every man who had been at the front as a fighting soldier. After all that was natural enough. The majority of the male population was civilian and once war was over they would bitterly regret that they had not gone. They would take it out on the ex-soldiers all right! [Ford, 1992, pp. 803–4].

(Ford's insight suggests that the alienation experienced by the returning war veteran is at least in part the alienation felt by the non-combatants toward the veteran.)

The generation that came of age during the Vietnam War era was the offspring of those who experienced World War II. They were a national population that was divided by an acrimonious difference of opinion about the necessity to fight in a very distant land that seemed to have little meaning to Americans apart from a few who grasped what they claimed was its geopolitical significance in keeping the Communist influence in check. It was important that there was so little said about the influence of trauma on the World War II combatants. In films, more often than not, the veteran of World War II was depicted as functional, but having to adjust to a dark, threatening world. Alcoholism was the disease of that generation, although it was rarely attributed to war trauma. Even the psychiatric diagnostic manual of the time buried the pathology of trauma, diverting it to disorders of hysteria (Rosenheck, 1986; Hyler & Spitzer, 1978). The impact on the offspring of those affected by World War II and the Korean War was manifested in intense feelings for and against engagement in more combat. And as Ford Madox Ford predicted, the veterans were blamed for the war and vilified for its traumatic impact. The emotional impact of trauma again became a disorder and the disorder itself (PTSD) was associated with flaws of character. Films depicting the Vietnam War era portrayed this impact by depicting war veteran characters who were at various times emotionally troubled, criminal, or, just as often (for such was the division), straight, powerful men of conscience who fought for justice. A few films, like *In Country*, *Cutter's Way*, and *Jacknife* addressed the complexity of adjustment. It is significant that the veterans of the current Wars on Terror are a select body of volunteers, men and women who are relatively few in number in proportion to the general population, and who, aside from the national tax burden, are left to absorb within their families the traumatic impact of combat.

There has been an ongoing denial that war — combat — is as traumatizing as it obviously is. At the end of World War II, director John Huston made his documentary about the psychiatric treatment of veterans. His documentary was shelved and a new one was created, one that blamed parenting for the psychiatric problems of veterans. After the Vietnam War veterans seeking a PTSD disability were repeatedly accused of malingering, and a DVA-IG investigation that showed minimal fakery did not offset the cynicism. Currently, in Washington State, there is an ongoing dispute that has surfaced in the news that the army forensic team has changed PTSD diagnoses of returning Iraq and Afghanistan war veterans, using unrealistic test guidelines, with the misguided belief, expressed openly, that a saving would result for the national treasury if the lifetime PTSD disabilities were reduced (Bernton, 2012a & 2012b). This denial seems to state that combat in wartime is not as bad (i.e., traumatizing) as veterans claim.

In all the wars that the United States has fought on foreign lands since the beginning of the 20th century, veterans of combat have returned home changed by their experiences to find that they do not fit as comfortably into the society they left, usually in marked contrast to how they may have idealized their homecoming. The alienation may dissipate, but it does not extinguish, and the war veterans experience its vestiges throughout their lives, hopefully softened to some extent by relationships and the veterans' participation in society and the presentation of their own narratives.

History tells us that none of this is new. Only technology changes. The enemy is still dehumanized. The killing is more efficient and the sensibilities of the combatants are damaged, if not traumatized, by the experience. The more remote the war, the more difficult it is to fit back into society, all the while remembering what it used to feel like to fit in socially and culturally.

Bibliography

Adams, M. C. C. (1995). Retelling the tale: Wars in common memory. In Gabor S. Boritt (Ed.), *War Comes Again: Comparative vistas on the Civil War and World War II*. New York: Oxford University Press.

Ahl, F., & Roisman, H. M. (1996). *The* Odyssey *reformed*. Ithaca: Cornell University Press.

Alexander, C. (2009). *The war that killed Achilles: The true story of Homer's* Iliad *and the Trojan War*. New York: Viking.

American Psychiatric Association (2005). *Diagnostic and statistical manual of mental disorders, fourth edition (DSM-IV)*. Washington, D. C.: A. P. A.

Angell, M. (2011, June 23). The epidemic of mental illness: Why? The illusions of psychiatry (7/14/2011). *The New York Review of Books*.

Austin, N. (1981). *Archery at the dark of the moon: Poetic problems in Homer's* Odyssey. Berkeley: University of California Press.

Baldacci, D. (1996). *Absolute power*. New York: Warner Books.

Bazin, A. (1967). *What is cinema?* Berkeley: University of California Press.

Bell, N., Hunt, P., Harford, T., & Kay, A. (2011). Deployment to a combat zone and other risks for mental health-related disability discharge from the U.S. Army: 1994–2007. *Journal of Traumatic Stress*, 24(1), 34–43.

Bergman, I. (1960). *Four screenplays of Ingmar Bergman*. (L. Malmstrom & D. Kushner, Trans.). New York: Simon & Shuster.

Bernton, H. (2012, April 22). New PTSD guidelines fault Madigan's screening tests. *Seattle Times*.

Bernton, H. (2012, May 24). Caseload bogs down military disability evaluations. *Seattle Times*.

Bierce, A. (2012). *The Devil's dictionary, tales, and memoirs*. S. T. Joshi (Ed.). New York: Library of America.

Borde, R., & Chaumeton, E. (2002). *A panorama of American film noir: 1941–1953*. (Paul Hammond, Trans.). San Francisco: City Lights Books.

Bram, C. (1995). *Father of Frankenstein*. New York: Penguin.

Briere, J., Hodges, M., & Godbout, N. (2010). Traumatic stress, affect dysregulation, and dysfunctional avoidance: A structural equation model. *Journal of Traumatic Stress*, 23(6), 767–774.

Briere, J., & Scott, C. (2006). *Principles of trauma therapy: A guide to symptoms, evaluation, and treatment*. Thousand Oaks, CA: Sage.

213

Buruma, I. (1996). Samurai of swat. In *The missionary and the libertine: Love and war in east and west.* New York: Random House.

Buruma, I. (2003). *Inventing Japan: 1953–1964.* New York: Modern Library.

Buss, R. (1994) *French film noir.* New York: Marion Boyars.

Cacioppo, J. T., Reis, H. T., & Zautra, A. J. (2011). Social resilience: The value of social fitness with an application to the military. *American Psychologist, 66*(1), 43–51.

Calohan, J., Peterson, K., Peskind, E., & Raskind, M. (2010). Prazosin treatment of trauma nightmares and sleep disturbance in soldiers deployed in Iraq. *Journal of Traumatic Stress, 23*(5), 645–648.

Capa, R. (2001). *Slightly out of focus.* New York: Modern Library.

Caplan, P. (2011). *When Johnny and Jane come marching home: How all of us can help veterans.* Cambridge: MIT Press.

Casey, G. (2011). Comprehensive soldier fitness: A vision for psychological resilience in the U.S. Army. *American Psychologist, 66*(1), 1–3.

Castner, B. (2012) T*he long walk: A story of war and the life that follows.* Garden City, N.Y.: Doubleday.

Chandler, R. (1981). *Selected letters of Raymond Chandler* F. MacShane (Ed.). New York: Columbia University Press.

Chu, J. A. (2010). Posttraumatic Stress Disorder: Beyond DSM-V. *The American Journal of Psychiatry, 167*(6), 615.

Clay, J. S. (1983). *The wrath of Athena: Gods and men in the* Odyssey. Princeton: Princeton University Press.

Cocteau, J. (1972) *Beauty and the beast: Diary of a film.* (Ronald Duncan, Trans.). New York: Marion Boyars.

Corman, R., Matthews, M., & Seligman, M. (2011). Comprehensive soldier fitness: Building resilience in a challenging institutional context. *American Psychologist, 66*(1), 4–9.

Curtis, J. (1998). *James Whale: A new world of gods and monsters.* Boston: Faber & Faber.

Daugherty, T. (2011). *Just one catch: A biography of Joseph Heller.* New York: St. Martin's Press.

Davis, J. E. (2000). Oliver Stone's *Born on the Fourth of July* experience. In R. B. Toplin (Ed.), *Oliver Stone's USA: Film, history, and controversy.* Lawrence: University Press of Kansas.

Davis, N. Z. (1983). *The Return of Martin Guerre.* Cambridge: Harvard University Press.

Denby, D. (2009, December 13). Review of *The Messenger. The New Yorker,* 97.

Denby, D. (2010, March 8). Out of the west: Clint Eastwood's long journey. *The New Yorker,* 52–59.

Desser, D. (1993). The wartime films of John Huston: Film noir and the emergence of the therapeutic. In G. Studlar and D. Desser (Eds.), *Reflections in a male eye: John Huston and the American experience.* Washington, D. C.: Smithsonian Institution Press.

Dickson, P., & Allen, T. (2004). *The Bonus Army: An American epic.* New York: Walter.

Dixon, W., & Foster, G. (2008). *A short history of film.* New Brunswick: Rutgers University Press.

Doherty, T. (1993). *Projections of war: Hollywood, American culture, and World War II.* New York: Columbia University Press.

Dower, J. (1999). *Embracing defeat: Japan in the wake of World War II.* New York: W. W. Norton.

Early, E. (1992). *The raven's return.* Brooklyn: Chiron.

Early, E. (2003). *The war veteran in film.* Jefferson, NC: McFarland.

Edelman, G. (2004). *Wider than the sky: The phenomenal gift of consciousness.* New Haven: Yale University Press.

Faust, D. G. (2008). *This republic of suffering: Death and the American Civil War.* New York: Alfred A. Knopf.

Festinger, L. (1957). *A theory of cognitive dissonance.* Stanford: Stanford University Press.

Figley, Charles R. (Ed.). (1978). *Stress disorders among Vietnam veterans: Theory, research, and treatment.* New York: Brunner/Mazel.

Ford, F. M. (1992). *Parade's End.* New York: Everyman's Library.

Fuller, S., with Fuller, C. L, & Rudes, J. H. (2002). *A third face: My tale of writing, fighting, and filmmaking.* New York: Alfred A. Knopf.

Fussell, P. (1975). *The Great War and modern memory.* New York, NY: Oxford University Press.

Fussell, P. (1988). Killing in verse and prose. In *Thank God for the atom bomb and other essays* (pp. 125–144). New York: Summit Books.

Gillingham, J. (1999) *Richard I.* New Haven: Yale University Press.

Gottman, J., Gottman, J., & Atkins, C. (2011). The comprehensive soldier fitness program: Family skills component. *American Psychologist, 66*(1), 52–57.

Greene, G. (1977). *The Third Man.* New York: Penguin.

Griffin, M., Resick, P., & Galoviski, T. (2012). Does physiologic response to loud tones change following cognitive-behavioral treatment for Posttraumatic Stress Disorder? *Journal of Traumatic Stress Studies, 25,* 25–32.

Grimm, J. & W. (1944, 1972). Bearskin. In *The complete Grimm's fairy tales* (pp. 467–472). (M. Hunt, Trans., J. Stern, Revised.). New York: Pantheon.

Grossman, D. (1995, 2009). *On killing: The psychological cost of learning to kill in war and society.* New York: Back Bay Books.

Halprin, M. (2012). *In sunlight and in shadow.* New York: Houghton Mifflin Harcourt.

Hamilton, I. (1988). *In search of J. D. Salinger.* New York: Random House.

Hemingway, E. (1925, 2003). Soldier's home. In *In our time.* New York: Scribner.

Herman, J. L. (1992, 1997). *Trauma and recovery.* New York: Basic Books.

Hexter, R. (1993). *A Guide to the* Odyssey*: A commentary on the English translation of Robert Fitzgerald.* New York: Vintage.

Hicks, M. H-R. (2011). [Editorial] Mental health screening and coordination of care for soldiers deployed to Iraq and Afghanistan. *American Journal of Psychiatry, 168,* 341–343.

Hillman, J. (1999). *The force of character.* New York: Random House.

Hillman, J. (2004). *A terrible love of war.* New York: Penguin.

Hinley, T. (1997). *Raymond Chandler: A biography.* New York: Atlantic Monthly Press.

Hirano, K. (1992). *Mr. Smith goes to Tokyo: Japanese cinema under the American occupation, 1945–1952.* Washington, D. C.: Smithsonian Institution Press.

Hoge, C. W. (2010). *Once a warrior always a warrior.* Guilford, CT: Globe Pequot Press.

Hoge, C. W., Castro, C. A., Messer, S. C., McGurk, D., Cotting, D. I., & Koffman, R. L. (2004). Combat duty in Iraq and Afghanistan: Mental health problems and barriers to care. *New England Journal of Medicine, 351,* 13–22.

Holm, T. (1966). *Strong hearts wounded souls: Native American veterans of the Vietnam War.* Austin: University of Texas Press.

Holt, J. C. (1982). *Robin Hood.* New York: Thames and Hudson.

Homer. (1996). *The Odyssey* (R. Fagles, Trans.). New York: Viking.

Horwitz, T. (1999). *Confederates in the attic: Dispatches from the unfinished Civil War.* New York: Vintage.

Hundt, N., & Holohan, D. (2012). The role of shame in distinguishing perpetrators of intimate partner violence in U.S. veterans. *The Journal of Traumatic Stress Studies, 25*(2), 191–197.

Hyler, S., & Spitzer, R. (1978). Hysteria split asunder. *American Journal of Psychiatry, 135*(12), 1500–1504.

Jakupcak, M., & Varra, E. (2010). Treating Iraq and Afghanistan war veterans with PTSD who are at high risk for suicide. *Cognitive and Behavioral Practice* [doi:10.1016/j.cbpra. 209.08.007].

Jones, E., Fear, N., & Wessley, S. (2007). Shell shock and mild traumatic brain injury: A historical review. *American Journal of Psychiatry, 164*(11), 1641–1645.

Jones, J. (1978). *Whistle*. New York: Open Road.

Jung, C. G. (1959). *Aion: researches into the phenomenology of the self,* vol. 9., pt. ii *Collected Works*. (R. F. C. Hull, Trans.). Princeton: Princeton University Press.

Jung, C. G. (1964, 1957). The undiscovered self. In *Civilization in transition,* vol. 10, *Collected Works*. (R.F.C. Hull, Trans.). Princeton: Princeton University Press.

Jung, C. G. (1969). A review of the complex theory. In *The structure and dynamics of the psyche,* vol. 8, *Collected Works*. (R.F.C. Hull, Trans.). Princeton: Princeton University Press.

Jung, C. G. (1971, 1936). *The archetypes and the collective unconscious,* 2d ed., vol. 9, pt. 1 *Collected Works*. (R. F. C. Hull, Trans.). Princeton: Princeton University Press.

Kardiner, A. (1941). *The traumatic neuroses of war*. New York: Harper & Bros.

Knight, S. (1994). *Robin Hood: A complete study of the English outlaw*. Cambridge: Blackwell.

Kuhn, E., Drescher, K., Ruzek, J., & Rosen, C. (2010). Aggressive and unsafe driving in male veterans receiving residential treatment for PTSD. *Journal of Traumatic Stress, 23*(3), 399–402.

Kurosawa, A. (1982). *Something like an autobiography*. (Audie Bock, Trans.). New York: Alfred A. Knopf.

Krystal, H. (1967). *Massive psychic trauma*. New York: International Universities Press.

Krystal, H. (1978). Trauma and affect. *The Psychoanalytic Study of the Child, 33,* 81–116.

Lanius, R. A., Vermetten, E., Loewenstein, R. J., Brand, B., Schmahl, C., Bremner, J. D., & Spiegel, D. (2010). Emotion modulation in PTSD: Clinical and neurobiological evidence for a dissociative subtype. *The American Journal of Psychiatry, 167*(6), 640–647.

Lanzmann, C. (2012). *The Patagonian hare*. (Frank Wynne, Trans.). New York: Farrar, Straus & Giroux.

Lattimore, R. (Trans.). (1959). *Hesiod*. Ann Arbor: University of Michigan Press.

Lifton, R. J. (1978). Advocacy and corruption in the healing profession. In C.R. Figley (Ed.), *Stress disorders among Vietnam veterans: Theory, research, and treatment*. New York: Bruner/Mazel.

MacShane, F. (1985). *Into eternity: The life of James Jones, American writer*. Boston: Houghton Mifflin.

Marlantes, K. (2009). *Matterhorn*. New York: Atlantic Monthly Press.

Marlantes, K. (2011). *What it is like to go to war*. New York: Atlantic Monthly Press.

Mason, B. A. (1985). *In country*. New York: Harper & Row.

Mauldin, B. (1945). *Up front*. New York: Henry Holt.

McBride, J. (2001). *Searching for John Ford*. New York: St. Martin's Press.

McCarthy, C. (2005). *No country for old men*. New York: Alfred A. Knopf.

McGilchrist, I. (2009). *The master and his emissary: The divided brain and the making of the western world*. New Haven: Yale University Press.

Melville, A. D. (Trans.). (1985). *Ovid metamorphoses*. New York: Oxford University Press.

Merwin, W. S. (Trans.) (2004). *Sir Gawain and the green knight*. New York, NY: Alfred A. Knopf.

Mettler, S. (2005). *Soldiers to citizens: The GI Bill and the making of the greatest generation*. New York: Oxford University Press.

Murnaghan, S. (1987). *Disguise and recognition in the* Odyssey. Princeton: Princeton University Press.

Negler, M. N. (1996). Dread goddess revisited. In S.L. Schein (Ed.), *Reading the* Odyssey (pp. 141–152). Princeton: Princeton University Press.

Nagy, G. (1996). *The best of the Achaeans,* rev. ed. Baltimore: Johns Hopkins University Press.

Nagy, G. (1999). *Homeric questions*. Austin: University of Texas Press.

Neupert, R. (2002). *A history of the French new wave cinema*. Madison: University of Wisconsin Press.

Otto, W. F. (1954). *The Homeric gods: The spiritual significance of Greek Religion*. (Moses Hadas, Trans.). New York: Pantheon.

Pash, M. L. (2012). *In the shadow of the greatest generation: The Americans who fought the Korean War*. New York: New York University Press.

Prince, S. (1991). *The warrior's camera*. Princeton: Princeton University Press.

Pucci, P. (1987). *Odysseus Polutropos: Intertextual readings in the* Odyssey *and the* Iliad. Ithaca: Cornell University Press.

Pucci, P. (1996). The song of the sirens. In S. I. Schein (Ed.), *Reading the* Odyssey (pp. 191–200). Princeton: Princeton University Press.

Reid, B., & Bringhurst, R. (1984). *The raven steals the light*. Seattle: University of Washington Press.

Remarque, E. M. (1930). *The road back*. (A. W. Wheen, Trans.). New York: Ballantine.

Renoir, J. (1973). *My life in films*. Paris: Da Capo.

Renoir, J. (1998). *Renoir on Renoir*. (Carol Volk, Trans.). Cambridge: Cambridge University Press.

Rhodios, A. (1997). *The Argonautika: The story of Jason and the quest for the golden fleece*. (P. Green, Trans.). Berkeley: University of California Press.

Richie, D. (1998). *The Films of Akira Kurosawa*, 3d ed. Berkeley: University of California Press.

Rogers, C. R., & Wallen, J. L. (1946). *Counseling with Returned servicemen*. New York: McGraw-Hill.

Rosenfield, I. (1992). *The strange, familiar, and forgotten: An anatomy of consciousness*. New York: Alfred A. Knopf.

Rosenheck, R. (1986). Impact of posttraumatic stress disorder of World War II on the next generation. *Journal of Nervous and Mental Disease*, 174(6), 319–327.

Ross, L. (1997) *Picture*. New York: Modern Library.

Salinger, J. D. (1953, 1991). For Esmé—With love and squalor. In *Nine stories* (pp. 83–114). New York: Little, Brown.

Sapolsky, R. (1998). *Why zebras don't get ulcers: An updated guide to stress, stress-related diseases, and coping*. New York: W. H. Freeman.

Saunders, M. (1996). *Ford Madox Ford: A dual life, Vol. II: The after-war world*. New York: Oxford University Press.

Schmidt, J. (1980). *Larousse Greek and Roman mythology*. New York: McGraw-Hill.

Scurfield, R. M. (2004). *A Vietnam trilogy: veterans and Post Traumatic Stress: 1968, 1989, 2000*. New York: Algora.

Selby, S. (1984) *Dark city: The film noir*. Jefferson, NC: McFarland.

Seligman, M. (2011). *Flourish: A visionary new understanding of happiness and well-being*. New York: Free Press.

Shakespeare, W. (1951) *Coriolanus*. In P. Alexander (Ed.), *The complete works*. London: Collins.

Shay, J. (1991). Learning about combat stress from Homer's *Iliad*. *Journal of Traumatic Stress*, 4(4), 561–580.

Shay, J. (1994). *Achilles in Vietnam: Combat trauma and the undoing of character*. New York: Simon & Schuster.

Shay, J. (2002). *Odysseus in America: Combat trauma and the trials of homecoming*. New York: Simon & Shuster.

Shephard, B. (2001). *A war of nerves: Soldiers and psychiatrists in the twentieth century*. Cambridge: Harvard University Press.

Slawenski, K. (2010). *J. D. Salinger: A life*. New York: Random House.

Sledge, E. B. (1981). *With the old breed at Peleliu and Okinawa.* New York: Ballantine.

Sledge, E. B. (2002, Autumn). *China Marine.* Tuscaloosa: University of Alabama Press.

Southwick, S., & Yehuda, R. (1997). Neurobiology of threat. *NCPTSD Clinical Quarterly.*

Stanford, W. B. (1992). *The Ulysses theme.* Dallas: Spring.

Stevens, A., & Price, J. (1996). *Evolutionary psychiatry: A new beginning.* London: Routledge.

Styron, W. (2009). *The suicide run: Five tales of the Marine Corps.* New York: Random House.

Sumption, J. (2009). *The Hundred Years War,* 3 vols. Philadelphia: University of Pennsylvania Press.

Szpek, E. E., Jr., & Idzikowski, F. J. (2008). *Shadows of Slaughterhouse Five.* New York: iUniverse Press.

Tedeschi, R. G., & McNally, R. J. (2011). Can we facilitate posttraumatic growth in combat veteran? *American Psychologist,* 66(1), 19–24.

Terr, L. (1987). Childhood trauma and the creative product: A look at the early lives and later works of Poe, Wharton, Magritte, Hitchcock, and Bergman. *Psychoanalytic Study of the Child,* 42, 545–572

Terr, L. (1990) *Too scared to cry.* New York: Harper & Row.

Thomson, D. (2010). The greatest show in town. In *The New York Review of Books,* 9/30/2010, p. 61. [Quoting Cecil B. DeMille in a review of *Empire of dreams: The epic life of Cecil B. DeMille* by S. Eyman.]

Thompson, F. T. (1983). *William A. Wellman.* Metuchen, NJ: Scarecrow Press.

Toplin, R. (Ed.) (2000). *Oliver Stone's USA: Film, history, and controversy.* Lawrence: University Press of Kansas.

Tracy, S. V. (1990). *The story of the* Odyssey. Princeton: Princeton University Press.

Vidal-Naquet, P. (1996). Land and sacrifice in the *Odyssey:* A study of religious and mythical meanings. In Seth L. Schein (Ed.), *Reading the* Odyssey. New Jersey: Princeton University Press.

Walker, C. (2010, November 22). War veteran barred from CCBC campus for frank words on killing. *Baltimore Sun.*

Walter, K., Palmieri, P., & Gunstad, J. (2010). More than symptom reduction: Changes in executive function over the course of PTSD treatment. *Journal of Traumatic Stress,* 23(2), 292–295.

Warner, M. (1994). *From the beast to the blonde: On fairy tales and their tellers.* New York: Farrar, Straus & Giroux.

Warren, R. P. (1961, 1998). *The legacy of the Civil War.* Lincoln: University of Nebraska Press.

Webster, G. (1981). *The Roman Imperial Army.* New York: Barnes & Noble Books.

Williams, J. E., Johnson, Anna, M., Heiss, G., & Rose, K. M. (2010). Association between exposure to combat-related stress and psychological health in aging men: The atherosclerosis risk in communities (ARIC) Study. *Journal of Traumatic Stress,* 23(3), 358–366.

Wilson, J. P., Friedman, M. J., & Lindy, J. D. (2001). Treatment goals for PTSD. In J.P. Wilson, M.J. Friedman, & J.D. Lindy (Eds.), *Treating Psychological Trauma & PTSD.* New York: Guilford.

Yeats, W. B. (1983, 1927). Sailing to Byzantium. In R. Finneran (Ed.), *The poems of W. B. Yeats.* New York: Macmillan.

Zipes, J. (Trans.). (1989). *Beauties, beasts, and enchantments: Classic French fairy tales.* New York: New American Library. (Mme. de Beaumont's story, pp. 233–245; Mme. de Villeneuve's, pp. 153–233.)

Zukoff, M. (2009). *Robert Altman: The oral biography.* New York: Alfred A. Knopf.

Movies Reviewed

Absolute Power, 1996. Director: Clint Eastwood. Cast: Clint Eastwood, Laura Linney, Gene Hackman, Ed Harris, Judy Davis.

The Adventures of Robin Hood, 1938. Directors: Michael Curtiz, William Keighley. Cast: Errol Flynn, Olivia de Havilland, Basil Rathbone, Claude Rains.

Alamo Bay, 1985. Director: Louis Malle. Cast: Ed Harris, Amy Madigan, Ho Nguyen, Donald Moffat, Truyen V. Tran, Rudy Young, Cynthia Carle, Martin LaSalle.

Army of Shadows, 1969. (France) Director: Jean-Pierre Melville. Cast: Leno Ventura, Simon Signoret.

Bad Day at Black Rock, 1955. Director: John Sturges. Cast: Spencer Tracy, Ernest Borgnine, Lee Marvin, Walter Brennan, Robert Ryan, Dean Jagger, Anne Francis.

The Ballad of Andy Crocker, 1969. Director: George McCowan. Cast: Lee Majors, Marvin Gaye, Jimmy Dean, Bobby Hatfield, Agnes Moorehead, Pat Hingle, Joey Heatherton.

Beauty and the Beast, 1946. (France) Director: Jean Cocteau. Cast: Josette Day, Marcel André, Jean Marais.

The Best Years of Our Lives, 1946. Director: William Wyler. Cast: Dana Andrews, Hoagy Carmichael, Fredric March, Harold Russell, Myrna Loy, Teresa Wright.

The Big Lebowski, 1998. Directors: Joel and Ethan Coen. Cast: Jeff Bridges, John Goodman, Julianne Moore, Steve Buscemi, Philip Seymour Hoffman.

The Big Red One, 1980. Director: Samuel Fuller. Cast: Lee Marvin, Robert Carradine, Mark Hamill.

Blackboard Jungle, 1955. Director: Richard Brooks. Cast: Glenn Ford, Anne Francis, Sidney Poitier.

Blessed by Fire, 2006. (Argentina) Director: Tristan Bauer. Cast: Gastón Pauls, Virginia Innocenti, Pablo Riva.

The Blue Dahlia, 1945. Director: George Marshall. Cast: Alan Ladd, Veronica Lake, William Bendix.

Bob le Flambeur, 1955. (France) Director: Jean-Pierre Melville. Cast: Roger Duchesne, Isabel Corey.

Born on the Fourth of July, 1989. Director: Oliver Stone. Cast: Tom Cruise, Willem Dafoe, Raymond J. Barry, Caroline Kava, Kyra Sedgwick.

Brothers, 2010. Director: Jim Sheridan. Cast: Toby McGuire, Jake Gyllenhall, Sam Shepherd, Natalie Portman.

China Gate, 1957. Director: Samuel Fuller. Cast: Gene Barry, Nat King Cole, Angie Dickinson, Paul Dubov, Lee Van Cleef, George Givot, Marcel Dalio.

Coming Home, 1978. Director: Hal Ashby. Cast: Jane Fonda, Jon Voight, Bruce Dern, Robert Carradine, Robert Ginty, Penelope Milford, David Clennon.

Coriolanus, 2011. Director: Ralph Fiennes. Cast: Ralph Fiennes, Brian Cox, Vanessa Redgrave.

Crossfire, 1947. Director: Edward Dmytryk. Cast: Robert Ryan, Robert Young, Gloria Graham, Robert Mitchum, Paul Kelly, Richard Benedict.

Cutter's Way, 1981. Director: Ivan Passer. Cast: Jeff Bridges, John Heard, Lisa Eichorn, Ann Dusenberry, Stephen Elliot.

The Dawning, 1988. (UK) Director: Robert Knights. Cast: Anthony Hopkins, Jean Simmons, Trevor Howard, Rebecca Pidgeon, Hugh Grant.

Dead Presidents, 1995. Directors: Alan Hughes, Albert Hughes. Cast: Larenz Tate, Keith David, Chris Tucker, N'Bushe Wright, Freddy Rodriguez, Rose Jackson, Michael Imperioli, David Barry Gray.

Desert Bloom, 1986. Director: Eugene Corr. Cast: Jon Voight, Annabeth Gish, JoBeth Williams, Ellen Barkin.

Distant Thunder, 1988. (U.S.-Canadian) Director: Rick Rosenthal. Cast: John Lithgow, Ralph Macchio, Kerrie Keane, Reb Brown, Janet Margolin, Denis Arndt.

Downfall, 2005. (Germany) Director: Oliver Hirschbiegel. Cast: Bruno Ganz, Alexandra Maria Lara, Corinna Harfouch, Ulrich Matthes, Juliane Köhler, Heino Ferch, Christian Berkel, Matthias Habich, Thomas Kretschmann.

The Dry Land, 2010. Director: Ryan Piers Williams. Cast: Ryan O'Nan, America Ferrera, Jason Ritter, Melissa Leo, Wilmer Valderrama.

Elevator to the Gallows, 1958. (France) Director: Louis Malle. Cast: Jeanne Moreau, Maurice Ronet, Georges Poujouly, Yori Bertin, Jean Wall, Charles Denner.

The Enchanted Cottage, 1945. Director: John Cromwell. Cast: Robert Young, Dorothy McGuire, Herbert Marshall, Mildred Natwick, Spring Byington.

Fairy Tale: A True Story, 1997. (UK) Director: Charles Sturridge. Cast: Florence Hoath, Elizabeth Earl, Paul McGann, Phoebe Nicholls, Peter O'Toole, Harvey Keitel, Tim McInnerny.

First Blood, 1982. Director: Ted Kotcheff. Cast: Sylvester Stallone, Brian Dennehy, Richard Crenna, David Caruso, Jack Starrett, Bill McKinney, Michael Talbott.

Forrest Gump, 1994. Director: Robert Zemeckis. Cast: Tom Hanks, Robin Wright, Gary Sinise, Sally Field, Mykelti Williamson, Michael Humphreys, Hanna Hall, Haley Joel Osment.

Frankenstein, 1931. Director: James Whale. Cast: Colin Clive, Mae Clark, Boris Karloff, John Boles, Edward Van Sloan, Dwight Frye, Frederick Kerr, Lionel Belmore, Marilyn Harris.

Gods and Monsters, 1998. Director: Bill Condon. Cast: Ian McKellen, Brendan Fraser, Lynn Redgrave, Lolita Davidovich, David Dukes, Keven J. O'Connor.

Gran Torino, 2008. Director: Clint Eastwood. Cast: Clint Eastwood, Christopher Carley, Bee Vang, Ahney Her, Brian Haley, Geraldine Hughes.

Grande Illusion, 1937. (France) Director: Jean Renoir. Cast: Jean Gabin, Pierre Fresnay, Erich von Stroheim, (Marcel) Dalio, Dita Parlo, (Julien) Carette, Gaston Modot, Jean Dasté.

Harry Brown, 2010. (UK) Director: Daniel Barber. Cast: Michael Caine, Emily Mortimer, Charlie Creed-Miles, David Bradley, Iain Glen, Sean Harris.

Hatful of Rain, 1957. Director: Fred Zinnemann. Cast: Eva Marie Saint, Don Murray, Anthony Franciosa, Lloyd Nolan, Henry Silva, Gerald S. O'Loughlin, William Hickey.

Heroes for Sale, 1933. Director: William A. Wellman. Cast: Richard Barthelmess, Loretta Young, Aline MacMahon, Robert Barrat, Grant Mitchell, Douglass Dumbrille, Charles Grapewin, Ward Bond.

Human Desire, 1954. Director: Fritz Lang. Cast: Glenn Ford, Gloria Grahame, Broderick Crawford, Edgar Buchanan, Kathleen Case, Diana DeLaire.

The Hurt Locker, 2008. Director: Kathryn Bigelow. Cast: Jeremy Renner, Anthony Mackie, Brian Geraghty, Guy Pearce, Ralph Fiennes, David Morse, Evangeline Lilly.

I Am a Fugitive from a Chain Gang, 1932. Director: Mervyn LeRoy. Cast: Paul Muni, Glenda Farrell, Helen Vinson, Preston Foster, Edward Ellis, Allen Jenkins.

In a Lonely Place, 1950. Director: Nicholas Ray. Cast: Humphrey Bogart, Frank Lovejoy, Gloria Grahame, Robert Warwick, Jeff Donnell, Martha Stewart.

In Country, 1989. Director: Norman Jewison. Cast: Bruce Willis, Emily Lloyd, Joan Allen, Kevin Anderson, John Terry, Peggy Rea, Judith Ivey, Richard Hamilton, Patricia Richardson, Jim Beaver.

In the Valley of Elah, 2007. Director: Paul Haggis. Cast: Tommy Lee Jones, Charlize Theron, Susan Sarandon, James Franco, Barry Corbin, Josh Brolin, Frances Fisher.

Indian Runner, 1991. Director: Sean Penn. Cast: David Morse, Viggo Mortensen, Valeria Golino, Patricia Arquette, Charles Bronson, Sandy Dennis, Dennis Hopper, Benicio Del Toro, Kevin Stabler.

The Invisible War, 2012. Director: Kirby Dick. Documentary.

The Jacket, 2005. (U.S.-German-Scottish) Director: John Maybury. Cast: Adrien Brody, Keira Knightley, Jennifer Jason Leigh, Kris Kristofferson, Daniel Craig, Kelly Lynch, Brad Renfro, Mackenzie Phillips, Jason Lewis.

Jacknife, 1989. Director: David Hugh Jones. Cast: Robert De Niro, Ed Harris, Kathy Baker, Sloane Shelton, Ivar Brogger, Michael Arkin, Tom Isbell.

Jacob's Ladder, 1990. Director: Adrian Lyne. Cast: Tim Robbins, Elizabeth Peña, Danny Aiello, Matt Craven, Pruitt Taylor Vance, Jason Alexander, Patricia Kalember, Eriq La Salle, Ving Rhames.

Jarhead, 2005. Director: Sam Mendes. Cast: Jake Gyllenhall, Jamie Foxx, Scott MacDonald, Peter Sarsgaard, Ming Lo, Lucas Black, Kevin Foster, Brian Geraghty.

Johnny Got His Gun, 1971. Director: Dalton Trumbo. Cast: Timothy Bottoms, Kathy Fields, Jason Robards, Donald Sutherland, Marsha Hunt, Charles McGraw.

Kansas City Confidential, 1952. Director: Phil Karlson. Cast: John Payne, Coleen Gray, Preston Foster, Neville Brand, Lee Van Cleef, Jack Elam.

Key Largo, 1948. Director: John Huston. Cast: Humphrey Bogart, Lauren Bacall, Edward G. Robinson, Jay Silverheels, Claire Trevor, Lionel Barrymore.

Lafayette Escadrille, 1958. Director: William Wellman. Cast: Tab Hunter, Etchika Choureau, Marcel Dalio, David Janssen, Paul Fix.

Land of Plenty, 2004. Director: Wim Wenders. Cast: John Deihl, Michelle Williams, Shaun Toub, Wendell Pierce, Richard Edson, Burt Young.

The Last Flight, 1931. Director: William Dieterle. Cast: Richard Barthelmess, Johnny Mack Brown, Helen Chandler, David Manners, Walter Byron.

Lawn Dogs, 1997. Director: John Duigan. Cast: Mischa Barton, Sam Rockwell, Christopher McDonald, Kathleen Quinlan, Miles Meehan, Bruce McGill.

Let There Be Light, 1945. Director: John Huston. Documentary. Cast: Walter Huston (narrator).

Lethal Weapon, 1987. Director: Richard Donner. Cast: Mel Gibson, Danny Glover, Gary Busey, Mitch Ryan, Tom Atkins, Darlene Love, Traci Wolfe, Jackie Swanson.

Little Lips (*Piccole labbra*), 1978. (Germany, Spain) Director: Mimmo Cattarinich. Cast: Pierre Clémenti, Katya Berger, Ugo Bologna, Michele Soavi, Raf Baldassarre.

Lonely Are the Brave, 1962. Director: David Miller. Cast: Kirk Douglas, Gena Rowlands, Walter Matthau, Carroll O'Connor, Michael Kane, George Kennedy, Whiskey (horse).

The Long Goodbye, 1973. Director: Robert Altman. Cast: Elliott Gould, Sterling Hayden, Nina van Pallandt, Mark Rydell, Henry Gibson, David Arkin, Warren Berlinger.

The Lucky Ones, 2008. Director: Neil Burger. Cast: Tim Robbins, Michael Peña, Rachel McAdams, Molly Hagan, Mark L. Young, Howard Platt, Arden Myrin.

Made in Dagenham, 2010. (UK) Director: Nigel Cole. Cast: Sally Hawkins, Geraldine James, Roger Lloyd-Pack, Miranda Richardson, Bob Hoskins, Daniel Mays.

The Majestic, 2001. Director: Frank Darabont. Cast: Jim Carrey, Martin Landau, Laurie Holden, Bob Balaban, Jeffrey DeMunn, Hal Holbrook.

The Major and the Minor, 1942. Director: Billy Wilder. Cast: Ginger Rogers, Ray Milland, Rita Johnson, Robert Benchley, Diana Lynn.

The Man in the Gray Flannel Suit, 1956. Director: Nunnally Johnson. Cast: Gregory Peck, Jennifer Jones, Fredric March, Lee J. Cobb, Ann Harding, Keenan Wynn.

The Manchurian Candidate, 1962. Director: John Frankenheimer. Cast: Frank Sinatra, Janet Leigh, Angela Lansbury, James Gregory, Laurence Harvey.

M*A*S*H, 1970. Director: Robert Altman. Cast: Elliott Gould, Donald Sutherland, Sally Kellerman, Tom Skerritt, Robert Duvall, Roger Bowen, Gary Burghoff.

The Men, 1950. Director: Fred Zinnemann. Cast: Marlon Brando, Teresa Wright, Jack Webb, Arthur Jurado, Everett Sloane, Richard Erdman, Virginia Farmer.

Mesrine: Killer Instinct, 2008. (France) Director: Jean-François Richet. Cast: Vincent Cassel, Cécile De France, Gérard Depardieu, Roy Dupuis, Elena Anaya.

The Messenger, 2009. Director: Oren Moverman. Cast: Ben Foster, Jena Malone, Eamonn Walker, Woody Harrelson, Samantha Morton.

Missing in America, 2005. Director: Gabrielle Savage Dockterman. Cast: Danny Glover, Ron Perlman, Linda Hamilton, Zoë Weizenbaum, David Strathairn, Timothy Webber.

Mrs Dalloway, 1997. Director: Marleen Gorris. Cast: Vanessa Redgrave, Michael Kitchen, Amelia Bullmore, Rupert Graves, Natascha McElhone.

Nightfall, 1957. (Sweden) Director: Jacques Tourneur. Cast: Aldo Ray, Anne Bancroft, Brian Keith, James Gregory, Rudy Bond.

No Country for Old Men, 2007. Directors: Joel and Ethan Coen. Cast: Josh Brolin, Tommy Lee Jones, Javier Bardem, Woody Harrelson, Kelly Macdonald.

Now, After, 2010. Director: Kyle Hausemann-Stokes (Blue Three Productions).

Oliver Sherman, 2010. (Canada) Director: Ryan Redford. Cast: Donal Logue, Garret Dillahunt, Molly Parker, Jamie Lyle, Duane Murray.

Powwow Highway, 1989. Director: Jonathan Wacks. Cast: A Martinez, Joannelle Nadine Romero, Gary Farmer, Amanda Wyss, Sam Vlahos.

Restrepo, 2010. Directors: Sebastian Junger and Tim Hetherington. Documentary. Cast: The men of 2nd Platoon, Battle Company, 503rd Infantry Regiment, 173rd Airborne Brigade Combat Team.

The Return of Martin Guerre, 1982. (France) Director: Daniel Vigne. Cast: Gérard Depardieu, Nathalie Baye, Maurice Barrier, Isabelle Sadoyan, Bernard-Pierre Donnadieu.

Ride the Pink Horse, 1947. Director: Robert Montgomery. Cast: Robert Montgomery, Fred Clark, Thomas Gomez, Rita Conde, Iris Flores, Wanda Hendrix, Grandon Rhodes.

The Road Back, 1937. Director: James Whale. Cast: John "Dusty" King, Richard Cromwell, Slim Summerville, Maurice Murphy, Andy Devine, Larry J. Blake, John Emery, Henry Hunter, Noah Beery, Jr. [Film is presumed to be lost.]

Robin Hood, 2010. (UK) Director: Ridley Scott. Cast: Russell Crowe, Max von Sydow, Cate Blanchett, William Hurt, Mark Strong, Oscar Isaac, Danny Huston, Eileen Atkins.

Ronin, 1998. Director: John Frankenheimer. Cast: Jean Reno, Robert De Niro, Natascha McElhone, Stellan Skarsgård, Sean Bean, Skipp Sudduth, Jonathan Pryce.

Rushmore, 1998. Director: Wes Anderson. Cast: Bill Murray, Jason Schwartzman, Olivia Williams, Sara Tanaka, Seymour Cassel, Brian Cox, Mason Gamble.

Le Samourai, 1967. (France) Director: Jean-Pierre Melville. Cast: Alain Delon, François Périer, Nathalie Delon, Cathy Rosier, Jacques Leroy, Michel Boisrond, Robert Favart.

Sanjuro, 1962. (Japan) Director: Akira Kurosawa. Cast: Toshirô Mifune, Tatsuya Nakadai, Keiju Kobayashi, Yûzô Kayama, Reiko Dan, Takashi Shimura.

The Searchers, 1956. Director: John Ford. Cast: John Wayne, Jeffrey Hunter, Vera Miles, Ward Bond, Natalie Wood, John Qualen, Olive Carey, Henry Brandon, Ken Curtis.

Seven Samurai, 1954. (Japan) Director: Akira Kurosawa. Cast: Takashi Shimura, Toshirô Mifune, Keiko Tsashima, Yukiko Shimazaki, Kamatari Fujiwara.

The Seventh Seal, 1957. (Sweden) Director: Ingmar Bergman. Cast: Max von Sydow, Bengt Ekerot, Nils Poppe, Bibi Andersson, Gunnar Björnstrand.

Shock Corridor, 1963. Director: Samuel Fuller. Cast: Peter Breck, Constance Towers, Gene Evans, James Best, Hari Rhodes, Larry Tucker, Paul Dubov, Chuck Roberson.

Shutter Island, 2010. Director: Martin Scorsese. Cast: Leonardo DiCaprio, Mark Ruffalo, Michelle Williams, Ben Kingsley, Max von Sydow, Emily Mortimer, Patricia Clarkson.

Le Silence de la Mer, 1949. (France) Director: Jean-Pierre Melville. Cast: Howard Vernon, Jean-Marie Robian, Nicole Stéphane, Ami Aaröe, Georges Patrix.

Snow Falling on Cedars, 1999. Director: Scott Hicks. Cast: Ethan Hawke, Yûki Kudô, Reeve Carney, Anne Suzuki, Rick Yune, Max von Sydow.

Some Came Running, 1958. Director: Vincente Minnelli. Cast: Frank Sinatra, Dean Martin, Shirley MacLaine, Martha Hyer, Arthur Kennedy, Nancy Gates, Leora Dana.

Somewhere in the Night, 1946. Director: Joseph L. Mankiewicz. Cast: John Hodiak, Nancy Guild, Lloyd Nolan, Richard Conte, Josephine Hutchinson, Sheldon Leonard.

Sommersby, 1993. Director: John Amiel. Cast: Jodie Foster, Richard Gere, Bill Pullman, James Earl Jones, Lanny Flaherty, William Windom, Wendell Wellman.

The Spirit of the Beehive, 1973. (Spain) Director: Victor Erice. Cast: Ana Torrent, Isabel Telleria, Fernando Fernán Gómez, Teresa Gimpera.

Spitfire Grill, 1998. Director: Lee David Zlotoff. Cast: Alison Elliott, Ellen Burstyn, Marcia Gay Harden, Will Patton, Kieran Mulroney, Gailard Sartain.

Stop-Loss, 2008. Director: Kimberly Pierce. Cast: Ryan Phillippe, Joseph Gordon-Levitt, Rob Brown, Channing Tatum, Victor Rasuk, Quay Terry.

Stray Dog, 1949. (Japan) Director: Akira Kurosawa. Cast: Toshirô Mifune, Takashi Shimura, Keiko Awaji, Eiko Miyoshi, Noriko Sengoku, Isao Kimura.

The Stunt Man, 1980. Director: Richard Rush. Cast: Peter O'Toole, Barbara Hershey, Steve Railsback, Allen Garfield, Alwx Rocco, Sharon Farrell, Adam Roarke.

Suddenly, 1954. Director: Lewis Allen. Cast: Frank Sinatra, Sterling Hayden, James Gleason, Kim Charney, Nancy Gates, Paul Frees, Christopher Dark, James O'Hara.

Sundays and Cybele, 1962. (France) Director: Serge Bourguignon. Cast: Hardy Krüger, Patricia Gozzi, Nicole Courcel, Daniel Ivernel, Anne-Marie Coffinet.

Taking Chance, 2009. Director: Ross Katz. Cast: Kevin Bacon, Tom Aldredge, Nicholas Art, Blanch Baker, Tom Bloom, Guy Boyd, James Castanien.

Taxi Driver, 1976. Director: Martin Scorsese. Cast: Robert De Niro, Jodi Foster, Cybill Shepherd, Harvey Keitel, Albert Brooks, Peter Boyle.

Thieves' Highway, 1949. Director: Jules Dassin. Cast: Richard Conte, Valentina Cortesa, Lee J. Cobb, Barbara Lawrence, Jack Okie, Millard Mitchell.

The Third Man, 1949. (UK) Director: Carol Reed. Cast: Joseph Cotten, Alida Valli, Trevor Howard, Orson Welles, Bernard Lee, Ernst Deutsch.

3:10 to Yuma, 1957. Director: Delmer Daves. Cast: Glenn Ford, Van Heflin, Felicia Farr, Leora Dana, Henry Jones, Richard Jaeckel, Robert Emhardt, Sheridan Comerate.

3:10 to Yuma, 2007. Director: James Mangold. Cast: Russell Crowe, Christian Bale, Peter Fonda, Logan Lerman, Gretchen Mol, Dallas Roberts, Ben Foster, Vinessa Shaw.

Till the End of Time, 1946. Director: Edward Dmytryk. Cast: Guy Madison, Dorothy Maguire, Robert Mitchum, Bill Williams, Tom Tully, William Gargan, Jean Porter.

The Tunnel, in *Akira Kurosawa's Dreams*, 1990. (Japan) Director: Akira Kurosawa. Cast: Yoshitaka Zushi.

Ulee's Gold, 1997. Director: Victor Nuñez. Cast: Peter Fonda, Jessica Biel, Vanessa Zima, Patricia Richardson, Christine Dunford, Tom Wood, Steven Flynn.

The Veteran, 2011. (UK) Director: Matthew Hope. Cast: Toby Kebbell, Brian Cox, Adi Bielski, Tony Curran, Ashley Thomas, Tom Brooke.

Vincere, 2009. (Italy) Director: Marco Bellocchio. Cast: Giovanna Mezzogiorno, Filippo Timi, Fausto Russo Alesi, Michela Cescon, Pier Giorgio Bellocchio.

Waltz with Bashir, 2008. (Israel) Director: Ari Folman. Animated.

The War, 1994. Director: John Avnet. Cast: Kevin Costner, Lexi Randall, Elijah Wood, Mare Winningham, LeToya Chisholm, Christopher Fennell.

Who'll Stop the Rain, 1978. Director: Karel Reisz. Cast: Nick Nolte, Tuesday Weld, Michael Moriarty, Anthony Zerbe, Richard Masur, Ray Sharkey, Gail Strickland.

Year of the Dragon, 1985. Director: Michael Cimino. Cast: Mickey Rourke, John Lone, Ariane, Leonard Termo, Raymond J. Barry, Caroline Kava, Eddie Jones.

Yojimbo, 1961. (Japan) Director: Akira Kurosawa. Cast: Toshirô Mifune, Tatsuya Nakadai, Yôko Tsukasa, Isuzu Yamada, Daisuke Katô, Takashi Shimura.

Index

www.ingramcontent.com/pod-product-compliance
Lightning Source LLC
Chambersburg PA
CBHW031129270326
41929CB00011B/1550